The Rushes of Tulsa

THE RUSHES OF TULSA
AND OTHER PLAYS

Sidney Goldfarb

Barrytown

Station Hill

Published by Barrytown/Station Hill Press, Inc., 120 Station Hill Road, Barrytown, NY 12507, as a project of the Institute for Publishing Arts, Inc., in Barrytown, New York, a not-for-profit, tax-exempt organization [501(c)(3)], supported in part by grants from the New York State Council on the Arts.

Online catalogue and purchasing: www.stationhill.org
e-mail: publishers@stationhill.org

Interior design by Tim Roberts
Cover design by Susan Quasha
Cover photo © 2008 Maceofoto | Dreamstime.com. Author photo on page ii by Suzanne Opton. Photo on page 158 © 2008 Beatriz Schiller, used by permission.

Library of Congress Cataloging-in-Publication Data

Goldfarb, Sidney, 1942–
    The rushes of Tulsa and other plays / Sidney Goldfarb.
    p.   cm.
    ISBN 978-1-58177-111-4 (alk. paper)
    I. Title.
PS3557.O36R87 2008
812'.54—dc22

                                        2008030967

Manufactured in the United States of America

Contents

The Rushes of Tulsa

The Rushes of Tulsa was presented in a staged reading at The Cherry Lane Theater, New York, in June 2004 by Dixon Place, Ellie Kovan, Artistic Director.

The cast:

DICK RUSH:	Roger Babb
ROSE RUSH:	Mary Shultz
KITTY AND WINNY RUSH:	Mary Bonner Baker
MO MENDOZA:	David Greenspan
BO NIXON:	William Badgett
JUANA WASH:	Sami Sargent
BOBBY WASH:	Terry Jones
EDUARDO:	Alberto Guerrero

Directed by Sidney Goldfarb

Cast of Characters

MO MENDOZA, ageless, Jewish, Kabbalistic massage therapist, owner of used clothing stores and whorehouses for the aged in Tulsa, Matamoros, and Denver, simultaneously, wears an old ten-gallon hat and large star of David

BOBBY WASH, 25, from Cortez, Colorado, half-Ute, half-Chicano, urban Indian, eventually, Winny's boyfriend

DICK RUSH, 40s, Tulsa oil and cattle magnate with an impeccable white suit, $500 Stetson, later decrepit wreck with huge oxygen tank

ROSE RUSH, 40s, Dick's wife, Belle of Tulsa, later Bo's lover

KITTY and WINNY RUSH, twins, 18, outrageous and outraged, played by one actress

TWIN STAND IN, female character, resembles twins, silent

BO NIXON, 40s, African-American, Drug "keeper" from Tulsa Keeper Academy, later heart surgeon and lover of Rose Rush

EDMUNDO SALAZAR, 25, handsome Venezuelan video artist, Kitty's boyfriend, also Chief of Federales in Matamoros, Mexico

JUANA WASH, 50s, Indian, Bobby's mother, Mo's maid, Rush's maid, later Mo's lover and fiancée

(1989 and after. Time is fluid. A three-level configuration of rooms. On the second level, a large central room, ordinarily the Rushes' living room. There are above rooms to either side of it, Edmundo's room SR, and Juana's room SL. The configuration should not be symmetrical. Below, a large room hung with old winter coats of every variety. A hanging sign: MO'S COATS AND PAWN: YOU WANT IT, WE GOT IT. Rough signs, arbitrarily nailed to the set, point to Tulsa, Denver, Matamoros. There are "crawl spaces" between and around all rooms, so characters can move quickly and visibly from room to room. The walls and floors of rooms and "crawl spaces" have openings covered with soft rubber membranes so that characters can push themselves into rooms head first, for instance. Characters may also pull one another into rooms, or leave each other dangling from ceilings or walls. Top level room SR, "Edmundo's room," later a Mexican Police Station, is cramped and cluttered with generic equipment and ersatz instruments, drugs, ritual satanic objects and statues including a large steel cauldron, etc. A large TV screen flashes in it. SL, top level, "Juana's room," is the maid's room, a room in a whore house, later, a room where Bobby and his mother live: very bare, just a cot, a table, a hot plate or stove. Above the two rooms a flat performing space. Below, the central room has some odd pieces of elegant, uncomfortable furniture, including a large rolling box that can serve as a dinner table, massage table, and a cof-

fin. An oversize statue of a golden bull, a prize for cattle production, glows upstage in the shadows. The rooms should be colored to give off a primary feel. The overall outline of the set should be well defined, as if indented in black space. It should suggest a brain or a heart, or a pulsating cell or hive, but should not symbolize anything in particular.

Native American music, heavy drumming, high-pitched singing, then sound of cattle in darkness, soft to loud to soft, as if a big herd were passing by. Goat sounds with bells, Mexican singing. Computer sounds in Edmundo's room, SR. Slowly visible images on TV screen, Edmundo at work, his Palo Mayombe (Satanic) collage documentary: a peasant exorcises a burning barn, Mexican police and dope smugglers digging skeletons out of the ground, etc. Lights grow from TV to encompass stage. Winny (Kitty) sits seminaked in maid's room SL, lazily puts on nun's costume, takes it off. After a while she leaves the room and is replaced by the twin Stand In. Edmundo continues working on his video. Images flash by as he works. But sometimes he sees images that shouldn't be there: flash forwards from parts of the play.)

EDMUNDO: What the fuck is this? How'd this shit get in here? Must be some kinda virus!

> *(Edmundo continues to be puzzled as he runs his video backwards and forwards. We see some images from his Satanic video, but also others that come from speeches, scenes, flash forwards, or doublings of scenes, Winny sitting on the bed, Mo and Bobby entering, etc. Mo and Bobby push through hanging coats on bottom level, each carrying an enormous pile of old coats.)*

BOBBY: I don't even know why you bother with these coats, Mo. You're just gonna give 'em away as soon as the weather gets bad. Every bum in Tulsa will be in here moanin' and groanin' that he needs a coat . . .

MO: Hey, how did I meet you, boychick?

BOBBY: I came in here moanin' and groanin' that I need a coat . . .

MO: And did I give you one?

BOBBY: You gave me this down parka, Mo. Saved my ass that winter. And then you gave me a job. But I don't see how you pay me. You buy these old coats. And then you give them away.

MO: The girls bring in the money, Bobby. The coats are just a front. Does this look like a whorehouse to you? Downstairs, coats. Upstairs, girls. If someone's shiverin' in December and they need a good coat, you give it to 'em. Maybe it's one less person who freezes to death. That makes me feel good. And my girls don't serve the general public. Only the old can get laid at Mo's. The prices are low, the girls are clean, and the Johns are too old to cause any trouble. You have to specialize in this world. It took me a while to get it all worked out. It isn't heaven, but what is? (*Mo buzzes a customer in. Enter old man, Dick, 40, looks 60, dragging a big oxygen tank behind him.*) Gotenu, what happened to you?

DICK: (*Wheezing heavily, extreme Texas accent.*) I had a heart attack about six weeks ago. Big operation. They cut on my ticker for most of a day. Quadruple bypass. (*Shows them enormous scar.*) So they give me this oxygen to keep me on my feet.

MO: You sure you wanna go upstairs? You look pretty weak.

DICK: Weak? I'm dead. After me, there's no more white people.

MO: No more white people. What will we do? You wanna go upstairs or not?

DICK: I miss the taste of a girl, Mo. The smell of a girl. I'll be O.K.

(Mo *pushes the buzzer. Stand In pulls curtain over room, SL.*)

MO: You take it easy. That's all I need is the last of the goyim' croakin' in my crib.

DICK: (*Wheezing with laughter, practically collapsing.*) The last of the goyim! The last of the goyim! A Jew can tell a joke, no lie! (*Catches his breath. Starts to go through the coats.*)

MO: You know where it is?

DICK: Are you shittin' me? My twins were born up there. (*He goes through coats, up crawl space. Barely visible, Stand In pulls him in through membrane. Mo and Bobby go back for more coats. Bo and Kitty enter quickly on middle level, central room. Bo is in his keeper uniform. Logos on cap and shirt say Tulsa Keeper Academy.*)

KITTY: I can't stand you followin' me around like shit on my shoes, Bo!

BO: As long as your daddy pays me to keep you away from drugs, Miss Kitty, your ass is my ass. Once an addict, is what we say at TKA.

KITTY: I'm not addicted to anything, Bo. I like getting off!
            Who doesn't?

BO: Now that's the first thing they angle you in on at
            (*Touching his cap.*) Tulsa Keeper Academy: as soon as
            they say they're not addicted, you know they are.

KITTY: This has got nothing to do with drugs. My old man
            is keeping me away from Edmundo. He knows I'm in
            love, and he can't stand the thought of some greaser
            copping pussy from his own flesh and blood. This
            house is a ranch. I'm just a cow. Well, he can try
            to lock me up in his barn. But he can't control my
            dreams!

BO: (*Taking out pen and notebook.*) Well, what kinda
            dreams you been havin' lately?

KITTY: I keep havin' these dreams that I'm at Edmundo's
            and we keep doin' hits of baster green. (*Garish light
            up on Edmundo. He prepares and does green hit as
            she describes it. Dick wheezes with Stand In behind
            curtain.*)

BO: Hits of green? What kinda green?

KITTY: They call it baster green. I'm not sure what it is . . .

BO: Tincture of O! I better get this written down!

KITTY: It isn't O, Bo. Our desires are a mystery to you.

BO: Just tell me how you do the shit . . .

KITTY: You do it in the ear with like this big turkey baster.
            (*Edmundo squeezes green liquid in his ear with enor-
            mous turkey baster, staggers around his room, danc-
            ing the pachanga.*)

BO: Turkey baster! You think I'm a fool!

KITTY: Look, every kid in Tulsa's been doin' baster green,
            Bo. Edmundo tilts my head to the side and pumps the
            stuff into my ear.

The Rushes of Tulsa   9

BO: You're serious . . . you shoot this shit in your ear. . . . Does it hurt?

KITTY: No, it feels great. It's like a warm vegetable blood right into your brain. And when you come you get this orgasm that's like completely green. You get a feeling for plant life you never had before.

BO: Wait a minute: this drug makes you come . . .

KITTY: Why else would you take it? It starts in your inner ear, see, and then you see this bright green glow flooding through your labyrinth. (*Edmundo writhes in ecstasy. Dick wheezes and moans behind curtain.*)

BO: What labyrinth?

KITTY: In your inner ear! You become your own TV set. Edmundo pumps the green in my ear and my set goes on and I see this vegetable protein pumping into my brain, like one part's shriveled like a big green chestnut and then another part looks like a gigantic green fig, and then all of a sudden the brain is like this pulsating green pond with all these beautiful ferns and vines swaying around it . . .

BO: This is unbelievable . . . (*Edmundo continues dancing.*)

KITTY: Wait, wait, I haven't told you the best part. 'Cause after your brain's like this rainforest pool, it starts to drip down to your chest. The pool becomes like this green cloud and it starts to rain down inside you, you don't know whether you're sky or earth, and then your heart starts glowing like this greenish red . . . it's all real slow, like evolution is happening inside you and you can see this green blood rushing down your arteries, and then you can see your organs secreting like these silken green threads, and I can see thousands of tiny green eggs in my ovaries like the world's most precious caviar, and then it starts to flow outward, you know. . . .

BO: You mean like onto your *skin*?

KITTY: First you notice it in your toenails, they get like this pinkish green, then my cunt hair is like this mound of turquoise moss, and then my nipples get like this purplish green, and then this stain flows along my skin like a wave and when it hits my clit it runs into this wave that's comin' from inside and I'm gone, only you feel very still like a small round pond of warm, green water on a day without a breath of wind . . . oh man, I'm due, I want some now!

BO: Wait a minute, wait a minute. I gotta get this down! (*Bobby and Mo enter quickly with another pile of coats. Bo writes and mumbles parts of what Kitty told him.*)

MO: These Shmatas are just a little compensation God dropped on us, Bobby . . . and you know why?

BOBBY: Why's that, Mo?

MO: Because we both come from tribes they tried to get rid of, the Jews and the Soos . . .

BOBBY: I'm not a Sioux, Mo. I'm a Ute. Part Ute, part Mexican. How many times do I have to tell you?

MO: Soos, Jews, Utes, Bantus! What difference does it make. We all want the same things: we wanna get laid, we wanta cruller and coffee, we wanta warm coat in winter, and we wanna fly through heaven 'til we see the empty throne . . .

BOBBY: You're crazy, Mo.

MO: You're not the first Indian who told me this.

BOBBY:	I don't even know why I care what you call me. It's been so long since I've seen my people, I don't belong to no tribe no more . . .
MO:	You can never, ever leave your tribe. Even if your tribe tells you you're a total goy, you always are what you always were . . .
BOBBY:	Wait a minute! Hold it! You just said that tribes don't matter at all.
MO:	So, it's a paradox. I contradict myself. So what!
BOBBY:	You ain't no Indian anyway, Mo. What the hell do you know about tribes?
MO:	Tribes? Tribes? You're asking me about tribes? Well, let me tell you. There was never a man so pissed on by his tribe as me. He's asking me about tribes! Is this the last load?
BOBBY:	The van is empty. I think I'm gonna go home early. Is that OK?
MO:	You're not feelin' good?
BOBBY:	I'm startin' to get one of those migraines. This one is a killer. . . .
MO:	Do you need the rub?
BOBBY:	I could really use the rub, Mo . . . if you got the time . . .
MO:	Bring out the table.
BOBBY:	I could really use the rub, Mo. It's been a while.
MO:	Well, the rub don't work unless you need it. (*Bobby exits through coats. Mo remains checking the coats, putting price tags on them. Bo looks up from writing.*)
BO:	OK, I got it all down. Now, what's Edmundo doin' while you're getting' off?

KITTY: You mean while I'm turning green? We're making love, asshole! What would you be doin' on a rush like that?

BO: (*Writing.*) Just tryin' to do my job!

KITTY: That's real white of you, Bo.

BO: You listen to me, Miss Kitty! I'm here to get the mambo monkeys off your back! This ain't just you. It's a whole country goin' under. They lay it all out at the Keeper Academy. South America wants North America, see what I'm sayin'? Edmundo is just a soldier in Fidel's Cuban Army.

KITTY: Edmundo's a Venezuelan, Bo.

BO: Whatever, Venezuelan, Dominican, Columbian, Peruvian, don't make no difference. Those are narco-countries. They want what we got. We're their habit.

KITTY: You know nothing about Edmundo. We've been workin' on a video together. . . .

BO: Video? You never said nothin' about no video! (*Writing furiously.*)

KITTY: Well, you remember that Texas student that disappeared down in Brownsville? And then they found out he'd been sacrificed by this dope dealer in Matamoros?

BO: No shit I remember! That dealer was into voodoo! He killed a pile of people . . .

KITTY: It wasn't voodoo. It was palo mayombe.

BO: Palo Mayombe: satanic arrest evasion. Very common in Miami. The Keeper Academy's got a whole unit on it.

KITTY: My sister sent me these tapes from Matamoros. She's tight with a narc down there. And he took these videos when they busted the dealer Patrón. They dug up

	the people he sacrificed, and they brought this brujo in to exorcise his shack! And now me and Edmundo . . .
BO:	You into voodoo!
KITTY:	It's not voodoo! It's video! Not voodoo, video, dick-head! I gotta get some coffee! (*She rushes from the room with Bo on her tail. Bobby and Mo enter with table.*)
BO:	Hold on! Wait up! You know the rules!
BOBBY:	(*Entering with table and Mo.*) Where the hell you get this table, Mo?
MO:	This table, this table I brought with me from Albuquerque when the rabbis down there run me out of town.
BOBBY:	You got run outta town?
MO:	It's a long story. . . . We was studying with this Zaddik in Albuquerque named Sholem Motel Zola in this coffee shop out on Central.
BOBBY:	What the fuck is a Zaddik?
MO:	A Zaddik is a medicine man. And this Sholem was the first one to say these two things: one, the empty throne cannot be approached alone and, two, the way to the empty throne is through the body. And ultimately this got us in a lot of trouble. Cause we was doing the rub for different people with excellent results: a lot of people saw the empty throne and was united with the universe, but then there was some complaints, some girl got rubbed the wrong way . . . it turned out this Sholem gave the rub to this girl he met in the Reform Synagogue parking lot, and rumors were flying, and it was a whole mess, and people said we were shtooping children which was completely untrue, and these rabbis threatened to kill us if we didn't get out of town,

so we had to leave for Mexico, Oklahoma, Colorado, you name it. That's why I don't do the rub now except for friends. Too risky, otherwise. They'll get you for this; they'll get you for that. It's not worth the tsuris. Are you comfortable? (*Bobby lies on narrow vertical table. Juana opens curtain in room, SL. She straightens out the bed, slowly puts on nun's garb.*)

BOBBY: Just bein' on the table makes me feel better, Mo.

MO: This is the curative effect of anticipation, hacholeh hachola . . . what might be is already . . . OK . . . you remember how this goes . . . this body is the tree of life . . . inside the body is God . . . we enter the body, we embrace the shekinah, the many female forms and the one female form of God who has no form and then we fly . . .

BOBBY: I do anything you say to get rid of these migraines.

MO: Now show me exactly where the pain is. (*Bobby touches temples with fingers.*) OK, those are the zim-zum contraction centers on the crude physical level. The flow of the universe through the brain is getting blocked by some bad pictures. Did you hit anyone this week?

BOBBY: I ain't hit anybody since my cousin burned my truck. Broke his goddamn jaw with a piece of firewood. But that was years ago. You know I calmed down since I been doin' the rub.

MO: This pain is old then, Bobby. We got to go lookin' for it.

BOBBY: Do it, Mo.

MO: We're gonna go up the tree now. If we hit some words, that's God's voice pushin' through. Don't let him

BOBBY: bother you. He's a pain in the ass, but he's all I got. You remember how it goes . . .

BOBBY: The words, the pictures, the fuckin' empty throne, put it on me, man . . .

MO: I'm gonna rub your feet, whatever happens just let me know. The feet are the Aleph of God. We been planted down here just like onions and potatoes.

BOBBY: My feet been hurting me a lot these last few weeks . . .

MO: Those rabbis in Albuquerque thought the devil would get in your head first. But the devil is a helluva lot smarter than that. (*Mo rubs Bobby's feet. Bobby moans.*)

BOBBY: That feels really good, Mo.

MO: The tree is like a ladder. Step by step we climb to the sky. I got a feeling we're gonna see the empty throne today. (*Kitty and Bo enter with coffee.*)

BO: OK now, lemme get this straight: you got a twin sister who's tight with this narc and this narc gives her this video about this dealer in Matamoros who's into human sacrifice, and you and Edmundo are making like this "video collage"! You expect me to put this in my report to the Keeper Academy? What's your sister really doin' down in Mexico?

KITTY: She's a singer.

BO: They don't got enough singers in Mexico? They got to import some white girls?

KITTY: They like country music down in Matamoros. Cowboys go down to get laid. Then they get homesick.

BO: Ever get any packages from her in the mail?

KITTY: All she ever sent was the video. She calls. On the first of the month.

BO:	So she'll call today?
KITTY:	If she don't, she's in trouble.
BO:	Well, we got a three-mile run ahead of us. (*They jog out the door.*)
MO:	I think I feel a picture coming . . . it's in the Shin shekin chakra, way up high in your neck. Can you see anything?
BOBBY:	It's where we used to live, Mo. When we were still out on the res. Oh, I know what this is. I don't want to see this. I feel like I got a big knot in my neck. Oh shit, there they are. I'm just a big blood clot rollin' down the road getting bigger and bigger.
MO:	I see the bloodclot. Slip the knot, boychick. Tell me what you see.
BOBBY:	Now I'm a boy. I'm walkin' home from school and these nuns pick me up . . .
MO:	Walking the dusty road. I can see it . . .
BOBBY:	And then these nuns come along in this station wagon . . .
MO:	I can see the nuns, Bobby. (*Juana is in nun's costume. Opens curtain. She comes to the front of her room and sits.*)
JUANA:	You're Bobby Wash, aren't you?
BOBBY:	Yes . . . sister . . .
JUANA:	You're the son of that drunk that got killed in Cortez.
BOBBY:	Someone killed my dad.
JUANA:	And do you know why he died?
BOBBY:	Some white boys beat him to death. That's what they say. Stripped him naked and cut his head off.
JUANA:	He died because he lied to you. He told you stories, and those stories were lies. He was a drunk and a liar

and he didn't believe in God the Father and Jesus, his only Son. And God punished him for lying to you.

BOBBY: They say some white boys killed him. Those white boys come from Farmington . . .

JUANA: He died because he said sisters and brothers fornicated and that's how the world began. He lied to you with those stories and God punished him.

BOBBY: They were stories, that's all . . .

JUANA: Do you want your mother to die, too?

BOBBY: Noooo.

JUANA: Well, you get every last trace of your father out of our house. Or your house will be cursed. And your mother will die.

BOBBY: I'm gonna fuckin' kill you! (*Juana pulls the curtain closed.*)

MO: What's the matter, boychick?

BOBBY: She pushed me out of the car. Right onto the road. That big blood clot was still there following me!

MO: This is the headache. Slip the knot.

BOBBY: My mother was savin' that coat for me, Mo. For when I got bigger. It's hangin' on a nail in the corner by the stove. I'm smellin' the coat, and the smell makes me crazy . . .

MO: We gotta spit out the sickness before we can travel.

BOBBY: I thought it was just the coat of my father, hanging on a nail in the corner by the stove. But there's a smell in that coat, Mo. A smell of sweat, a smell of smoke, a smell of wine, a smell of deer, a smell of cigarettes, Mo. There's the smell of my father in this coat, Mo.

MO: No Mo now, Bobby, just your heart.

BOBBY: A smell too old for a coat to get over! The blood clot was gone. It's just me and December and it's windy

and my father's coat is empty, Mo! Why are there so many coats in the world?

MO: Because the world is cold, and God made us naked. Go figure.

BOBBY: Why is my mother so poor? Why is my father dead? Why is his head all gone up there? Why did they take his clothes off, Mo?

MO: I don't know, boychick. Nobody knows. Not even God.

BOBBY: I'm trying to crawl inside the sleeves. Why am I tearing his coat apart?

MO: Go into the darkness. Tell me what you see!

BOBBY: I see a white guy, Mo. He's in a real fancy suit.

MO: A white guy in a suit? I must be tappin' inta someone else's rub!

BOBBY: There's a white guy in our house. He's got my old man's head in his hands. (*Edmundo is videoing himself in a white suit placing human head in cauldron. Dick, looking twenty years younger and healthy, enters on second level, in the same white suit as Edmundo.*)

MO: I better go back to the bottom and start over. I musta fucked this rub up. I think we're pickin' up an outside story.

DICK: Did she call you yet, Kitty? I want her back here!

KITTY: Don't you think my keeper would have told you if she called?

DICK: She'd kill herself just to embarrass me. It'll be the talk of the stock show. I've got to have the two of you here. One is meaningless to me without the other. You understand that, don't you, Kitty?

KITTY: Like a bull understands a cow!

DICK:	(*To Bo.*) You see there's always been the two of them. They weren't two separate people. When you were talking to one, you were talking to the other. When you were touching one, you were touching the other. Because you always knew if one was away, the other would be there. And you could never be sure which one it was. You didn't want to be sure. 'Cause whatever you did, you didn't know who you'd done it to. They weren't really people, they were clones. A stable herd needs no changes! I started out with a dozen cows. And in ten years I had the biggest ranch in Oklahoma. In twenty years I was floatin' in oil. I'm not gonna lose it to the jungle. I almost lost one! I'm not gonna lose two, am I, Mr. Nixon?
BO:	Any loss to the jungle is too much, Mr. Rush.
KITTY:	I want to speak to Winny alone when she calls, dad.
DICK:	You bring her back here, Kitty.
BO:	I advise against privacy here, Mr. Rush. She's callin' from Matamoros. Could be into voodoo down there!
DICK:	I don't think there can be any drugs transferred over the phone.
BO:	You the boss, Mr. Rush. But if you really want this girl to remain drug free, I suggest all calls be censored absolutely. (*Barely visible behind curtain in Juana's room Stand In dials and waits. Phone rings. Bo grabs the phone. Kitty struggles with him to answer.*)
KITTY:	Do I get to answer my own phone calls or no, Dad! Am I going to be allowed any privacy at all? Can I piss alone? Do I get to put my tampax in by myself?
MO:	That's not our phone, Bobby. That's the whorehouse upstairs. Just relax.

DICK:	I think Kitty can be allowed to speak to her sister alone, Mr. Nixon.
KITTY:	Let me have this phone, motherfucker! I'll kick your nuts up in your nose!
DICK:	I think you better come with me, Mr. Nixon.
BO:	I think I better stay right here, Mr. Rush.
KITTY:	(*Phone gets louder.*) Gimme the fuckin' phone!
BO:	This is a drug call! I can feel it!
KITTY:	Maybe Bo wouldn't mind slidin' my tampax in! I know guys who get off on that!
DICK:	Kitty! I think you should keep a few of the sordid details of your life in reserve. Why waste them in meaningless outbursts. (*Phone gets louder.*)
BO:	That's where I think you're wrong, Mr. Rush. That's one of the first things they angle you in on at the Keeper Academy.
DICK:	(*Pulling phone away from Bo.*) I don't want to hear about your keeper training right now, Mr. Nixon.
BO:	There's a whole section in the first Keeper Cadet Module, The Outburst Event: how to observe, record, and make use of the keepee's outbursts. (*Picks up notebook and begins writing.*)
KITTY:	Give me the phone, dad! I know it's Winny! (*Stand In hangs up. Ringing stops. Kitty slaps at Dick, tears at him violently.*) I hate you! I fuckin' hate you! I'd like to pull your dick off and stuff it in your mouth! (*Dick manages to pin her arms.*) Why don't you just tie me up, Dad. Like the old days. Too bad Winny's not here. Then you could do both of us. (*Dick releases her. She runs from room, enters crawls space, crawls to Edmundo's. Stand In exits. Juana enters, straightens room.*)

DICK: That's what they always say these days. Try to keep them from killing themselves, and they just accuse you of incest!

BO: (*Writing furiously.*) Oooo, this is gettin' really rich! Do you want me to chase her down?

DICK: Let her go! The house is clean, isn't it?

BO: The house is clean as a nun's bush, Mr. Rush. (*Juana changes from nun to maid.*)

DICK: I was brought up by nuns, Bo. So I will thank you to show respect to women who . . .

BO: You ever do push-push with a nun, Mr. Rush?

DICK: (*Sitting in massive chair, loosening tie, opening collar.*) Nuns are married to God, Mr. Nixon. They go places with him you and I never dreamed of. Look, I need to get something fresh in my blood. (*Bo checks his stash.*)

MO: What do you see now, Bobby, anything?

BOBBY: I'm pushing my head up the sleeve of my dad's coat, Mo! But I look like a girl. And the sleeve is long. It's long as a hall and wide as a water pipe.

MO: The girl is a mini-shekinah, lowest level, but we're back on track. Follow the girl to the goat pen; you'll see your mother.

BOBBY: The rub feels really good, Mo. It's just like a drug.

BO: Here's what it is: I got up, down, sideways, inside out, the usual. Then there's the Mauritanian pod you liked, and this new shit from Bucaramanga they call Dead Man's Float. Comes in two forms, smokeable and enema.

DICK: No enemas for me today. I'll take a neck hit, sideways puncture, a good straight shot. (*Bo prepares Dick for "neck hit," opening his collar, tying his neck with a*

	cord to make jugular stand out, loading impossibly large syringe with a black liquid, etc. Sound of goats. Light on Juana. She holds a torn-up leather coat. Kitty's head pops down through Edmundo's ceiling. Edmundo pulls her down. They slowly undress and do baster green and make love.)
BOBBY:	I can see my mom now, Mo. She found the coat I tore up and she's coming out of the house!
JUANA:	Why'd you tear up your dad's coat, you bad boy! Your dad was a good man. This coat was all I had left of him. I was savin' this coat for you this winter. Well, you act like a goat; you can live like a goat! I'm gonna put this rope around your neck and tie you up and you can stay out here with the goats all night!
BOBBY:	*(Bo is tying up Dick.)* She's tyin' that rope around my neck now, Mo. I can barely breathe! And she's tying the other end to a post in the goat pen, and the goats are comin' all around me to sniff. And it's really cold, Mo. Just after sunset. Don't leave me out here all night, I'll freeze!
JUANA:	Where'm I gonna get another coat like that! *(Bo shoots needle into Dick's neck. He groans and gets up out of the chair, shaking.)* You take that rope off your neck, I'll whup you so hard you'll wish you were never born!
BOBBY:	Don't leave me out here! *(Bobby cries softly. Sounds of goat bells, wind. Bo gets Dick back into chair.)*
MO:	Rest in the night, boychick. I'll keep you warm.
DICK:	*(Loosening slowly as Bobby becomes quiet. Edmundo and Kitty make love. Rose enters second level and stands watching as Dick babbles and Bo stands with*

huge needle in hand.) Mnnnn. I owe a lot to you, Mr. Nixon. The way you've kept the goats in their pens!

BO: Can't have them randy goats roamin' around with Miss Kitty in heat!

DICK: I know perfectly well that I can still kill perfectly calmly the way we did in Dam Binh To, you remember Dam Binh To, don't you, Bo?

BO: Is pig pussy pork, brother Rush. I was there!

DICK: Tropical diseases spread the fastest! Can't let a plague like that run wild! Hitler knew the secret. Pipi pipi pip! Gas! Gas! Gas! And there's your pile!

BO: More jobs for the brothers!

DICK: Exactly. Thomas Jefferson, Sam Houston, pasture, feed, and pussy. All you need.

BO: Put your face in it!

DICK: Have you ever castrated a calf, Mr. Nixon?

BO: Are you yankin' my snake?

DICK: It's not as bad as you think, Bo. Course I started at seven.

BO: You de-balled a doggie when you were seven years old!

DICK: You don't like it at first, cause you got your own balls you see! You got those calf nuts right there in your hand, and your own little kid nuts shrink up the size of pinto beans!

BO: My dick would fall off and crawl to El Paso!

DICK: My dad broke me in, see, doin' horn removal first. We used them Leavitt Clippers to snip the horns off. And, of course I done branding, you do 'em all at once you see, castration, dehorning and branding, best use of time and best for the animal. We used them Leavitt clippers cause our calves were already a year and a half on up to two years, and that's a pretty substantial little booger and those horns are pretty good sized by then. If you get 'em younger you can use that Barnes Dehorner, but with these bigger calves that Barnes Dehorner won't get down to the root!

BO: Wouldn't want to leave any horn in there!

DICK: That's exactly right, cause that horn can grow back!

BO: You know it will!

DICK: But with that Leavitt Clipper you get the horn out right down to the root. Course the calves are bawling and struggling and shooting snot like hot soup all over the place, and the cows are bellowing in the pasture, it's the first time the moms and kids been separated, see. And the air is full of dust and smoke so you hardly know what you're doing, but when you get that scrotum in your hand for the first time, all of a sudden, you know! And we didn't have those Burdizzo Pincers back then, just a sharp old jackknife and you got the scrotum in one had and the jackknife in the other, and my dad showed me where to cut. You cut the bottom third of the scrotum clean through, and you get a hold of one testicle and the other comes right along. First time I did it they just fell right out and landed on my boot and my dad's yellin', "Good job, Dick, you're a cowboy now!" And I said shit, I just cut the balls out of this calf, and the blood was pumping so hard in my head, I nearly fell over with . . . with . . . with . . . joy! There's no other word for it!

BO: You're making me jealous, Mr. Rush!

DICK: Course it's not such a big deal you use them Burdizzo Pincers, see, 'cause you don't cut. There's no blood, them Burdizzo Pincers just crimp the spermatic cord, see. It's a helluva lot simpler, you just crimp that cord with those pincers and you don't de-ball the calf at all . . .

ROSE: (*Enters.*) Dick, you promised me you wouldn't drink before dinner! I won't have talk like that around this house. What if Kitty should hear you?

BO: (*Seeing Rose and panicking.*) Why, Mrs. Rush, we weren't expecting you 'til after six. Have you seen the new scarf I got for Kitty? (*He pulls drug-soaked scarf from his stash and puts it over her mouth, she collapses on Bo's shoulder.*) This should erase the last few minutes.

ROSE: (*She begins rushing from the drug-soaked scarf.*) I had a black appaloosa when we lived out in Stillwater, and I named him Jack Daniels (*snuggling against Bo's neck.*) and that was freedom to me, that's what I wanted my life to be, all the time, all the time. The neck of that horse. (*Awakening.*) Oh, excuse me. I felt a little faint there.

BO: No harm done, Mrs. Rush. Kitty was just in here looking for you. I think she really needs you right now.

ROSE: Oh the poor thing. Is she in her room? (*Bo nods. Rose exits and wanders through crawl spaces looking for Kitty, calling out for her.*)

ROSE: Kitty, Kitty, where are you dear . . .

DICK: Who was that, Mr. Nixon?

BO: Hooker on the stroll, Mr. Rush. No one we know. (*Rush laughs.*)

DICK: The gobble girls wiggle in their chambers, Mr. Nixon! A little room in Matamoros! I was just a boy. My Uncle Forrest made sausage out on his ranch. Squirt it in and tie it up and slice it up and fry it.

ROSE: Kitty. Kitty. Kitty, where are you?

DICK: We ate it all! Roast cow, roast pork, roast goat, roast dog, roast lamb, roast snake. Everything tastes good when it's roasted, Mr. Nixon!

BO: I'll take it roasted, and I'll take it toasted, Mr. Rush.

DICK: Fuck, it's goin' too fast now. Can you slow me down!

BO: How slow do you want to go, Mr. Rush?

DICK: Slow as you can go.

BO: (*Begins preparing neck shot downer. Ties Rush up, etc.*)

MO: Can you see the night now, Bobby?

BOBBY: I can see it all real clear, Mo. I'm tied up in the goat pen, and all night I'm outside while the wind whips down off the mesas and the goats keep nibbling at my feet, and I try to kick them away, and one time I forget I got the rope on my neck and I run hard at the goats to get them to leave me alone and I'm really running fast when the rope runs out and chokes me. It cuts at my neck so hard it knocks me off my feet, and I lie down in the goat pen just crying like a baby. (*Bo shoots Dick in neck with needle during the speech. Dick slumps down in chair. Bo enters crawl space on way to Edmundo's. Dick mumbles occasionally through the following scene.*)

DICK: Roast lamb, roast dog, roast pork, roast goat!

JUANA: You feel cold, bad boy, well you sleep under this!

BOBBY: And she comes running out of the house with my father's coat, the one I just tore to pieces when I come home from school, and she throws it at me. And I lie there all night in the goat pen with my father's coat over my neck and shoulders. And I could smell my father's body in that coat. It was like I was lyin' in my

	father's grave. My neck had a burn so bad from the rope I could hardly catch my breath from the pain. You can still see the scar on my neck from that burn.
MO:	I can see it, Bobby.
DICK:	I learned about women from cattle, you see.
BOBBY:	Every woman I've known likes to kiss that scar. But I never let them.
MO:	Someone did.
BOBBY:	I don't think so, Mo.
MO:	Maybe you'll remember.
BOBBY:	Oh, that's sore down there.
MO:	We'll go real easy. Is that OK?
BOBBY:	It's a little sore, but it feels really good.
ROSE:	(*Just above Juana's room. Looks down into it.*) Kitty. Kitty. I know you're around here somewhere. (*Bo reaches Edmundo's. Presses buzzer. Pushes head through membrane. Edmundo pushes Kitty up into crawl space. Kitty escapes as Bo dangles in.*)
EDMUNDO:	Quien?
BO:	It's me, Bo, buzz me in.
EDMUNDO:	Yo no conozco a ningún Buzz. . . .You got the wrong apartment!
BO:	I'm Bo, Edmundo. Wake up. Fly right! Bo! Bo! Bo!
EDMUNDO:	Oh, Bo! Whineyousayso! (*Buzzes him in. Bo's head pops though membrane. Edmundo pulls him into room.*)
ROSE:	Kitty! Kitty! Don't play games with mommy, now!
BO:	(*Getting to floor, immediately sees large, steel cauldron with 18 blue sticks protruding, looks down into it, staggers back. . . .*) Oh no, oh no. Help me, Jesus! What is that?!

EDMUNDO: That? That's my nganga. Very convincing, que no! That's where the Patrón put all them brains from those people he sacrificed on down in Matamoros! It's best if you kill them when they're alive. The more brains you have in the pot, the more hearts, the more power you have against the narcs.

BO: Oh man, you ain't doin' no palo mayombe in here! I gotta get this shit written down right now!

EDMUNDO: I'm not doin' it, Bo! This is for my video! You think I'm a dealer! I do video! There's the Patrón! (*Points to image of Patrón on TV screen. It's Edmundo in white suit.*) I'm shootin' these mockups to fill in what I don't got. I got my nganga . . . got my goat head . . . (*He pulls objects out of nganga.*)

BO: I'm gonna be sick!

EDMUNDO: Exactly. That's Art! Got my nail! Got my horseshoe! Got my brains in here!

BO: Oh no! Oh no! I can't handle this!

EDMUNDO: Calm down, man! I got 'em at a hobby shop! This guy pulled real ones right outta people's heads! (*Pointing to screen. He runs images forward.*) Here's his temple of sacrifice. Here're the cops diggin' up the headless skeletons. Then they brought in this exorcist to burn down the temple! I'm gonna get a Guggenheim when I get this thing finished! Here, hold this baby, and spit this rum on it. This is satanic initiation! (*He videos Bo spitting rum on doll. Bo seems helpless to refuse. Image of Patrón as a baby on TV screen.*) Beautiful! Perfect! One take!

BO: OK, enough with your video, your art, your Guggenheim, whatever, man. Kitty told me you had some kind of liquid she got this heavy orgasm off of . . . said you squeezed it in her ear.

EDMUNDO: Yeh, it's new stuff we got up from Colombia . . . they call it baster green . . .

DICK: We'd slaughter a steer and roast the intestines!

EDMUNDO: It's in a big green bottle . . . (*Rummaging around.*)

ROSE: (*Kitty as Winny emerges from crawl space above. Rose comes out of another crawl space.*) Oh, Kitty, there you are! Why didn't you answer me?

WINNY: I'm not Kitty, Ma. I'm Winny.

ROSE: Of course you're Winny.

WINNY: We got a show to do. (*They begin setting up on top level for Winny's show, put on costumes, etc.*)

EDMUNDO: Oh here it is, but I only got the red!

BO: Is it as good as the green?

EDMUNDO: Better! You get a totally hot trip!

BO: But you shoot it in the ear?

EDMUNDO: (*Shows enormous turkey baster.*) Same deal. Baster Red.

BO: Well, give me a hit, will you. (*Edmundo loads baster. Bo leans his head on Edmundo's lap.*)

EDMUNDO: Whatever you say. (*Squeezes liquid into Bo's ear.*)

BO: Oooooo . . . mmmnnnnn . . . ohhhh . . . mmmmm . . . they're takin' off my skin, man. Are you there, Edmundo?

EDMUNDO: Open your eyes, man!

BO: I can't open my eyes! They've blinded me. What I see now is what I'll always see!

EDMUNDO: Try opening your eyes, man! I can't sit here with you on my lap all day.

BO: I don't have any eyes, man! Can't you see what they did?

EDMUNDO: What who did?

BO: The Apaches workin' the coatroom that's who!

EDMUNDO: What coatroom! What Apaches?

BO: You know what I'm talkin' about!

EDMUNDO: Bo! Open your eyes!

BO: Top floor, bullshit! This is a white club, man! Check your skin at the door! Roll you up on the floor!

EDMUNDO: You're supposed to be keepin' people, now! You ain't supposed to be freakin' out! What if the little Kitty's gettin' off right now? (*Bobby moans. Phone rings in main room. Bo's beeper goes off, suddenly waking him out of his freak-out. General scramble like air raid drill.*)

BO: Dick is gonna wake up and find me gone. (*Twangy Western music. Edmundo changes into Jefe Edmundo Salazar costume. Puts video camera on himself. Bobby moans loudly. Sounds of a bar. Rush staggers around trying to find telephone. Phone goes on and off.*)

MO: What is it, Bobby? Something's coming up out of your chest.

BOBBY: I don't know. Another girl.

MO: Let her come back all the way, Bobby. That's the one that kissed the scar.

ROSE: (*In Matamoros club, Top Level.*) Sure do wanna welcome you boys down here to Matamoros, Mexico, land of sunshine and romance. I know you've been out there in this wonderful town, so full of surprises and exotic delights, the food, the people, the wonderful rugs and baskets, and I know some of you young men have been havin' an especially good time meetin' some of the lovely Mexican girls down here. But I know that sometimes, when all the drinkin' and ballin' is over, and you send your little brown-skinned girl home with a few of your hard-earned American dollars, and you're layin' out there in the El Rito Motel with your pickup parked outside the door, there might be a girl up there in Snyder, Texas or Henrietta, Oklahoma who crosses your mind. A girl you knew a long time ago who seems to come back to you in those empty moments when the partyin's over and you yearn for someone you really cared about, a long time ago up north across the border. Ladies and Gentleman . . . Miss Winny Rush!

WINNY: *(Sings.)*
WHEN YOU LEFT ME THE STARS
SHININ' OVER THE PRAIRIE
WERE SHARP AND AS COLD
AS THE BLADE OF A KNIFE
I WATCHED THE LIGHTS OF YOUR PICKUP
DISAPPEAR ACROSS THE RIVER
AND THE NIGHT MADE ME SHIVER
FOR THE REST OF MY LIFE

(They all sing chorus.)

I DON'T COME EASY
I'M JUST NOT THAT WAY
I'D RATHER WAIT FOR THE RIGHT ONE
THAN GIVE IT AWAY

YOU KISSED ME HARD
YOU KISSED ME LONG
YOU WHISPERED ME
A TENDER SONG

YOU KISSED MY LIPS
YOU TOUCHED MY HEART
BUT I COULDN'T GIVE YOU
MY SOFTEST PART

(*Chorus.*)

I STOOD ON THE PORCH
AND I COULDN'T STOP SHAKING
DARK CLOUDS WERE BREAKING
THE MOON IN THE SKY
THE RAIN BEAT THE DUST
IN THE ABILENE DARKNESS
YOU KNOW THAT I'M NO VIRGIN
AND I AIN'T AFRAID OF SIN

(*Chorus.*)

(*Edmundo as Jefe Salazar in Matamoros dials Dick.*)

DICK: Dick Rush speaking . . .

EDMUNDO: (*Winny slides through ceiling and sits on his lap.
           He videos himself. He's in full Federales regalia and
           speaks in a Mexican accent. He's playing with Dick.*)
           It's Jefe Edmundo Salazar in Matamoros.

DICK: Edmundo . . . I assume you're keeping your eye on my
           daughter down there.

EDMUNDO: Like a cockroach on an enchilada. Because the prees
           down there started a comboostion, you know what I
           mean?

DICK: The priest down where, Edmundo?

EDMUNDO: The prees in El Salvador, we was carryin' out your orders in the Mass when he had to say bye-bye.

DICK: The priest down where, Edmundo? I was worried she was mixed up with that human sacrifice deal!

EDMUNDO: I'm talkin' big picture. You unnerstan' what I'm trine to say? The wafers we was sellin' before all gone! Se acabaron! Se acabaron after the las huracán! Aid money came back to us from Miami then, see what I say. We had a series of pooblic relaciones disasters from Chile to Chicago. I can arez you Weeny any time.

DICK: No arrests. What we want is zero publicity.

EDMUNDO: Had to make them nuns say bye-bye también. The problema is always more . . .

DICK: We got into a lot of trouble with nuns that last time. And voodoo's hard to handle. But it's my daughter I'm worried about.

EDMUNDO: They din bury them deep enough, Dick. It won't happen again.

DICK: Is anyone in control down there?

EDMUNDO: We got those computadoras. And a lot of garlic. I can see your little girl rinow! (*Winny snuggles closer.*)

DICK: (*Bo is squeezing himself out of crawl space into Rushes, through rubber membrane.*) Texas will always be Mexico no matter who rules it!

EDMUNDO: Your girl is my girl, Dick!

DICK: Thanks again.

BO: (*Snuggling up to Rose.*) Was it her that we heard, or was there a brand on the word, Dicky-Wicky, huh, huh?

DICK: Excuse me, Mr. Nixon . . .

BO: That was some rack job, Dick: What you do, cook up a batch in the coatroom and let it slide down through the heat vents? You promised me a black room to glide in Dickie!!! Not some crib fulla boilin' oil! My balls swelled up like refritos for this little enchilada here!! What you stuffed with, honey! Somethin' sweet!

ROSE: Is he trying to tell me something, Dick?

BO: I needed a white coat to keep from goin' totally charcoal!

DICK: I didn't understand a word he said . . .

BO: No meat on her either.

ROSE: Dick, I think Mr. Nixon is teasing me!

DICK: (*Realizing that Bo is loaded.*) Oh, I don't think you've got that right, Rose. Mr. Nixon here brought you a nice scarf. (*Takes drug scarf from Bo's stash bag. She sniffs the scarf. Kitty's head pushes through membrane. Rush presses scarf against Rose's face. Rose rushes, then collapses in chair.*)

ROSE: (*Heavy, sudden deep Oklahoma accent from her childhood in Stillwater.*) I was doin' my student teaching when Dick knocked me up. Second grade. And you can't imagine how much joy it gives you watchin' little kids learn to read. I didn't know I had it in me. And I was good at it! Course in those days you come to school and your belly starts poppin' out and you ain't married, they give you your walking papers faster'n a weasel sucks down duck eggs. That hurt me bad. So I don't regret what we got. (*Fades out. Dick puts her in a chair.*)

KITTY: What are you doing to Mom, Dad?!

DICK: Your mother is feeling a little faint, Kitty. Could you get her a glass of water, please? (*Kitty exits. Bo and Rush eye each other.*)

BO: You the Lone Ranger, Dick! Foes feed and done for a coupla caps. Thas mighty, mighty greedy. I ain't a warnin' Warren or no shit like that . . . (*Dick moves toward Bo with scarf, threateningly.*)

DICK: I warned you not to slip into that language, Mr. Nixon . . .

BO: (*Frightened, knowing he's too loaded to resist.*) Don't cop my tongue, Dick. When all the other juice runs out, it's all the grub I got left in the fridge. (*Rush comes toward him with the scarf.*)

DICK: Keepers are supposed to speak English, Mr. Nixon. That's the language we speak here in Tulsa, Oklahoma . . .

BO: (*Rush forces scarf against Bo's face. Bo resists weakly.*) I can get my words back. I can seal the dog . . . (*Bo weakly sings "Nature Boy," slowly fades out.*)

DICK: (*Putting him in second chair.*) Why don't you seal the dog right over here. (*Puts scarf back in Bo's bag. Kitty enters with water.*)

ROSE: Oh, Dick, I thought I was in a used clothing store! How strange! (*Kitty offers her water. Bo stirs.*)

BO: Anybody see my coat?

DICK: Which coat is that, Mr. Nixon?

BO: It's an old herringbone tweed I bought down at Mo's. You know Mo's Coats? I thought I had it on . . .

ROSE: Do we know Mo's Coats?

DICK: We certainly do.

ROSE: Now, Kitty, when your father was still in Tulsa Christian, and we didn't have a cent . . .

KITTY: I've heard this story, Mom, about four thousand times.

ROSE: Well, your dad worked at the cattle auction for his spending money, and we had this iddy biddy apartment upstairs from Mo's Coats, and when the cold weather came your dad would save up a few dollars and we'd go downstairs and we'd say, "Mo, we want the very best coat we can get for 5 bucks." And this Mo, he always had those Indians workin' for him. And this Mo, there were a lot of rumors floating around about him, like we used to hear from those prostitutes that were right next door that Mo had been a Rabbi back out in Albuquerque, but they'd kicked him out for practicing some sort of black magic. Well, I never got the story straight. And then one time we come in down the back stairway, and sure enough he had this Indian up on this old rickety table, and Mo was massaging this Indian and talkin' to him, and this Indian was moanin' and groanin', and we couldn't understand a word. But that Mo always treated us well, and he'd find your dad the best coat he had, and he would never take a penny from us, and that was where I got pregnant with you and Winny. I'm sure Mo must be gone by now . . .

BO: (*Coming around.*) Ol' Mo's still out there.

ROSE: Oh, Richard, we've got to visit Mo. Wouldn't he be surprised after all these years?

DICK: Oh, I'm sure he would, Rose. (*Juana enters as Rush's maid.*)

JUANA: Señores, señora, señorita, dinner will be ready at seven o'clock.

DICK: I'm going to go to the club and get a little rubdown before dinner.

(*Bo exits crawl space SR, Rush in crawl space SL. Rose exits rear. Kitty goes through ceiling into Mo's. Mo helps her through. She is now Winny. She sits next to Bobby.*)

BOBBY: I can see that girl again, Mo. I seen her before.

MO: Where is she, Bobby?

BOBBY: She's in this bar where me and my brothers used to go to out in Colorado. I never seen a girl in that bar before. I was workin' for the Park Service, one summer at Mesa Verde. Cleanin' up garbage. All those people come out from everywhere to look at where those Indians lived a thousand years ago. All I wanted to do was die as soon as possible. Those kids killed my father. And they all got off. Me and my mother was livin' on cornmeal and lard. And I'd come to this bar after work and I had this garbage collector's stink on me. I didn't even care how I smelled. And there was this girl sittin' there. And it was real quiet in the bar. Cause women never came in there. Especially not an Anglo girl. And this girl couldn'a been more than 18 or so. And she sat right down on the stool next to mine.

WINNY: How 'bout I buy you a beer?

BOBBY: Sure, why not?

WINNY: Boy do you stink! I kinda like it though.

BOBBY: Hey, whatever gets you off! You got Indian fever?

WINNY: I drove down from Denver to look at the cliff dwellings.

BOBBY: Is that right? Well, that's where I work over there at Mesa Verde. Maybe you'd like me to show you around?

KITTY: What are you over there, some kind of Park Ranger?

BOBBY: Yeah, I'm a Park Ranger. Smokey the Bear.

KITTY: It must be strange to work where your ancestors lived a thousand years ago.

BOBBY: I don't think they was really my ancestors. I don't give a fuck.

KITTY: Well I wish I could give you my white blood and take your Indian blood.

BOBBY: Oh yeah, whatya wanna be an Indian for?

WINNY: I hate my blood. I hate my father's goddamn cracker blood. (*Brief pause. She quickly kisses his scar.*) Did someone try to cut your head off?

BOBBY: My mom kinda tried to hang me once . . .

KITTY: Well, if my old man had tried to hang you, you'd be hung.

MO: Follow the movie, boychick. (*Winny leaves. Enters crawl space and goes to Juana's room.*)

BOBBY: I followed her back to Denver. She could really kiss.

MO: Another mini shikinah. Middle level. We gettin' close.

ROSE: (*From second level, calling to Dick, who's disappeared from crawl spaces into darkness.*) Don't stay at the club too long now, Dick.

DICK: I'll be back in plenty of time. (*Knock on crib door. Rush with oxygen tank, aged seemingly 20 years, pushes head through membrane. Behind partly open curtain, he is pulled in by half-dressed Winny. Bo buzzes at Edmundo's.*)

WINNY: Come on in . . .

EDMUNDO: Quien?

BO: It's me, Edmundo, Bo! Buzz me in!

MO: I think there's one last thing stuck in here . . .

DICK: (*Winny pulls Rush out of membrane.*) Hey, you don't look like no Mexican girl to me.

EDMUNDO: There's no Buzz here, man.

BO: Why do I have to go through this every time? (*He buzzes again.*)

WINNY: Don't you like what you see?

DICK: Well, you're not too bad lookin'.

WINNY: What brings you to Matamoros?

DICK: A little fun. (*They embrace.*)

EDMUNDO: I tol' you there's no Buzz in here!

BO: It's Bo! Bo! Bo, Edmundo!

EDMUNDO: Oh, Bo, whineyousayso! (*He buzzes him in. Bo's head pops through membrane. Edmundo pulls him out slowly.*)

WINNY: People like the service at Mo's.

DICK: Hard to find a place'll do a guy with a tank.

WINNY: We'll take it nice and slow. Are you holdin'?

DICK: (*Pulling red and blue bottles from his bag.*) Got the red and I got the blue, right over the counter.

WINNY: Should we have a little squeeze before we get friendly?

DICK: You bet. (*Winny fills the basters while Rush undresses.*)

BO: (*Finally reaching the floor of Edmundo's room.*) Get me down off that red shit, man!

EDMUNDO: You got your keepers kit.

BO: I don't even know what the red shit is, how'm I supposed to counter it?

EDMUNDO: OK. OK. Just do one more thing for this video. Put on this Doctor's stuff for a still. (*Bo puts on green doctor's smock, stethoscope, head mirror, etc. Edmundo videos him. Bo leaves medical stuff on.*) This doc was gonna do plastic surgery on Patrón when he was on the run from the Federales. Maybe we should try some of the blue stuff. That might cool you down.

BO: You got baster blue too?

EDMUNDO: Now what the fuck did I do with it?

MO: (*Having worked up to Bobby's forehead.*) There seems to be something up here, Bobby. Right under your third eye. You got a big dent in your forehead . . .

BO: It's a good thing you're not a doctor, Edmundo . . .

EDMUNDO: Hey, you're the Doctor!

MO: I think this is where the movie is, boychick . . .

EDMUNDO: Me a doctor, that's good. You're a funny man.

WINNY: Just the fucking sight of this shit makes me high . . .

MO: Can you see anything yet?

BO: Dr. Bo Nixon, M.D.!

DICK: Watch out you don't spill it now!

BOBBY: It's a place I got hurt workin' out in a snowstorm, Mo. (*Snow starts to fall on cow in central room.*)

MO: Where is that, boychick?

BOBBY: Winter of 1987. There was this five-day blizzard at 10 below and the cattle started to freeze in the fields. Those steers would die and hump up against the fences in a pile. Big Black Angus bulls all covered with snow up next to this rancher's fence . . .

MO: This is the movie, boychick.

BOBBY: There's my brother, Ray, there's Bunkie, we all got this job, see! Cause them dead cattle would freeze and roll over by the fences and make a pile and the live steers'd

The Rushes of Tulsa   41

walk on over them, live bulls go right over dead bulls right over the fences, and then them live bulls'd get out there and just wander straight down the highway, and that snow was comin' down so hard you couldn't see 'em. And some of them bulls would just freeze solid standin' straight up on all four legs. There's a big bull (*Light up on bull.*) that me and Bunkie are hitchin' up to right now. We got this tractor from a rancher, cause this bull is frozen solid see, right in the middle of the highway. That's how we got this job. Cause one of them ranchers run into a frozen bull comin' home at night from a bender in Durango. He's in this big Cherokee doin' about 60 miles an hour on that road. Now them bulls weigh a thousand pounds, so this rancher in his Cherokee hit half a ton of frozen bull at 60 miles an hour, and all they found was the pieces. The bull was still in one piece, but that guy and his Cherokee was all over Colorado. So we got this job, see, pullin' them bulls off the road. But this one here don't want to move, Mo!

MO: The frozen bull don't want to move, that's bad.

BOBBY: We got the ropes all around this bull, and it's snowin' like a sumbitch! (*Snow falls harder in central room.*)

EDMUNDO: Here's the red. Now what did I do with the blue . . .

BOBBY: Bunky throttles up that tractor and me and Ray are pushin' like a sumbitch, here we go! (*Grunts as if pushing.*) Aww, shit!

MO: Whatsamatta?

BOBBY: The bull's so frozen to the road the tractor can't move him.

MO: So whatya do now?

BOBBY: We're gettin' out axes from the ditch, Mo!

MO: You gonna chop up a frozen cow?

BOBBY: Bunky yells, we're gonna chop that bull's legs right off at the hoof. I'm just a kid, now, Mo! And I'm liftin' my axe as high as I can, and I swing that sucker as hard as I can and Wannnggggg! The axe just snaps back up at me and hits me right in the forehead!

BO: I can't believe you lose your own dope!

BOBBY: Right here, Mo, where I got this dent.

MO: A dent in the head!

BOBBY: I'm out cold now on the road to Durango. I can hear Bunky yellin' to me. But I just can't move. Bunky's yellin', "Gettup, buddy, you gonna freeze." But his voice is comin' from way up in the sky. And I'm tryin' to talk, but my lips won't move . . .

MO: What are you tryin' to say, Bobby!

BOBBY: I can't move, motherfucker! You got me pinned down here under your frozen fuckin' bull!

WINNY: I'll get us a couple of beers.

MO: What's happening now, Bobby?

DICK: This red shit gives me the dry mouths.

BOBBY: They're movin' me, Mo. I'm in a motel room now. I never been in a motel before. And my head hurts really bad. But all I can hear is this woman's voice in the room next door.

MO: The walls are always thin . . .

BOBBY: . . . but I can't hear what she's sayin' . . .

MO: (*Rubbing Bobby's head. Puzzled.*) Hnnnnnnn. Strange.

DICK: Always work the same motel?

WINNY: Started at the Alamo. But I've been at the El Rito for quite a while.

MO: Where is this motel, Bobby?

BOBBY:	El Rito Motel. U.S. 160.
MO:	Are you sure it's not in Mexico, Bobby? It feels like Mexico to me.
BOBBY:	I been in New Mexico. And I been in Texas. And Oklahoma, which is where we are now. . . . (*Bobby is suddenly frightened.*) This is Oklahoma, ain't it, Mo!
MO:	Of course it's Oklahoma! Don't worry about it. Sometimes you feel like you're in two places at once. Just rest in the bed in that motel.
BOBBY:	I'm in the motel, Mo.
MO:	Just rest on the bed 'til your head feels better.
BOBBY:	I'm resting, Mo.
DICK:	Doin' OK?
WINNY:	I just want to get loaded.
DICK:	Well, what'll it be, the blue or the red?
WINNY:	Let's start with the blue. (*She puts her head on his lap, etc.*)
EDMUNDO:	Hey! I knew it had to be around here somewhere!
WINNY:	Mnnnnnn. Makes me really cool. Like a rush of the ocean over my back. Want me to do you now?
DICK:	(*Lies on her lap.*) Gimmee a good squeeze.
WINNY:	Pleasant dreams.
BO:	Squirt that shit in my ear, Edmundo. It'll balance off that other rush . . .
DICK:	Feels like I got a little icy brook runnin' through the top of my head and right out my asshole . . .
WINNY:	Mind hittin' me with a shot of the red?
DICK:	Hey, you can't do both at once, it'll kill you!
WINNY:	I been doin' the two together for years. Come on, be a sport. (*He gives her a red hit. Edmundo and Rush squeeze at the same moment. Winny and Bo moan. Winny and Rush get into bed.*)

MO:	You should see the throne of heaven now, Bobby.
BOBBY:	Can't see no throne, Mo.
MO:	Well, what do you see?
BOBBY:	I can see a bed.
MO:	A bed? God's got to sleep somewhere. But he shouldn't be sleepin' now!
BOBBY:	Is that God I'm seeing? That can't be God, Mo!
MO:	Why not, Bobby?
BOBBY:	Cause he's in bed with this white girl, Mo. And some dopers are gettin' loaded in the room next door. I never knew God knocked off pussy before!
MO:	You mean the guy you see is gettin' laid?
BOBBY:	He's puttin' it to this white girl, Mo.
WINNY:	Now take it slow. No need to rush.
DICK:	Can't go much slower.
MO:	Maybe we're in the wrong motel! Do you recognize the girl?
BOBBY:	It's hard to tell, Mo. The dude's on top of her . . .
MO:	See if you can get a look at her face . . .
BO:	I feel like half of me had a stroke. How about doin' the other side . . .
WINNY:	What's your rush? Lemme slow you down . . . (*She gets on top.*)
EDMUNDO:	Well, turn your head over then . . .
BOBBY:	I can see her now! She's the girl come in with Edmundo.
MO:	Edmundo? The one goin' with Kitty Rush?
BOBBY:	Yeah, that one.
MO:	That was Dick Rush's girl . . . the twin . . . How'd I screw this up? I never got off the track with you before . . .

BOBBY: Maybe it's my fault, Mo . . . maybe I was goin' too fast . . .

MO: You weren't going too fast, Bobby. We just run into some stuff that is actually happening, that's all. Your past has stumbled into someone else's present. That's the last thing I want: to get you stuck in someone else's life. There's no cure for that pain. I'm gonna work down to the middle and start over, OK?

BOBBY: Anywhere you wanna take me. (*Winny and Bobby sigh together. Winny is almost still on top of Rush.*)

DICK: Hey! You're not fallin' asleep on me, are you?

WINNY: (*Very softly.*) Oh, I'm not fallin' asleep.

DICK: Little girl got to give me some moves.

WINNY: I feel so warm and safe here.

DICK: Oh, don't get weird on me, baby!

WINNY: . . . Kitty . . . Kitty . . . Kitty . . . (*She dies.*)

DICK: Hey, don't play games now . . . fuckin' drugs (*He shakes her.*). Come on! Wake up! (*She remains limp as a rag doll. Shakes her harder. Realizes she's dead.*) Jesus, Jesus God, you're not breathin'! (*Bolts from bed. Slaps clothes on. Grabs money from table. Exits.*)

EDMUNDO: How's it goin', Bo? Are you alive down there?

BO: I'm doin' good, my man. That shit puts you in a really low gear. Like bein' in a world of ice . . .

MO: You should be back in that motel now, Bobby . . . Just gettin' warm after they brought you in from the cold . . .

BOBBY: Bunky just put another blanket on me, Mo.

MO: Let's just stay there for a while . . . 'til we get good and warm.

EDMUNDO: You better get back.

BO: *(Staggering up, in slow motion, barely able to move, frozen like a robot, still in medical smock, stethoscope, etc.)* Thanks, Edmundo. I'm so cool I can barely move. *(Juana comes in through "crawl space" and sees Winny sprawled in bed. Bo attempts to get in "crawl space" and slides out.)*

EDMUNDO: Let me help you, Bo.

BO: That blue shit really slows you down . . . *(Edmundo manages to squeeze him into crawl space.)*

JUANA: *(Waits at door for a moment, then enters.)* Ah, estas durmiendo, chica . . . *(She comes closer to adjust the sheet.)*

MO: You good and warm now, Bobby?

BOBBY: I'm good and warm now, Mo.

JUANA: Déjeme hacerle mas cómmoda . . . *(She adjusts sheet. Notices that something is wrong. Sees drug basters. Picks them up one at a time. Suddenly realizes what has happened.)* Ay comó siento el olor de la muerte!
Con hongos con liquidos con fuego con sangre!
Enredada en la ropa de la miseria inevitable!
Sucurso multifacial mutilacion sin fin!
El cuerpo duerma mas que las rocas!
Y la petrificacion del odio y las hormigas
Matan el amor debajo de la gran piedra!
Y todos los paranoias de las culebras del mundo
Sudan mierda en la coca y cortan los drogadictos!
Y matan los gringos y matan los niñas!
Y crespán en la madrugada sobre las cascada de las cabezas!
Y una de los dos es muerta y una de los otros es perdida!
Donde venden el sexo y vivimos sin poder!

(*She dials the phone. The phone rings in Edmundo's office.*)

EDMUNDO: Mandé?

JUANA: Hay una muchacha muerta, señor.

EDMUNDO: Con quien estoy hablando?

JUANA: Soy una criada, en una casa de la zona.

EDMUNDO: Cual casa?

JUANA: El Rito Motel, señor . . . es una de las muchachas de la casa que se murio . . .

EDMUNDO: Comó se llama?

JUANA: Se llama Weeny Roosh, señor.

EDMUNDO: Weeny Roosh!

JUANA: Si señor.

EDMUNDO: No toca a nada. Ya vengo. Weeny!

MO: How's it feel, Bobby?

BOBBY: I can see a woman. It's like I'm standin' right next to her.

MO: You can't see yourself, Bobby?

BOBBY: I'm standin' right next to this woman, Mo. And my mother's standin' beside me.

MO: Is she sleepin' now?

BOBBY: I don't think she's sleepin', Mo . . . She isn't breathin'.

MO: Can you sit up?

BOBBY: (*Looking around.*) This is the store. These are the coats.

MO: You see I have another store sometimes . . .

BOBBY: Another store?

MO: Down south of the border. Everything's the same.

BOBBY: But this one is real, Mo? We're in the same place?

MO: We're in the same place, but it's different, too.

BOBBY: Are you talkin' about your whorehouse, Mo?

MO: Well, it's my whorehouse, Bobby. But it's in Mexico (*They enter Winny's room by crawl space.*)

BOBBY: Mexico? (*Seeing Winny.*) This is the place I was seein' in my movie, Mo.

MO: (*Bending over Winny.*) She's dead. Listen, Bobby. The cops are gonna be here real soon. Just let me do the talkin'.

BOBBY: Whatever you say, Mo. (*Edmundo as Federale and Juana enter through membrane.*)

EDMUNDO: (*Looks at Winny. Touches her.*) Weeny! Mi Weeny! (*Starts to lose it. Catches himself.*) Y quiénes son estos hombres? (*He whispers with Juana. Dick, Edmundo, Juana, Bobby, Mo, are all crowded into crib.*)

EDMUNDO: (*Looking at them in turn.*) Un indio. Un vendedor de chalecos usados. Una criada en una casa de la zona. Y una gringa bellisima, recién muerta. Ayudenme. (*They lift the dead body from the bed and put it into a coffin on rollers, then close the lid. They roll the coffin into the central room.*) Muy bien . . . dejala aqui . . . Voy llamar a los parientes. Pueden salir ahora. (*They exit through door at rear of room. Juana changes into the Rush maid costume putting on apron and cap, etc. She enters again bringing in the dinner settings and places them on coffin as dinner table. Mo takes Bobby back to clothing store down crawl space, parts coats, puts him back on table.*)

BOBBY: Were we in Mexico, Mo?

MO: God gave me that set-up down there you see, in case they need me . . .

BOBBY: In case they need you where, Mo?

MO: South of the border. This is the way God wants it. Same set-up everywhere. Pawn shop downstairs, whorehouse upstairs. Cheap apartment for rent next door.

BOBBY: That dead girl was the girl who kissed my scar, Mo. I'm fucked up!

BO: (*Finally sliding from "crawl space" into central room.*) Man, that shit coats you down so slow you feel like a frozen snake. I don't know if my jaw can move enough to chew at all. (*Enter Dick and Rose, dressed for dinner. Bo sits heavily, barely able to hold his head up.*)

ROSE: Now when Winny calls, Dick, I want you to tell her to come back home.

DICK: (*Sitting down and slapping the coffin hard as he speaks.*) Winny is already back, Rose. Can't do without her!

BO: I feel like something's froze right under my nose . . . or maybe my nose is froze . . .

DICK: She's made her own bed, Rose. And now she's got to lay in it.

ROSE: I just want to have my family together again!

BO: (*Slowly pulling head up from table.*) That's the first thing they angle you in on at the Keeper Academy. No dope. No motive. (*Slumps down again.*)

DICK: Where the hell is the food!

ROSE: Juana won't serve it 'til Kitty is here. (*Kitty enters naked to the waist with a big bloodstain down her face and chest. Bobby moans.*)

MO: Easy, Bobby, easy.

BOBBY: It's the dead girl, Mo.

MO: They don't see what you see, Bobby.

ROSE: You look wonderful, Kitty. Staying away from those drugs has done you a world of good.

KITTY: If I don't get some food in me I'm gonna croak! (*Juana carries in a stack of bloody meat. Bobby moans loudly.*)

DICK: (*Picking up a large bloody steak on a fork.*) Here's a nice piece of meat and it's done to a turn! (*Bobby moans.*)

BOBBY: They're eatin' raw meat, Mo.

BO: Wooo, this fork is so cold, I can barely hold it in my hand. I better put my mittens on. But maybe it's really my hand that's cold. (*Touches his hand to his face. It freezes to his cheek. He tries the other but it freezes too.*) But my face is cold too. I wish I could get this hot meat in me to warm me up. (*Slumps down again. Gets up. Manages to put face to meat. Tries to get large piece of meat into his mouth. Fails. Falls to table after it, etc.*) I can't seem to get my jaws to move . . .

ROSE: Oh this meat is delicious, Juana. Is this a Mexican dish? (*Juana is pouring Valvoline into fancy wine glasses. All drink with great pleasure.*)

JUANA: Yes, that dish comes from my own home town.

ROSE: Oh it has just a very special flavor. (*She starts to slump down.*) It reminds me of something we used to eat out in Stillwater.

DICK: (*He starts to slump down.*) I wonder why it is that blood makes me feel so calm . . .

BO: (*Barely getting head off table.*) Meat is the oldest drug . . . there's a whole section . . . (*slumps down again.*)

ROSE: (*Lifting her head. Looking at Kitty.*) It's so good to have you back with us, Winny.

KITTY:	I'm not Winny, mom. I'm Kitty.
ROSE:	Now stop it, Winny. You can't fool me! I know the difference between you two just by your voices. (*Slumping down.*) Isn't it good to have Winny back with us, Dick?
DICK:	(*Barely lifting head.*) I always liked the taste of Winny, Rose.
ROSE:	(*Lifting head.*) What are you saying, Dick? You tasted our twins? (*Slumping down.*)
JUANA:	Your sister is dead, Kitty.
KITTY:	I knew it would happen today.
BOBBY:	Do we have to go to Mexico again, Mo?
MO:	It's on the way to the throne of heaven.
KITTY:	I'll have to go with Bo.
BO:	(*Lifting head from table.*) I gotta get this written down. (*Slumps down. Light on Edmundo dialing phone.*)
KITTY:	The phone is going to ring, now. (*Phone rings, very softly.*)
JUANA:	(*Picks up phone.*) Si, si, si, si, si sisi.

END OF ACT ONE

ACT TWO

(Juana's room, SL, whorehouse crib in Matamoros. All characters are present, crowded into tiny space. Table is coffin.)

EDMUNDO: *(As Jefe Salazar in Federales uniform.)* You are . . . Miss Catherine Roosh? You have a striking resemblance . . . I can barely keep from . . .

KITTY: She was my twin sister.

EDMUNDO: That's very disturbing . . .

KITTY: Well, excuse me . . .

EDMUNDO: Forgive me if I am not under . . . control. The case we just concluded, thirteen men sacrificed alive by the Patrón Adolofo de Jesus Hernandez in the ritual of Palo Mayombe, one of them a twelve-year-old boy in a ragged shirt of the Miami Dolphins, digging up the skeletons, exorcising the shed where this unspeakable desecration has taken place, this has shaken me. To you the Federales are a kind of joke. But you don't see what we see every day. There are many things that happen in the work of the police . . . because of the many things that are breaking down . . . things falling apart and becoming cruel . . . in the breaking of the rules . . . on both sides the same . . . in my country and in yours . . . we are like sisters, too, you see, on both sides of the border . . . we are the great rivals in destruction . . . nobody kills as many people as we do . . . that's a kind of distinction . . . I've become obsessed with it . . . the level of destruction . . . and these two sister countries . . . so much the same, and yet so different. (*Lifting the lid of the coffin and looking in. Sincerely.*) Weeny! (*Pause.*) Like you and your sister. Exactly the same, except she, the one in here, is dead. Weeny! And the one out here . . . you . . . are alive. How much difference does death make between two beings who are otherwise exactly the same? (*Reaches into coffin.*) The bones of your cheek are exactly the same . . . and if I open the eyes of the deceased in here, so recently shut for good . . . I see that you have the very same green eyes, a very deep green, almost like the leaf of the algodon in spring . . . the eyes, unlike the skin, do not change immediately after death . . . very beautiful eyes . . . your sister had them and now you have the same . . . so it is almost as if she hadn't died, however it was that she died, because the same eyes, if I did not know she was dead, are now looking at me, because looking into your eyes, they are the eyes of Weeny Roosh, eyes which (*Looking back and forth between the corpse and Kitty.*) by the way, I got to know very well over the years . . . Weeny! I am obsessed with these things, you see . . . the impossible paradoxes that are never resolved . . . as in a crime where there is no criminal . . . but victims are everywhere. I think this is why there is so much interest in the crimes of the criminal . . . because it takes the mind from the question of the crime without criminals . . . who are all these other people being killed by? There is no clear answer . . . so in the case of your sister here . . . it was perhaps auto-destruction, but what led her to this act of auto-destruction? (*He continues to look back and forth between the two.*) . . . we cannot say . . . and she cannot tell us now . . . Weeny! (*He continues to look into the coffin from time to time. Begins to close coffin lid, leaves it open. Looks into coffin.*) Your sister was very provocative, very beautiful, but also very disturbing, as you, as well, are beautiful, provocative and disturbing. Any object, in any circumstance, could be treated with love or with cruelty, or, if living, could treat themselves with love or cruelty . . . so . . . we have come to this inquest thinking that something will end here in Matamoros, Mexico . . . and here is the cast of characters: a dead twin, Winifred Roosh, the last person to see her alive, a gringo from Tulsa, Oklahoma . . . A customer who had already paid for sex and found himself embracing death. Is that not so, señor?

DICK: I swear I didn't kill her, chief.

EDMUNDO: I believe you, señor. Though the fact that you are from Tulsa, Oklahoma and bear a certain strange resemblance to the deceased is very disturbing and very provocative. And this is the maid of the establishment who found the body. And this man has the store next door . . .

BO: (*Still in his medical gloves, stethoscope, mirror on forehead.*) What the fuck are you doing down here, Mo . . .

MO: Quiet, I'm begging you, Bo.

BO: There's some weird shit happenin' here.

EDMUNDO: (*Looking at Rose.*) And this woman was your sister's employer. (*Looking at Bo.*) And this man . . . he is a member of your family?

KITTY: He's my . . . bodyguard . . .

BO: Bo Nixon, Chief.

EDMUNDO: You are a Doctor. You'll be guarding these two bodies. (*Lifting the lid of the coffin.*) Weeny! Excuse me. This dead one in here, and this living one out here . . . (*To Kitty.*) But I would like you to come with me and make an official identification.

KITTY: Oh, Winny . . . Winny . . . she's so pale . . .

EDMUNDO: (*To Bo.*) Have a look, Dr. Nixon. Very disturbing and . . . at the same time . . . very, very beautiful . . .

KITTY: Do you have any idea how this happened?

EDMUNDO: Death, what is it that causes death? (*Picking up the turkey baster syringes.*) The red and the blue together are always fatal . . .

KITTY: Oh my God, Edmundo!

EDMUNDO: How did you know my name?

KITTY: I was thinking of . . . of someone else . . .

EDMUNDO: (*Bending over coffin again.*) And yet the resemblance is very provocative . . . Weeny!

KITTY: (*To Dick.*) Did you give her the drugs?

DICK: I was just after a little lovin'.

ROSE: Jefe, we knew she was using drugs for a long time. You know us, we're like family . . .

KITTY: I don't have any family now. She was it.

ROSE: Oh, I feel you're my little girl just like she was.

EDMUNDO: I think we can close the coffin now . . . although the provocation of the two of you here together is hard to . . . to . . . bring to . . . an end . . .

KITTY: Will you stay here with the body, Bo?

BO:	I'm not supposed to let you out of my sight . . .
EDMUNDO:	I assure you that Miss Roosh will be safe with me . . .
BO:	(*To Kitty. Looking at Mo.*) There's something fishy about this whole set-up . . .
MO:	(*Whispering.*) Let her go, Bo, I'm in control.

(*They begin to move simultaneously, dance-like gestures.*)

JUANA:	(*Putting her arm around Bobby, forcibly pulling him with her.*) Ven conmigo, hijo! Vamos a la casa . . .
BOBBY:	What's she saying to me, Mo? Are we in the rub or out of it?
MO:	It's your mother, Bobby. Don't you recognize her?
JUANA:	Ven . . . Ven . . .
BOBBY:	My mother? What the fuck are you talkin' about, Mo? My mother wasn't no Mexican! She was a Ute!
MO:	She'll be a Ute by the time you get home . . . (*Bobby and Juana circulate through all the crawl spaces.*)
ROSE:	(*To Dick.*) I'm very sorry your visit to my place has caused you so much trouble.
DICK:	You girls have always treated me good, Miss Rose. (*Rose comes close to him.*)
BOBBY:	I don't want to go home now, maw . . .
JUANA:	You come home with me . . . you think you can just tear up your dad's coat like that and nothing's gonna happen!
BOBBY:	That was a long time ago!
MO:	It's OK, Bobby. I'll find you later.
ROSE:	Maybe I can repay you personally for your patience.
DICK:	Why that would be right kind of you . . .

BOBBY: I'm coming . . . don't hurt me! (*The three couples turn out of the room leaving Mo and Bo alone. Edmundo and Kitty enter tube for room SR, disappear in darkness so Kitty can enter coffin from back. Juana and Bobby leave for room SL. Rose and Dick climb ladder to upper level.*)

BO: Are you riding that damn magic carpet of yours again!

MO: I tried to help you when you worked for me.

BO: I'm a doctor now, Mo.

MO: If you don't see the empty throne, nothing matters.

BO: Yeah, well I never seen no empty throne with you!

MO: That's because you left the path to nothing too soon.

BO: Nothing, my ass! You wanted to make me some bullshit black Rabbi! (*Other characters move to rooms or levels during this exchange. Stand In moves with Edmundo.*)

MO: The last place does not exist, but we can't know that 'til we get there. And even the letters that form my words are just little formless points of eternal nothing. Because nothing stays in one place for more than an immeasurable moment. All mystery, no God! You'll see eventually.

BO: Yeah, well what about the body in this coffin, Mo. When someone croaks that's the last move they make. (*Coffin lid behind him begins to lift slowly. Dick and Rose appear on upper level and dance in very dim light to a soft 1940's version of "Where or When." They are in their 20's. Winny twists and turns as she rises, as if she's being born. Edmundo and Stand In move slowly toward "police station."*)

MO: Is that so, Bo? Well look behind you . . .

BO: Ahhhh! Kitty! Kitty! Shit for a second . . .

WINNY: I'm not Kitty, Bo. I'm Winny!

BO: Winny, bullshit! How'd you get in that box, Kitty?

WINNY: I'm not Kitty! (*She climbs down from coffin. Bo rushes to coffin. Looks in.*)

BO: It's Winny, Mo!

MO: I know it's Winny, Bo.

BO: But she was dead just a minute ago, Mo. I saw her dead!

MO: I told you nothing ever dies, and I told you nothing is born, but did you believe me?

BO: This is one of your Rabbi tricks! She ain't real! (*He touches her, steps back horrified. Winny pulls him back. She gently takes his hand to her face. She enters "crawl space" for Edmundo's, catches up with Edmundo as Stand In disappears in shadows.*)

JUANA: (*From crawl space.*) Your dad couldn't find no work. We was livin' on handouts. Don't you understand?

BOBBY: I do now, mom. I was scared.

JUANA: And those white boys took advantage of him. They knocked him cold and pulled his clothes off and had sex with him, all four of them, and then they cut his head off. That's the memory I have to live with of the man who was your dad. The man who loved you.

EDMUNDO: (*Getting Kitty out of membrane.*) I never thought your father would let you out again . . .

KITTY: What you know about my father? (*Edmundo ignores her.*)

EDMUNDO: Just come out real slow so you don't hurt yourself . . .

JUANA: (*Lifting tattered coat in air from crawl space.*) Look at his coat.

BOBBY: I'm sorry, Maw. I didn't mean to!

KITTY: (*Getting to her feet somewhat dazed.*) Just give me that release to sign, and I'll go . . .

EDMUNDO: I got a hit of green all ready.

KITTY: (*Seeing the bottle of green.*) I wouldn't mind a hit of green though . . .

EDMUNDO: Now what the fuck did I do with my baster . . .

KITTY: This place is pretty messy for a police station . . .

MO: I'm gonna try to find Bobby, Bo. You better find Kitty and let her know that Winny's on the loose. We got a whole different story now.

BO: It's always a different story with you, Mo! (*They enter crawl spaces SL and SR. Edmundo pulls Kitty onto his lap.*)

KITTY: I don't want to get so fucked up I can't sign the release . . .

EDMUNDO: You'll get plenty of release . . . you know you're acting really strange today . . . like you don't know where you are . . .

KITTY: I am a little disoriented . . .

EDMUNDO: This will clear your head . . . (*He gives her a squeeze of green.*)

KITTY: This is really weird, gettin' off with a cop. (*She groans as the green hits. He has positioned her in front of the video screen. He snaps the screen on and Palo Mayombe video begins, tinted with green. Leaves and vines come down slowly from the top of room, flowers. Mo and Bo move very slowly in crawl spaces.*)

EDMUNDO: Easy does it, OK, we gotcha now . . . let's do the poem. I got the tape recorder all ready . . .

KITTY: Poem? Tape recorder? Who are you!

EDMUNDO: Just lock on the screen and rap, baby! (*Video starts. He rolls her up next to it.*)

KITTY: Wo . . . Wooooo! That green is strong! (*Finally overcoming confusion and locking on screen.*) It's the thunder that flutters in the green that is my mother!

EDMUNDO: (*Whispers.*) Beautiful. You can say that again!

KITTY: It's the thunder that flutters in the green that is my mother. I know it from the needles I've held in my hand . . .

EDMUNDO: (*Deep whisper.*) Rush, baby, rush!

KITTY: Where the firelight of the father keeps flashing into blackness . . .

EDMUNDO: (*Whisper.*) Firelight! Father! Blackness!

KITTY: And she accepted the current while pretending to be mad . . .

EDMUNDO: P'alante!

KITTY: Growing weaker than an emerald while storing up my dream . . .

EDMUNDO: (*Whispers.*) Weaker emerald dream . . . that's beautiful . . . (*Video continues to run.*)

KITTY: And I can tell that I am bark from the beetles that pierce me
And I can tell from my smell that my sap is running clear
I know there are pools where my bones are at the bottom (*Whispers.*)
I know that my leaves have nothing to fear

EDMUNDO: What! What! I didn't hear you!

KITTY: And I know that my leaves have nothing to fear

EDMUNDO: That's very far out! You're unbelievable!

KITTY: Nothing will grow without water
Our days grow cool in a circle of fern fingers

The shadows of braids and mazes drink the sun
Let the rain come down my lover
Turn the soil around my slender green members
But don't disturb the worms around my waist!
And let loose your green flakes of fish scale and
　　murmur
Your little steamy flagon of sweat
I will meet you with all that my helix can render
No end to my end then or image of my demise

(*Kitty slumps over in Edmundo's lap as if she has fainted.*)

EDMUNDO: Hey, that was the most amazing one so far. Are you OK?

KITTY: I think I'm OK. Where am I anyway?

EDMUNDO: Where do you think you are?

KITTY: I thought I was in Mexico for a while . . .

EDMUNDO: Mexico?

KITTY: I thought I was in Tulsa and Winny died . . . Jesus . . .

EDMUNDO: Tulsa? What would we be doin' in Tulsa?

KITTY: Well, I was born there, you know.

EDMUNDO: I know you was born there, but . . . Look, come over here. (*Takes her to edge of level.*) What do you see out there?

KITTY: A bunch of winos . . .

EDMUNDO: So where are we?

KITTY: Denver. Colfax and Logan.

EDMUNDO: Good girl! Now you're gonna lie down for a while. (*Putting her down on a couch, light fades on Edmundo's room. He plays tape softly. Bobby and Juana finally reach her room.*)

JUANA: (*Putting the rope on Bobby's neck.*) So go ahead. Explain.

KITTY: (*Rising up suddenly off Edmundo's lap. She puts scarf over her head, nun-like.*) You're the son of that drunk that died last month, aren't you?

EDMUNDO: Take it easy, just rest . . .

BOBBY: (*Sadly.*) My dad died. Yuh. That's right.

KITTY: And do you know why he died?

EDMUNDO: Jesus, this must be the after-poem . . . I better record this too . . .

KITTY: He died because he lied to you. He told you stories about sisters fornicating with brothers to make the earth. God heard his lies, and he punished him for his sins. There's only one God, and he had only one son, Our Lord Jesus Christ, son of the Virgin Mary.

BOBBY: He told us some stories, that's all . . .

EDMUNDO: The shit just comes rushing out of her . . .

KITTY: Do you want your mother to die?

BOBBY: Nooo! Please! Don't hurt her!

KITTY: If you don't get every trace, every smell of your father out of your house. As long as there's one bit of him left, you'll remember the lies he told, and Jesus will strike your mother dead and turn her skin to fire for a million years! Is there anything of your dad that's left in your house?

BOBBY: Just an old coat my mom was savin' for me!

KITTY: That coat is gonna drag your mother down to Hell! That coat is cursed. It smells of the lies your dad told you! You better tear that coat up, or your mother will die before tomorrow night! (*She sinks back down.*)

BOBBY: So I tore the coat up and prayed to Jesus to help me!

JUANA: This coat was all I had left of him. Well, you act like a goat; you can live like a goat! (*Chases him with rope. She catches Bobby. They struggle. She pulls noose tight around his neck.*)

BOBBY: I can't breathe, Ma!

JUANA: You believe those nuns before you believe your own dad! You're not an Indian, you're nothing! (*Dragging him off. Intense sound of goats.*)

BOBBY: Don't leave me out here all night, I'll freeze!

JUANA: Where am I gonna get another coat like that!

MO: (*Pushing his head and arms through membrane.*) Here! Wait! (*They freeze. Goats are silent.*) This is your dad's coat, Bobby. Give it to your mom.

JUANA: Who are you? How did you get in here?

BOBBY: (*Taking coat from Mo. Helping him in.*) It's Mo, Ma. The guy I work for.

JUANA: Work! What the hell are you talking about? (*Rushing at Mo, yanking Bobby away from him.*) You get the Hell out of here, you devil!

MO: Wait! Wait! This is your husband's coat. (*Bobby shoves the coat at her.*)

JUANA: (*Looking at the coat, shocked.*) Who are you? How'd you get in here?

BOBBY: It's Mo, Ma. The guy I work for.

MO: Smell the coat! It's your husband's coat!

JUANA: (*She smells the coat.*) It's your dad's coat, Bobby. How can that be?

MO: This is the real coat. Believe me. If there's one thing I know, it's coats.

BOBBY: I'm workin' for him now, Ma. His name is Mo.

JUANA: You're workin' for him? What kinda work?

BOBBY:	He's got a pawnshop out on Colfax. Mostly old clothes.
JUANA:	Colfax's up in Denver. You're lyin'.
BOBBY:	We're in Denver now, Ma. Don't you remember? I work in a pawnshop.
JUANA:	You work in a pawnshop?
BOBBY:	Look out this window, Ma. What do you see?
JUANA:	Oh my goodness, there's a lot of traffic goin' by out there. But it don't look like Albuquerque . . . or Gallup . . .
BOBBY:	It's Denver, Ma. We got this little house here on Lincoln and Fourth.
JUANA:	This is Denver . . . well I'll be darned . . . I always wanted to live in Denver. We got a lot of relatives up here . . .
BOBBY:	I told you about Mo, Ma. He helped me stop drinkin' . . .
JUANA:	I musta got confused . . . I'm getting old . . . this is your boss? Is he a Mexican?
BOBBY:	He's a Jew, Ma. But he don't talk to his people. You got somethin' on the stove?
JUANA:	(*To Mo.*) Are you hungry?
BOBBY:	You bet I'm hungry. I've had a long day.
JUANA:	(*She looks at coat for a minute.*) Would you like to eat with us, Mr. Mo? It's just goat stew . . .
MO:	Stew would be fine . . .
JUANA:	Well you two sit down. I'll get you some iced tea.
BO:	(*Looking around in crawl space.*) Shit, this entry looks just like Edmundo's . . . (*He buzzes.*) It's me, chief, Bo . . . buzz me in!

EDMUNDO: Yo no conozco a ningún Buzz . . . you got the wrong apartment!

BO: It's Bo! Bo! Buzz me in!

EDMUNDO: Listen, hombre, there's no Buzz here. You got the wrong number!

BO: I'm Bo, Edmundo, Dr. Bo Nixon!

EDMUNDO: Oh, Dr. Nixon, whineyousayso! (*Buzzes him in. Bo's head pops through membrane.*)

BO: (*Hanging out of membrane, looking around.*) This is definitely not a police station! There are enough drugs in here to stock a pharmacy!

EDMUNDO: Is everybody crazy today? Nobody knows where they are!

KITTY: Oh, he's always like that, Edmundo . . . He just acts weird so you'll offer to get him off . . .

EDMUNDO: Well, he ain't gettin' no more red offa me . . . he went fuckin' crazy the last time!

BO: Listen you two, I don't know what game you think you're playing, but your sister is alive, I've seen her myself!

KITTY: You know, Edmundo . . .

BO: Edmundo! Your name is Edmundo!

KITTY: I think we really ought to fix Dr. Nixon here a batch of red. He gets all the hospital dope he wants! But we know what he's doing here.

BO: Well, now that you mention it, a little red, before surgery, always seems to make my sutures just a bit more . . . elegant.

EDMUNDO: Slide your ass over here, my man. (*Bo pulls over. They hit him with red. Bo moans, staggers around the room and goes out. Juana has put stew on the table. Mo has tasted.*)

MO: This stew is very tasty, Juana . . . (*Bo groans in crawl space.*) It's a long time since I had a home-cooked meal.

JUANA: Don't you have a wife, Mr. Mo?

MO: Me? A wife? Who could put up with me?

JUANA: Oh, I don't know . . . you seem OK. And you ain't too bad lookin' . . .

BOBBY: Hey, you're makin' Mo blush, Ma. You better get him some more iced tea.

MO: (*Embarrassed.*) Err . . . what's in this goat stew?

BOBBY and JUANA: Goat! (*They laugh.*)

JUANA: You be quiet, Bobby. Don't make fun . . .

MO: I deserve it. I'm a funny old man . . .

JUANA: You are a little funny . . . but you're not that old . . . (*They look at each other. Mo eats again.*)

BO: (*In crawl space.*) This operation will be exquisite! (*Kitty exits, becomes Winny below.*)

DICK: (*Coming quickly out on middle level, pulling Winny behind him.*) Hurry up now, we don't have much time . . .

WINNY: I'm not gonna do it again, Dad. You can't make me. I won't!

DICK: What's the matter with you, Kitty? Don't you love me? (*Mo suddenly rises up from table, nearly spilling stew.*)

WINNY: I'm not Kitty, Dad. I'm Winny and you know it!

JUANA: What's the matter, Mr. Mo? Are you OK? (*Mo looks around confused.*)

MO: No . . . I thought I heard something . . .

DICK: Come on, just give your daddy a little hug . . .

MO: Are we in the rub, Bobby!

WINNY: Kitty! Help me!

DICK: That's my nice Kitty.

WINNY: (*Struggling with him, but more softly.*) I'm not Kitty, dad, I'm Winny . . .

DICK: You know you like it . . . (*Enter Rose.*)

ROSE: You'll keep an eye on the girls while I'm gone, won't you, Dick? (*Winny looks away.*)

DICK: Take all the time you want, dear.

ROSE: Now Kitty you'll get your homework done.

WINNY: (*A whisper.*) Winny . . .

ROSE: What did we say, Kitty?

WINNY: Sure, mom, I'll do it.

ROSE: I'm not going to have you two getting knocked up and dropping out like I did, just cause some dickbrained shitkicker got you blotto on beer!

WINNY: Sure, mom. I'll get right to it.

ROSE: They've both gotten so boy crazy, it's a wonder they haven't flunked out already. (*Rose exits.*)

DICK: She'll do her homework. (*Grabs Winny very hard.*) What was she talking about? Do you have a boy-friend? (*Mo jumps up again.*)

WINNY: It's none of your fucking business, dad!

MO: (*Dick shakes her. Mo staggers around the room con-fused.*) I've got to go. There's something wrong.

BOBBY: Is it at the store, Mo? I'll come with you.

DICK: Who is he?

WINNY: None of your fucking business . . .

MO: Go to the store, Bobby . . .

DICK: Who is he! Tell me! (*Mo goes into crawl space above and drops down into room where Winny and Dick are.*)

WINNY: It's just a guy for crissake . . .

BOBBY: I'm on my way, Mo . . .

DICK:	Who is he?
JUANA:	(*Mo slides into crawl space.*) Your boss is flying, Bobby . . . does he always fly?
BOBBY:	(*Plunging through floor into crawl space.*) I'll be right back, Ma. Keep the stew warm.
DICK:	Who is he!
WINNY:	He's an Indian. (*Rush comes to a dead stop.*) He's got a scar on his neck right here. And I love to kiss it!
DICK:	Did you have sex with him, Kitty?
WINNY:	As much as I can. Every day. I love him! I really love him, Dad!
DICK:	(*He begins to strangle her.*) I'll kill you! You'll never leave this house again! (*She pulls a knife from her pocket and slashes at his shoulders. Mo tries to pull them apart. Winny rushes out to store, through floor membranes and crawl spaces.*)
MO:	I knew this would happen. (*Dick pushes Mo to edge of level and dangles him over the edge. Juana sees him hanging there and helps him. Bobby emerges carrying big pile of coats as in first scene. Looks around, sees no one. Then goes behind coats. Rush exits.*)
JUANA:	Mr. Mo. You're back. Would you like a cup of coffee and a piece of cherry pie?
MO:	Coffee and pie would be fine. I'd like that very much. (*Mo sits at table eating coffee and pie.*)
JUANA:	(*Joining Mo for pie and coffee.*) I've always thought that something unpredictable was going to happen to me at the very last moment . . .
MO:	What do you mean, the very last moment?
JUANA:	I just mean, just when you think all the kinds of things that can happen have happened. Like one day your dad says he's going into Farmington to sell his calves.

And then he don't come back. Ever. Or you go to the Indian rodeo in Gallup with your sister and her husband. And then you meet a guy in the fry bread line, and you don't even know if he's a Navajo or a Hopi or what. He might even be a Mexican.

MO: I understand you completely . . .

JUANA: The clouds are the clouds you're used to seeing . . . the little dust devils have always been there . . .

MO: The coats hang in the store. There's a new batch to be sorted in back.

JUANA: Exactly . . . the yellow dog pees on the piñon stump . . . the black dog pees on the boulder by the corral . . .

MO: And then . . .

JUANA: Then . . . (*They stare at each other.*) How old are you?

MO: I don't know. Lost my birth certificate.

JUANA: Would you like to see the rest of the house . . .

MO: The rest of the house? There's more?

JUANA: Oh, there's a lot more. (*She takes his hand. They exit into shadows.*) It looks small from the outside. But once you're inside, it goes on forever . . . (*Winny slides through ceiling membrane down into Mo's. Bobby enters with big pile of coats. He catches her and helps her down.*)

BOBBY: Winny . . . what the hell are you doing here?

WINNY: He tried to do me again!

BOBBY: I'll kill the son of a bitch!

WINNY: Oh, don't worry about him! (*Shows him bloody knife.*) I got him good . . .

(*Dick falls through the membrane with a knife and runs at Bobby. Bobby kicks it out of his hand. Bobby kicks Dick in chest. Dick has heart attack. Clutches at his heart, staggers out.)*

WINNY: (*Watching Dick stagger out.*) I woulda killed him if Mo hadn't showed up.

BOBBY: Mo? Are you talkin' about my Mo? He was just at my house!

WINNY: I don't even know how he got in there. It looked like he came right up through the floor. I really need to lie down for a while.

BOBBY: Well use the table over here. (*She lies on holy table.*) Here, let me put this pillow under you. (*He puts a coat under her, covers her with a large coat. As she begins to rest he piles more coats on her 'til she's invisible. She makes it to crawl space, becomes Kitty. Kitty's head pops through membrane as she knocks on Juana's door. Mo comes out in his underwear.*)

KITTY: Mo! What the hell are you doing here? In your underpants!

MO: Well, life is very unpredictable. The forces of nature, the forces of chance, the desire to desire . . . (*Enter Juana.*)

JUANA: Oh, Kitty, come on in. And you put some clothes on, Mo! You look like an old goat sitting in your underwear like that!

KITTY: I didn't know you two were . . . oh never mind! Have you seen Winny?

JUANA: Maybe she's with Bobby. He's at the pawnshop.

JUANA: Bobby's got the shop now. (*Kitty withdraws head, moves backwards into crawlspace. Tinkle of door at Mo's. Rose slides through ceiling. Bobby comes out. Mo and Juana amorous. Bo is operating on Dick on upper level. Juana and Stand In are nurses, Edmundo assisting. Blood flies.)*

BOBBY: Can I help you with something?

ROSE: Is Mo here?

BOBBY: Mo's not here anymore. I run the store now. My name's Bobby Wash.

ROSE: Why, nice to meet you, Bobby. Just call me Rose.

BOBBY: I know who you are. Winny showed me your picture.

ROSE: This is rather embarrassing . . . You see, years ago, my husband and I used to live upstairs. And sometimes I'd have a lot of back pain . . . when I was pregnant with my twins. And Mo, well, he used to give me a massage from time to time . . .

BOBBY: You mean the rub . . .

ROSE: That's right . . . he always called it the rub. There was one place in particular: he said my stories always got stuck there. You don't know how to do the rub, do you?

BOBBY: Me? Hell no!

ROSE: You've never seen Mo do it?

BOBBY: Well, sure I seen him do it. He's been doin' it on me the last coupla years.

ROSE: He hasn't been telling you how it works?

BOBBY: Yeah, well he kinda tells me while he's doin' it. I mean most of what he says just sounds crazy to me.

ROSE: Oh, it won't take long with me.

BOBBY: Well, I don't know.

ROSE: If it doesn't work, no harm done . . . is that the holy table under the pile of coats? Here, let me help you clear them off . . .

BOBBY:	No, no, that's OK. I can handle them. (*He scoops up coats and the sleeping Winny. Puts them on counter.*) You just lie on the table.
ROSE:	Oh my God, it's just like old times . . .
BOBBY:	You want me to start with the feet . . .
ROSE:	No, no, my feet are fine. It's right here over my heart.
BOBBY:	Wo! Something really hard in there. I can barely feel your heart beating.
ROSE:	Oh my God, that's sore!
BOBBY:	That's God's mouth right under this plate! Just let him talk.
ROSE:	There's three square rooms in the middle of my head.
BOBBY:	What's in the rooms?
ROSE:	There's an old man in one with the head of a goat. (*Mo has on goat head.*) He's sitting at a table with an Indian woman. But she doesn't notice the goat head at all. And there's a room with a big pile of coats and Kitty is sleeping under them. What are you doing there, Kitty?
WINNY:	(*Rises up from under coats.*) It's Winny, Ma. Winny . . . (*Falls back asleep.*)
ROSE:	And a black man's taking Dick's heart out! Why is he doing that? (*Bo holds Dick's heart in the air. Licks it clean, kisses it, puts back in his chest.*)
BOBBY:	It's God's movie, Rose, don't be afraid . . .
ROSE:	And now they're lying down on the floor to sleep in one big pile of coats, and Kitty is crawling under them! (*All Doctors and Nurses rest in pile of coats.*)
WINNY:	(*Rising up.*) It's Winny, Ma. Winny . . .
ROSE:	There's no air for her to breathe!
BOBBY:	Don't worry about it, Rose, it's just God's TV show!

The Rushes of Tulsa   73

ROSE: I can see myself upstairs when I was pregnant with the twins.

BOBBY: You mean Winny was born here?

ROSE: Yes, and I can feel the two of them kicking inside me. I could already tell that they were different, cause one would sort of float on top, and one would sort of kick up from the bottom. (*Winny kicks from under coats and Stand In begins to sink down through membrane in ceiling.*) I can see them as living persons, and I talk to the one on top and call her Kitty . . . and I say, "Little Kitty, I sure hope we can get out of this place before you're born. Cause I'm so scared for my little girls." And then I can hear the beds start to creak right next to my head. And I see Dick in all of those beds. And I know. I just know. Even before they're born. Even though I didn't really know such things existed. (*Pause.*) That's better. That's much better. I can breathe now.

        (*All characters take crawl spaces to second level. Second level becomes stage. Dick, Rose, Bobby, Juana, and Mo sit at small round table as if in audience. Loud sounds of performance club, as if 200 people are present. Rose is sitting with Bo. He is elegantly but tastefully dressed. His clothing should be in very clear contrast to what we have seen previously. Rose seems several years younger.*)

ROSE: Don't you think you're a little overdressed for a place like this? It's very casual in here!

BO: You mean maybe I should have put on my slumming clothes? Or maybe you're ashamed to be seen in public with your ex-husband's heart surgeon!

ROSE: Oh, stop it, Bo. We've been together for a year! No one's going to be shocked by us! (*Brief pause. Looking around nervously.*) Is he here yet?

BO: Listen. You're worried about absolutely nothing. Dick is so debilitated from the procedures that he can hardly breathe. Hardly any assets left after the settlement fees and all the judges he paid off. He's not going to risk his demise. Besides, we've had numerous encounters since we've been together, and he's been relatively sane. (*Nibbling her ear.*) Settle down. Enjoy the show. (*Dick enters pulling a heavy oxygen tank. The wheels creak. Bo and Rose sit down without seeing him. Dick clumsily rushes across the room to Bo.*)

DICK: Dr. Nixon! Dr. Nixon!

BO: Easy now, Mr. Rush.

DICK: Dr. Nixon! It's so good to see you!

ROSE: Stop it, Dick! Not here, not tonight!

DICK: Could you turn the oxygen up a little? I'm feeling a little faint.

BO: If I turn it up any higher you might burst into flame.

DICK: Just a taste. (*Bo turns oxygen up.*) That's much better.

ROSE: You've got enough oxygen in there to last you a week.

DICK: Well, tonight's pussy night, Rose. After the show, it's off to Mo's.

ROSE: I thought Juana made him close that whorehouse down!

DICK: Mo's doing me a special favor. It's hard to find a girl who'll do a guy with a tank. (*Mo, Bobby, Winny, and Juana enter. Rose gets up quickly and rushes to embrace Juana.*)

ROSE: Juana, Juana, I'm so happy for you. Bobby told me about the wedding.

JUANA: Well, I hope you can come, Rose.

ROSE: Wouldn't miss it for the world.

JUANA: Mo closed the whorehouse down. And he promised not to go off flying anymore, and that was enough for me. It's just coats now. Bobby's running the store. (*As Juana's back is turned, Dick slides furtively over to Mo. He whispers heavily.*)

DICK: Are we set up for later on, Mo? I got a full tank . . .

MO: This isn't the time or the place, Dick. (*Musical introduction to Edmundo's video. Edmundo takes mike.*)

EDMUNDO: Ladies and Gentlemen! My name is Edmundo Salazar. I am originally from Tucupitu, Venezuela, and when my mother dies in a mud slide I move to live with my aunt in Maracay, where we were selling arepas de lengua and guasacaca, and when she and my uncle move, I go to study at the Universidad in Merida with Miguel Neo, El Chino Valera, and Tarik Suki, and then I come here to live with my cousins and win a scholarship at the Rocky Mountain College of Art and Design. Thas it. My story. I would like to thank Dr. Larry Feinberg for keeping my diabetes under control. This is the last video of the night, and the poem that accompanies the video was written by Kitty Rush. The title is "Palo Mayombe Baster Green." The poem will be read by the Rushes of Tulsa. (*Room goes dark. On TV screen we see Edmundo's video speed by incredibly fast.*)

KITTY, ROSE, STAND IN: (*In shadows, almost invisible, reading overlapping.*)

> It's the thunder that flutters in the green that is my
>   mother!
> I know it from the needles I've held in my hand
> Where the firelight of the father keeps flashing into
>   blackness
> And she accepted the current while pretending to be
>   mad
> Growing weaker than an emerald while storing up
>   my dream
> And I can tell that I am bark from the beetles that
>   pierce me
> And I can tell from my smell that my sap is running
>   clear
> And I know there are pools where my bones are at
>   the bottom
> And I know that my leaves have nothing to fear
> Nothing will grow without water
> Unless our days grow cool in a circle of fern fingers
> And the shadows of braids and mazes drink the sun
> Let the rain come down my lover
> Turn the soil around my slender green members
> But don't disturb the worms around my waist!
> And let loose your green flakes of fish scale and
>   murmur
> Your little steamy flagon of sweat
> And I will meet you with all that my helix can render
> No end to my end then or image of my demise

(*Loud applause. Crowd disperses. Kitty and Winny talk in near darkness. Kitty does both voices with little shifts to indicate two voices.*)

KITTY and WINNY: You know, it's really strange: tonight I thought your voice was my voice. There was a kind of country thing, a darkness, like a saw-toothed fishing knife, either side could cut you, even in a whisper, and you know, don't fuck around with this muttering, listen or split, but don't lean back and scan the curves, or sit there dripping when you lock on the nipples, thinking maybe, maybe not, maybe, maybe not, maybe, maybe not, no, with this knife it's in or out, stay or leave, but don't stand in the doorway, asshole, other people are waiting. (*Pause.*) That's interesting. I like it. Well, I felt that there was something funny too, something like a hole in my voice, like it was over finally, he was gonna die, when I felt my body slide through yours, it was like putting on a sock, and when your foot gets to the toe you just keep on going, your toe goes through, your foot goes through, your ankle goes through, your calf, your knee, your hip, your vagina, and then it's both sides of you, your ribs, your tits, your shoulders, your eyes, and then the top of your head just gently slips out of its scalp, and you're flipped completely. You slide out of yourself like hot butter from a bowl, and when you come out the other end it's your sister's body you're standing in, and when I bend my head, I'm reminded of the comfort of my feet in singing, in yodeling, in noodling, in knowing the darkness where little children including ourselves are sold to the highest bidder for use or just abused with a bar or a door or a soiled piece of cloth, fading out of life as a moth falls after touching a flame, and death is so close, and pain is so close you might as well fall from a plane as be born, except in this particular moment you look down and see that your feet are entirely clad in comfortable shoes, and though the black, black canyon is so dark below I cannot see a river, neither sister or river or self or forgiver, it's at that moment that I know that it's your feet in my socks or my toes in your shoes, and it's done. I mean it's really over. He's gone. (*Pause.*) Yeah, I know. I felt that too. (*Total darkness, the Denver night goes by. Stars fly across the mountains. Dim light. Rose and Bo become visible in bed on the second level. Juana's room has become their bedroom. For a moment they are in deep sleep. Soft spot on their faces. Then Rose wakes up and looks around nervously. This wakes up Bo.*)

ROSE: (*Soft knocking on door.*) It's him. I knew it . . . heart attack or no heart attack . . . (*Knocking again, a little louder this time.*) You don't divorce Dick. You have to kill him! (*The knocking gets louder.*) Maybe I can get rid of him.

BO: I'll come with you. (*He gets out of bed and begins to put his bathrobe on.*)

ROSE: You stay right where you are. The last person he needs to see is you. (*Bo continues to get dressed. He pulls a gun from his bathrobe.*)

BO: Never sleep with a divorcee without a baretta in the bathrobe. I learned that in Medical School.

ROSE: Jesus Christ, Bo! Put that away!

BO: I'll stay out of sight. (*Knocking again. This time quite insistent. Rose goes across to door.*)

ROSE: Who's there? (*Dick's head is sticking through membrane.*)

DICK: It's me, Rose, open up . . .

ROSE: Dick, it's six in the morning.

The Rushes of Tulsa 79

DICK: I'll just take a minute. (*She pulls him in, dragging his enormous oxygen tank behind him, dressed in a bloody butcher's smock.*)

ROSE: You know you're not supposed to come here without calling first! (*She sees his bloody butchering smock.*) Oh my God! What have you done, Dick!

DICK: I was just goin' out to butcher a steer up in Longmont; I was gonna give the kids some steaks and freeze up the rest.

ROSE: The kids don't want no steaks from you.

DICK: I couldn't find my knife. Double-handed cleaver was right where I left it! (*He pulls an enormous cleaver from a hook on his belt. Bo is moving toward them and becomes visible just now.*)

ROSE: Oh my God, Dick, put that thing away!

DICK: But I couldn't find my big butcher's knife. I was drivin' out there, and I come by here, and I thought, well, maybe Rose has seen it.

ROSE: Dick, it's been two years since you left this place. You went over it then with a fine-tooth comb.

DICK: I thought maybe I left that knife in some corner of the basement.

ROSE: Oh for God's sake go and take a look! (*Dick walks past her revealing an enormous butcher's knife hanging from the back of his hip. Rose sees it.*) Dick . . . stop . . .

DICK: What?

ROSE: Reach your hand around behind you. (*Dick feels the knife and unhooks it. Bo is slowly closing in.*)

DICK: Well I'll be darned.

ROSE: How did you drive out here without noticing it, Dick?

DICK: I ain't got too much feeling in my hip these days. Oxygen don't get that far. (*Bo becomes visible in the hallway as Dick raises his knife in the air like a sacred sword.*) This is a day I've been waiting for for a long, long time. They said I couldn't do it, but this blade'll be deep in a belly fulla guts before long . . .

ROSE: Stop it, Dick!

DICK: . . . cutting and slicing so fast and so clean, the whole room'll be full of steaming meat before you know it! (*Bo sees Dick with his knife in the air, assumes he's about to kill Rose. He steps quickly into the room.*)

BO: Put the knife down, Dick.

ROSE: Put the gun away, Bo! You got it all wrong!

BO: Don't try to defend him, Rose!

ROSE: Gimme the gun, Bo. It isn't what you think!

BO: I'll give you the gun when he drops the knife!

DICK: Gun! Does someone have a gun?

ROSE: Bo's got a gun in his hand, Dick! Can't you see it?

DICK: I don't have my glasses on! Looks like he's holding an egg roll from over here!

ROSE: He can't see the gun, Bo! You're threatening a blind man!

BO: I'll put it where he can see it, then! (*Bo sticks the gun in Dick's face.*)

DICK: Now you can shoot me, Doc, but I know where your heart is at!

BO: Put the knife down, Dick.

ROSE: He wasn't threatening me at all, Bo. He was on his way to Longmont to butcher a steer. (*A knock on the door.*)

ROSE: (*She opens the door.*) Come on in. It can't get any worse. (*Mo enters through membrane with gun in hand. Though he is holding it in an unthreatening manner, the sight of the two armed men cause him to raise his gun reflexively.)*

MO: Dick, you got me in a lot of hot water.

BO: Put the gun down, Mo.

ROSE: Mo's got a gun, Dick. Put the knife down.

DICK: What are you talking about, Mo?

MO: I'm gonna be fast here, Dick. Cause Juana's comin' in. You promised me you'd keep our deal on the Q.T. You know I promised Juana no more whores. So five-thirty this girl rings the doorbell . . .

DICK: What girl is that, Mo?

ROSE: Would all you fools just put down your weapons, please!

BO: I'll put mine away when Dick drops the knife.

MO: You left your gun in the room Dick.

DICK: I can't really see it, Mo, without my glasses!

MO: It's your gun, Dick. I swore to Juana that all the apartments were rented now. No more girls. And then my doorbell is ringing at five-thirty, and why is that, Dick? Because the girl needs to find you, Dick. The fucking girl who you don't even fuck . . .

DICK: Shut up, Mo . . .

MO: So this child molester can get a little conversation, I put my marriage in danger. Why?

DICK: Shut up, Mo!

KITTY: *(Edmundo and Kitty enter with video. Edmundo films scene.)* Oh my God!

DICK: *(To Edmundo.)* Get that bazooka outta my face! I just wanna butcher a steer!

ROSE: It's not a bazooka, Dick, it's a video camera!

EDMUNDO: You get it on tape, it never goes to trial.

KITTY:	You're not supposed to be here!
ROSE:	He was on his way to Longmont to cut you and Edmundo some steaks.
DICK:	This is my goddamn butcher's knife. You got eyes, don't ya? (*Dick thrusts knife into air in front of Kitty. Juana comes through a door with a huge bag of donuts. She sees the knife and screams at the top of her lungs. This makes Bo and Mo raise their guns again, just as they were finally relaxing.*)
JUANA:	Don't shoot him, Mo.
ROSE:	Nobody's gonna kill anyone, Juana! It's all just a big mistake! Now if you'll all just calm down, I'm gonna make us some coffee. (*Rose exits to kitchen.*)
JUANA:	(*Circling toward the armed men, first to Dick.*) You think I don't know who you are, big man with the big knife? You think I don't know what you did to your girls? As far as you know, I wasn't even there. But I watched you. I saw you lookin' over your shoulder every time that you peed. You think I don't know what was what. I knew. And I ain't going to forget. No way. These pictures I got of you are gonna stay in my blood. Even after I die, someone will remember. Cause my blood's gonna rise like steam from a pool, and any person around can just suck them pictures up. You know what you are, Mr. Rush. You're gossip. You're just a little slimy rumor people pull under the door.
MO:	Take it easy now, Juana. (*To the others.*) She's a different person than I thought she was . . .
JUANA:	You shut up, Mo! (*She moves toward Bo.*) And you. You think I don't know all the things you been? Just cause you look like a big doctor now. I know what

The Rushes of Tulsa   83

you been stickin' in people for a long time. One prescription's same as the next. Don't turn your head! You can't stand anyone lookin' at you now. Well that's too bad! Nobody forced you to do what you did. You just did it to be the boss of your hill. Little tiny boss of your little tiny hill.

MO: That's enough, Juana. (*She turns sharply to him.*)

JUANA: Enough! You think you can tell me when something is enough! Just cause I'm with you don't mean that I'm stupid. You drive a big Lincoln! Well I know how you got that car. I ain't been out on the res all these years, you know! I was a maid in Mexico! I was a maid in Tulsa. In a big ranch house with people takin' dope, spending money, rushin' around like hungry dogs. You think I bought this little act of yours! Phony Baloney, Holy Man! Like you never seen a gun before. Look at the way you're holdin' that gun. You been livin' off the small change of killers all your life.

MO: This gun ain't even loaded. (*Mo raises the gun and pulls the trigger. A thunderous explosion. Everyone hits the floor except Mo and Juana. Rose swings in from kitchen with an enormous coffee maker, cups, creamer and sugar on a rolling cart.*)

ROSE: I hope nobody's dead in here, cause the coffee is ready. Oh, good, just a little misunderstanding. That was one good thing about living with Dick all those years: you got used to the sound of gunfire. Kitty, go get some plates for the donuts. Those are donuts you got in the bag there, Juana?

JUANA: Yeah . . . donuts and crullers. I bought enough for the week at the day-old store on Federal. They were just opening up.

MO: I broke my promise.

JUANA: Well, you eat your donut, cause we're gonna get married. (*Others have poured themselves coffee and have seated themselves at long table facing audience as much as possible. Weapons are stored away. Suddenly the scene is very calm, ordinary, and conversational; they talk news and weather. People drink coffee and eat crullers.*)

DICK: (*To Bo, a little loud.*) You know, Doc, there's been one thing I been wanting to ask you about my operation . . . (*They suddenly become quiet.*)

BO: I hope you're not going to ask me what your face looked like when I operated on you.

DICK: How'd you know that I was gonna ask you that?

BO: Everyone wants to know that. A person is put under a very powerful anesthetic. People they don't know very well open them up and mess with their insides for several hours. Sometimes they come very close to dying, but they don't even know! Even conventional procedures have touch-and-go moments. These are moments of extreme tension, for the whole operating staff, but especially for the surgeon. You feel the ebb and flow of the patient's life right under your fingertips . . .

MO: Oy . . . oy . . . I can't listen to this . . .

DICK: Well, doesn't that scare you?

BO: Damn straight it scares you! Sometimes my heart is pumping so hard and I'm sweating so bad . . . You can't believe the rush! It's like pure adrenaline is hitting your brain through a two-inch stainless steel pipe! I got so freaked out when I was cutting you open that the scalpel flew right outta my goddamn hand!

DICK: Now why was that, Doc?

BO: (*Pause*.) I suppose it was because I'd become attracted to your wife. So the sight of your beating heart just under my fingers . . .

DICK: I see what you mean . . .

BO: Can you imagine what it's like to feel someone's living, beating heart under the spread of your fingers?

DICK: Well I've taken the heart out of a freshly killed steer . . . would that be similar?

MO: This conversation is making me a little dizzy. I'm starting to get some shooting pains down in my legs.

BO: Well the steer is dead, isn't it?

DICK: Well, it depends on what you mean by dead. (*Mo moans here and continues to moan from time to time throughout this conversation*.) I've shot a steer right in the brain, but when you open it up it seems like the heart is still . . . well, like shivering . . .

BO: Palpitating . . .

MO: Oy . . . oy . . . gotenu . . . you're going to kill me!

BO: Well, I've never seen the palpitating heart of a freshly killed steer.

DICK: Well, what I really wanted to know was about my face . . .

BO: I never look at the faces.

MO: If this pain gets to my back I'm gonna die!

DICK: So let me ask you this, Doc . . .

BO: Is the heart like a face? Is that what you want to know?

DICK: Something like that . . .

BO: When I look down, do I see in the array of ventricles, valves, scars and pumping meat, a symbolic representation of that person, that's as particular as a face . . .

DICK: Yeh . . . that's it exactly . . .

BO: A heart is much more particular than a face. A heart wears no make-up. Decorates itself with no particular cut of hair. The heart is the hidden face. The part of the person that can't be disguised. All the crimes done to a person are visible there . . . scars of anguish . . . accumulations of greed and rage . . . holes big enough to put your little finger in. You can see how long the dog's been slobbering along, how many days have rushed through these pumping skins of bad intentions. You can see the blood-encrusted pulp of savagery. Dermis worn thin by yearning. And you see the little nubs and creamy bars left behind by all those slabs of rare sirloin rubbing and rippling and corrupting the blood.

MO: You can't talk about this anymore.

DICK: We've all got to face it sooner or later . . .

BO: That's why I always make sure to kiss every heart before I stitch my patient up.

DICK: (*Completely panicked.*) You what!

MO: (*Twisting and trying to hold his back.*) I . . . I beg you . . . please . . .

DICK: Are you saying that you . . .

BO: I kiss the hearts of my patients before I sew them up!

DICK: (*A high-pitched moan.*) You kissed my heart! You put your fat . . . lips on my beating heart! I'll kill you! (*He tries to stand up, but the first of a wave of heart attacks hits him. He quickly sits back down, moaning, breathing with great difficulty and clutching his chest.*)

BO: Just before I stitched you up, I looked down and for the first time I really took your whole heart in. I saw a

The Rushes of Tulsa   87

seething, insecure, bullying, bulbous, steaming heart, bent out of shape by so many contrary rushes of blood that the purplish, phlemy dripping edges looked like they'd been bitten by a tribe of hyenas who'd taken a couple of swallows and then changed their minds, because the taste was so sour, so putrid, so gristly and cheap, that they gagged and spat out what they couldn't swallow . . . (*Dick staggers up out of his seat again screaming in pain.*) And then I saw the eyes of the heart, the place where the beating comes from, and they stared up at me like two colorless globs of a viscous, bluish, disappointed tint, old cracker eyes that once stared into a sunset of black necks snapped like palmettos in a hurricane, eyes empty of meaning when there's nothing in sight to be killed or consumed . . . You following me so far, Dick? (*This sends Dick into a spasm of rage.*) Cause that's when I saw what I was looking for. I saw the mouth of your heart, Dick, little, worn-down, blackened, indented teeth, chewing away at your meatless, ragged pancake of heart gristle, and a tiny, sucking, puffing hole, dripping and drooling like a baby spitting up milk, trying to shape words but unable to shape them, a mouth all desire but no definition (*Dick tries to speak, but cannot shape words.*) . . . unable even to say what it wants, just a little, begging, pullulating sore calling out for help . . . if there ever was a heart that needed to be kissed it was yours, Dick . . .

DICK: (*Barely able to articulate.*) Mama! Mama, help me! (*The others see Dick's heart attacks but don't care.*)

BO: I looked down at my work, the gouging and scraping and cutting and sewing that let the blood rush free in you again . . . and I bent over and pressed my lips to your scraggly heart, and I held them there for a long time, a good deep kiss, Dick. And before I pulled my mouth away, I let my tongue push out of my mouth, and I licked your heart, Dick, like a cat licks its own face, I licked your heart 'til it was good and clean . . . (*Dick falls to floor. Slowly becomes still.*) I can remember the taste of your heart right now. I guess it's a kind of privilege. With all the talk we do about the heart, hardly anyone knows that it's really there. But I do. I've kissed the human heart several hundred times. But I've only licked one heart clean, Dick. And that was yours. I wanted to do the job right. (*Dick is still. Mo moans a deep moan of deepest pain. No one pays any attention to Dick's death.*) What's the matter with you, Mo?

JUANA: He's probably having a heart attack!

MO: I am not having a heart attack!

BO: Well, what's wrong, then?

MO: I got pain in twenty places!

BO: Well, we can give you the rub, Mo . . .

MO: Whadya mean you can give me the rub, don't be ridiculous . . .

JUANA: Oh he just needs the rub, thank God! Why didn't ya say so, Mo?

ROSE: Let's get this stuff cleared off . . . (*They begin clearing the table so they can do the rub on it.*)

EDMUNDO: We all know the rub, Mo. We're not barbarians . . .

KITTY: Here . . . somebody give me a hand . . . (*Mo acquiesces to being lifted onto the table. Dick remains very still on the floor.*)

MO: I had no idea you knew the rub . . .

KITTY: Oh, for God's sake, Mo! You can't get out of second
           grade without learning the rub these days!

MO: But you can't do the rub without God's table!

EDMUNDO: You don't need God's table to do the rub. Not in
           Venezuela.

MO: I got so many things goin' around in my head. I get
           confused sometimes. So much pain there is. Winny in
           Mexico yet, and they send the body back. But then
           she's alive. And Dick has a heart attack and drops
           dead. But does Dick ever die? (*They have Mo stretched
           out on the table. Characters station themselves next to
           parts of Mo behind the table, facing the audience.*)

JUANA: Pain gives him nightmares.

EDMUNDO: Lemme get these shoes off. Here, you do the feet,
           Kitty. (*Kitty rubs his feet, but the others continue
           to rub gently the rest of him to the top of his head.
           Silence. Then Mo begins moaning softly.*)

MO: It's a baby, and he's alone. He's on the floor of the
           store and he's crawling around on a big pile of coats.

KITTY: Who is it, Mo? Can you see its face?

MO: It's a baby crawling through a big pile of coats. It's a
           coat store but it's not mine. And this kid is happy. He's
           lookin' at me like he's my son. But I never had a son.
           And now this kid is getting bigger. Every time he smiles
           it's like a year goes by. Every breath he's bigger.

BO: Take it easy, Mo. It's just God's movie comin'
           through!

MO: He puts a coat on. He takes a coat off. As soon as he
           gets the coat on it's too small for him. And his hair
           is gettin' longer and longer. And now he's really mad
           he's got this old leather coat, and he's tearin' it to
           pieces!

JUANA: It's Bobby! It's Bobby, Mo!

MO: It's not Bobby! It's an Indian, but it's not Bobby! He's so big the coats don't fit him now! He's growin' so fast, the coats just pop right offa him. And now Dick's comin' through the door? What the hell is he doin' back there in Newark?

BO: Newark! You never said nothin' about Newark, Mo!

MO: He's gonna kill the Indian with that knife! Where the hell's my uncle!

ROSE: Your uncle? What's this got to do with your uncle?

MO: It's my Uncle Norm's store in Newark! Dick's cuttin' this Indian open. But then another Indian baby is born outta that Indian! I can't stand this! It's gonna happen all over again! Get me outta here! Get me outta here! I see it all! Go up to my penis!

ROSE: He wants us to rub his penis! This is too much!

MO: (*Rises up slightly from table.*) What am I dealing with, amateurs here? You know what the order is, Rose! Feet, penis, heart, head! When I had to rub your clit did I do it?

JUANA: I'll do the penis, Rose, don't worry about it! (*They massage him gently, quietly.*)

MO: (*He becomes quiet, then moans softly as Juana begins to rub his penis.*) That's right . . . that's good . . . but that soil is dry . . . it looks like it hasn't rained for five years . . . no that's good . . . there was just a little rain . . . I can see the steam coming out of the crack . . . well what ya know! I think I'm gonna like this for a change: to be a tree and nothing but a tree! All the green sap waiting . . . cause it's storing up, it's storing up . . . but five lifetimes 'til everyone's pain catches up! Gennug shen! That's what I say! There's the green finger pushing up through the soil, just a little confused shoot with a head of steam, and a twig that thickens, that's very good, don't stop, now . . .

JUANA: I'm not gonna stop, Mo, don't worry about it!

MO: . . . and branches from branches come, whoa, take it easy not too fast, I've never been a goddamn trunk before. You think these leaves don't tickle? And every leaf has a word written on it! I'm a growing tree of words that never stop . . . only now the leaves are fall-ing . . . it's like all of my life in every breath! One leaf says diamond, another one says horn, another one says eye, another says water . . . house leaf, door leaf, bread leaf, head leaf, wind leaf . . . and now the leaves are stopping . . . all the leaves have flown away and I'm just bare and standing there. Just a big bare tree with no name . . . silent . . . still . . . sha . . . sha . . . sha . . . it's gone . . . sha . . . sha . . . sha . . . alone . . . alone . . . sha . . . sha . . . a little rain . . . a few flakes of snow . . . (*They pause and become very quiet, let-ting him rest from the vision. They must seem very professional, like they've done this a thousand times before.*)

BO: I'm gonna move to your heart now, Mo. Is that OK?

MO: You the doctor now, Bo. I'm in your hands . . .

BO: Just one more step, Mo. We're gonna go right through your heart to the empty throne . . . (*Bo gently rubs his heart. They become very quiet. After a while Mo begins to moan very softly.*) What is it, boychick?

MO: It's Winny, Bo. And she's older than me.

BO: Just let it come through.

MO: It's Winny with white hair, and she's sittin' on a park bench . . . she's feeding the birds . . . little kids go by . . . and they stop and talk to her . . . they look like they all know her from before. Like they come by her bench every day to say hello. She's got a little bag of candy for them . . . it looks like she's givin' them little Tootsie Rolls . . . it's in City Park in Denver . . . it's in the spring . . . she didn't die, Bo. She's alive! But how did she get so old so fast? She's talking to those kids but her voice sounds like water. She's got a nice spring coat. It's one I gave her. It still looks good on her. A long time ago I gave her that coat.

BO: Just stay right with it.

MO: Oy veyz mir. This is the future that never happened. That never could happen, because . . . dying, dying, dying . . . so many of them . . . just one big pile . . . because I . . . I lived my life . . . mit der tatte geshtorbin, and der mama geshtobin. (*Silence. Kitty rubs his forehead.*)

KITTY: It's OK now, Mo. You got through the tears right down to the bottom. And your words come back, the words you were missing, all this time.

MO: Gut . . . gut meine kin . . . meine shvester . . . meine tochter . . . shluffen gayen . . . ein fenster . . . ein teer . . . die eyen mit mazel . . . (*He babbles on in Yiddish in a whisper 'til he fades out. Quiet. A long pause.*)

KITTY: You should see the empty throne now, Mo. (*Pause.*) Mo . . . Mo?

JUANA: He's asleep. Time comes to see the empty throne, and he's asleep . . .

ROSE: If he's asleep, he needs to sleep . . . (*They stand touching him for a moment.*)

KITTY: Let's go home, Edmundo.

ROSE: You think he'll be OK there?

JUANA: I'll stay with him. (*Rose and Bo go back to bed as Kitty and Edmundo exit. An empty simple chair floats above Mo and Juana. Winny and Bobby enter.*)

WINNY: What happened to Mo?

JUANA: Fell asleep.

BOBBY: What's with that chair up there?

JUANA: (*Looks at floating empty chair.*) Could be one of Coyote's tricks. Or it might be the empty throne Mo's always talkin' about. Only it don't look like much of a throne to me. What do you think, Winny? You're the quiet one. But I can tell you're always thinkin'.

WINNY: I think it's just a chair.

BOBBY: What kinda chair?

WINNY: That's the chair you put up next to the window and look out on the street, the shittiest chair in the shittiest room looking out on the shittiest street in Matamoros. That's the chair you sit in when you cry, and you don't care who sees you cryin'. I've cried in that chair so hard my heart's just sunk down through my chest and dropped out my ass. Everyone who's been trapped has sat in that chair. That's why it's empty. We don't need to see anyone in it. We all know what it is. It's when you run out of sadness, and there's nothing left but emptiness. The clouds stop in the sky, the drunks spit out their mescal, mothers stop giving birth, sleepy night stalkers lose their nerve, a little piece of old newspaper is suspended in the air, and you see it, floating like an empty chair in the air over the groaning earth of pain. And in that emptiness you realize that every breath of every person is infinitely precious. That's what I think the empty chair is. Course, those are just my thoughts. (*The three have come close together, surrounding Mo. The chair floats gently in the air. Slow fade to black.*)

Orange Grove

Presented by Manhattan Theater Club, Lynn Meadow, Artistic Director, at City Center Stage, Downtown/Uptown Festival, curated by Matthew Maguire. Performed by Otrabanda Company in March 1991.

The cast:

BILL:	Roger Babb
PHIL:	William Badgett
IRENE:	Mary Shultz
MYRA:	Louise Smith
MRS. AVAKIAN:	Ellen Maddow
MONA:	Suzanne Baxtresser
THE GIRL IN THE WINDOW:	Rocky Bornstein

Directed by Roger Babb
Choreography by Rocky Bornstein
Music by "Blue" Gene Tyranny
Set by Nick Fennel

Characters

BILL, white, mid-thirties
PHIL, black, Bill's brother, late thirties
IRENE, Bill's longtime lover, early thirties
MYRA, pregnant Highway Patrolwoman, early thirties, childhood
       friend of Irene's
MRS. AVAKIAN, the landlady, a crusty western woman, mid-sixties
MONA, Phil's lover, mid-thirties, very pregnant
THE GIRL IN THE WINDOW, a silent character

A large central room of a run-down house in an orange grove, formerly used to house migrant workers, now rented to Bill and Irene. There is a large picture window or double windows stage left, and next to it a screen door, looking out on the orange grove. Stage right of the door there is a funky upright metal shower stall. Mid-stage left, a large rectangular table with a hotplate for cooking. Mid-stage against the wall, a small table and chair covered with maps. Maps on the wall beside the table. Dog wind music in the dark, sound of Irene chopping vegetables for chili. Lights come up fast. Intermittent sounds, very soft, of various forms of water.

BILL:	(*At small table, pouring over maps. Irene cooking.*) I can't make heads or tails of this damn thing. I thought I remembered every bit of the trip perfectly.
IRENE:	When Phil comes he'll figure it out.
BILL:	Phil. Phil?
IRENE:	Phil's better at remembering things than you are. He has a photographic memory.
BILL:	Irene, are you talking about my dear brother Phil? Because if you are, you're talking about a man who frequently can't remember how to walk.
IRENE:	That's got nothing to do with it. He can remember where he's been. (*Pause.*) I wish you'd stop worrying

about that map and start worrying about where we're going to live when Avakian kicks us out of here!

BILL: It's not sure yet . . .

IRENE: It's sure. I can tell you when a landlord has made up his mind. His eyes bug out when he looks at your furniture.

BILL: He's just worried he won't get enough wetbacks to pick his oranges.

IRENE: He keeps asking vague questions about our future plans . . .

BILL: But there's always gonna be enough wetbacks . . . this new law means nothing.

IRENE: He could sell this place any time he wants . . .

BILL: The man is sick, Irene. Look, here's where we parked the pickup at the edge of the barrio. Remember, there was a sugary whiff of that ramshackle refinery in the air?

IRENE: Right.

BILL: A slight mist coming off the lake. The pontoon bridge to the floating bar. Remember, you asked me why they'd want to float a bar, and Phil said, to make the customers think they were sober. Remember that?

IRENE: I remember every bit of it, Bill, the sugary whiffs, the floating bar, ask me anything.

BILL: And then we followed a little path past that house with the big guard dogs behind that elaborate wrought-iron fence . . .

IRENE: The wrought-iron fence . . .

BILL: And those dogs were ill! Remember, they had something that looked like psoriasis, though the light was too dim to see. I remember they seemed ill, because

Phil growled at them to get a rise out of them, and they opened their mouths to growl at us, but no sound came out! They were too weak to bark! Don't you remember that?

IRENE: I remember the ill dogs, Bill, and I remember Phil growling at the same ill dogs . . .

BILL: You'd never expect to see such sick dogs behind an elegant fence like that. And those dogs were dry! You could hear water lapping all around us, the air was full of moisture . . .

IRENE: The air was full of moisture . . .

BILL: But those dogs' tongues hung out of their mouths like ladles . . .

IRENE: They were hanging out like ladles, Bill, the tongues of those ill dogs . . .

BILL: I couldn't figure it out. Were they once healthy dogs who were suddenly struck sick? Had their once-wealthy owner met his sudden demise? But the fence was freshly painted. The lawn was freshly cut . . . (*Sound of a car.*)

IRENE: Oh, it's Phil! It's Phil and nothing is ready! Why can't you help me instead of bending over that map all day? Coming, Phil! I'll be right there! (*Exits to unlock gate for Phil.*)

BILL: None of us could put it together! The moon
was the color of cantaloupe, the breeze
hissed in the palos verdes, the wharves behind us
creaked and ruffled the little waves, and we
supplied the missing element, the water, which we
knew was everywhere, but which we could not see.

(Myra and Irene pass by window during Bill's speech and enter at end of it. Myra is in her Highway Patrol uniform, Smoky the Bear hat and mirror glasses. She carries gun, walkie-talkie, etc.)

IRENE: *(Coming in.)* It isn't Phil . . .

MYRA: *(Coming in behind her.)* So blame me for not being Phil. That's karma. Cause and effect. The right place at the wrong time. The wrong place at the right time.

IRENE: You could have at least changed out of your uniform, Myra. Nothing gives me the willies like a pregnant cop.

MYRA: I brought a change of clothes. I came straight from work.

IRENE: Work! What'd you do this morning? Raid a turkey farm for wetbacks?

MYRA: *(Unpacking groceries and beer for meal.)* Actually, I arrested a sixteen-year-old girl for drowning her father. *(Girl appears in window. Stays a moment.)*

IRENE: Did she drown him?

MYRA: She did. Knocked him cold and dumped him in their swimming pool. Thought it'd look like an accident.

IRENE: Why'd she do it?

MYRA: She says he was fucking her. And she was afraid he was gonna start with her younger sister.

IRENE: Did you believe her?

MYRA: Yup.

IRENE: How come?

MYRA: She was one of the most honest-looking people I've ever seen. You get to know what the liars look like. *(Girl is gone.)*

BILL: (*Who has continued bending over maps.*) Myra, come over here and take a look at this map. It's from the trip. There's something here that doesn't make sense . . .

IRENE: Yeah, go over there and help Bill, Myra. He's trying to find his way into the present.

(*Myra moves toward Bill, gun drawn. He turns around, faced with gun and cop.*)

BILL: Jesus!

MYRA: (*Laughing.*) I guess I should go through it again. I just got off work. I got a nice change of clothes. My maternity leave begins today! I'm off duty! Off duty!

BILL: Look, here's where we parked the pickup . . .

MYRA: Right . . . there's the lake, Lago Viejo . . . the little trail . . . there's the curve where that big house was with the sick dogs . . .

BILL: Right, but here it shows us crossing a bridge . . .

MYRA: We did cross a bridge.

BILL: We did?

MYRA: Of course we crossed a bridge. It was an old wooden bridge, big thick planks, but no railing at all. And it kind of scared you, cause it was almost dark by then, and you could barely see the water, but you could hear it, and it felt deep. Deep and steady . . .

BILL: I don't recall a bridge. I don't remember it at all.

IRENE: Don't pay too much attention to him, Myra. This is what he does when the pressure is on. Starts fixating on some goddamn irrelevant detail, when we don't even know where we're going to live tomorrow!

MYRA: Did Avakian kick you out already? I thought he was still in the hospital . . .

BILL:	He hasn't decided yet.
IRENE:	That's what his wife says, that's not what he says . . .
BILL:	Avakian's nearly dead, Irene! He's not gonna boot us out with his very last words. He'll die. There'll be a lot of financial complications. Mrs. Avakian's not gonna kick us out in the meantime. I'm the only one she's got to turn the irrigation on and off. Look at this will you, Myra? Here's where we passed the house . . .
MYRA:	Where we saw those dogs so sick they couldn't bark . . .
BILL:	Right.
IRENE:	And then that tiny man came out of the house and spoke tons of Spanish . . .
MYRA:	Oh, remember him!
IRENE:	He was barely as tall as those dogs!
MYRA:	(*Imitating the man.*) Estos perros no son malos. Son perros buenos. No molestan a nadie. No son peligrosos.
IRENE:	You can remember that, can't you, Bill?
BILL:	(*Girl comes up in the window. She leans in and looks at Bill.*) I just can't remember any bridge . . .
MYRA:	Look, Bill, what is the problem with this bridge? The main thing is we met that little girl on the other side. You can remember that, can't you?
BILL:	Of course I can remember that!
MYRA:	Well, if you can remember meeting that little girl, then what's the problem? If you can remember the main thing of an experience, why get so involved in some missing detail?
IRENE:	(*Girl is gone.*) I told you, Myra, this is what he always pulls when we've got something real we have to face. I can't stand this living day to day without knowing

whether we have to leave the orange grove or not, and I keep begging him to check around to see what he can find. He's got the time. I don't! I work! I have to be at the dog track every day at eleven. He sits there reading those damn maps all day!

BILL: You don't call what I do work! Well, who put you in charge of the definitions! There isn't a person in this world that works harder than I do! Just because the work I do isn't what most people call work, does that mean I should be shunned and insulted like a common malingerer?

IRENE: Help him with the map, Myra. I can feel him winding up . . . (*Sound of a car.*) Oh, thank God, it's Phil! (*Running out.*) Coming, Phil! I'll be right there!

MYRA: Listen, we went over a couple of low hills . . .

BILL: This is my work, Myra . . .

MYRA: I understand that, Bill, you don't have to explain . . .

BILL: I'm as dedicated to my work as you are to yours . . .

MYRA: I believe you, Bill.

BILL: We're not going to leave this orange grove. (*Enter Irene and Mrs. Avakian.*) I can feel it in my bones. Avakian's going to die.

IRENE: It isn't Phil. It's Mrs. Avakian. (*Stage whisper.*) Now you ask her, Bill!

MRS. AVAKIAN: I'm very sorry to bother you, but I don't know who to talk to.

BILL: Come on in, Mrs. Avakian. You know our friend Myra, the pregnant cop. We're just cooking a little chili. How's Mr. Avakian?

MRS. AVAKIAN: He's very bad, very, very bad. All the water has gone out of him. Ernie's all dried out. Desiccated.

BILL: Well, sit down. Stay awhile.

MRS. AVAKIAN: You see, Ernie's system is not running properly. This is what the doctors tell me. Some fluid's supposed to be going downhill, but it turns around on its own and starts going uphill, and that's where it runs into the young drops and the tubes start to burst. They showed me on a picture and it looked like leaves, big drops of water sliding off leaves, but pointed wrong, see, when that flow reverses. They want to poke some holes in there and get it to drain before it turns around, but Ernie says, "No! No one's pokin' any holes in me!" That's my husband Ernie. I can't understand a word of it. They say the body is like a field and the tubes are like ditches to help me, but I'm no good at it. Send me down here to turn a valve, sure I can, and if there's dripping, like here, you remember?

BILL: Of course we remember. How could we forget?

MRS. AVAKIAN: You were almost washed out when that pipe let go. Well, that's the way it is. I can fix a pipe, a pipe's got joints, joint's got solder, you pump on one end or the tank's up the hill. But when the damn stuff starts turnin' around on its own and runnin' into the young stuff, I'm lost. They showed me on a screen, see: . . . we were all lookin' right through Ernie, and you never saw a guy look so emptied out as Ernie did in that picture. The old doc, the one from Salt Lick, says it's cause of this too-little skin on the veins, you see. And then the new intern, he's an Indian from over there in India, he says it's supposed to go in a circle and filter out, but the stuff backs up, and when that unit starts backin' up in there, the tubes are too stiff to hold the flow and the suckers burst and that's the end of Ernie. Well, thanks for listenin' to an old woman. I got to get to the hospital. Now that that damned daughter of mine's moved up to Visalia, if I don't have the TV on, all I hear is the water sloshin' in the ditches, and I just get scared.

BILL: I'm glad you came by, Mrs. Avakian. You don't want to let things build up.

MRS. AVAKIAN: That's right. Well, it's a help there are people you can talk to in this world. How's that pipe holdin' up? Still got a little leakage back here I see.

BILL: Oh don't worry about that pipe. We got so used to the sound of that dripping, we'd be kind of lost without it . . .

MRS. AVAKIAN: Well, that's very generous of you, Bill. It's good to have tenants who understand reality. Goodbye. (*Exits.*)

BILL: Say hello to Ernie for us!

MRS. AVAKIAN: (*Passing window.*) I will. If he's still alive.

IRENE: You didn't ask her, Bill. You didn't even remind her.

BILL: (*Already returned to maps.*) I don't remember any bridge at all . . .

MYRA: Listen, we went over a couple of low hills. It was nearly dark . . .

IRENE: (*Chopping onions.*) Even I remember that. In that kind of darkness, after you've been exposed to those barkless, scab-covered, dry-mouth dogs, and you feel this wooden bridge under your feet, and you meet this little girl just standing there on the other end as if she'd been waiting for us . . . AAAcccchhhh!!!!! This onion is strong!

MYRA: Run cold water! Run cold water!

IRENE: Run cold water?

MYRA: Run cold water, it's a cure!

IRENE:	You're crazy! I'm dripping like a faucet!
MYRA:	Run cold water. Throw salt on a pillow. Hammer a fish flat and whistle. All those work . . .
BILL:	Where the hell are those paper towels? Didn't I buy paper towels? I know I bought them and I put them right here, right where I always put them. Don't put your fingers in your eyes!!
IRENE:	I hate it when I can't stop crying like this!
MYRA:	Warm a pot of sand on the stove! Talk to a bird like a dog! Take a bath in a tub of fresh grass!
BILL:	You make such an effort to figure out where everything should go, just so this kind of emergency comes along, you know where to look. You carry around a mental picture of the place in your home where you agreed the stuff should be . . .
IRENE:	STOP! STOP! Both of you! I'm fine now.
BILL:	Oh, here they are. I thought we'd agreed to keep them over there next to the liquid wrench and the joint compound. (*Hands paper towels to Irene.*)
IRENE:	I'm fine now, Bill, thanks, really . . .
BILL:	(*Embracing Irene.*) You sacrifice so much for the rest of us . . .
IRENE:	I'm fine. I wish Phil would get here . . .
BILL:	But you just said nothing's ready. What's the point of having someone appear before his time?
IRENE:	We didn't just invite Phil here to eat, Bill!
BILL:	We didn't? What'd we invite him for? (*Pause. Accusingly.*) Is there something Phil's coming over to do you haven't told me about?
IRENE:	MAYBE HE'D GET YOU OFFA THINKIN' ABOUT THAT GODDAMN BRIDGE!!!! (*Bill staggers back to maps.*)

MYRA:	Look, Bill. Think of the water running under us . . . Picture the girl at the end of the bridge . . .
BILL:	I'm ready to believe there was a bridge if you say so . . .
MYRA:	These are U.S. Geological Survey maps, Bill. Every little broken-down wharf and collapsed miner's cabin is recorded right here. And this map shows that bridge over Big Cuchara Creek.
BILL:	I remember Little Cuchara Creek as clear as day . . .
IRENE:	Oh, who wouldn't remember Little Cuchara Creek. I got soaked!
MYRA:	Soaked! You nearly drowned!
IRENE:	Oh, I didn't nearly drown . . .
MYRA:	Irene, if you didn't have long hair back then, Phil could never have pulled you out!
IRENE:	Oh I would have got out! I can swim, you know!
MYRA:	I know you can swim . . .
IRENE:	I just didn't realize it was that deep, that's all . . .
MYRA:	You'd think they would have had a bridge across a stream that deep . . .
IRENE:	(*Myra begins changing out of her uniform into her party clothes.*) I wasn't even paying attention . . . I thought it was just one of those big logs they lay across just to keep your feet from getting wet, so when I slipped off the edge, I thought I'd hit ground right away, but instead I went straight down, and the shock of suddenly being over my head! I can't explain it! You know what kind of a swimmer I am! It just startled me so much I was afraid I couldn't get my breath, and I opened my mouth and swallowed a lot of water . . .
MYRA:	You really looked like you were drowning . . .

IRENE:	I forgot how to swim! I forgot how to float!
MYRA:	Oh, Irene, you were flailing around like you'd never been in the water before!!!
IRENE:	It's amazing how your body can forget like that . . . I couldn't stop shaking when I got out.
BILL:	(*Pause.*) It wasn't so bad though. You warmed up real quick. It's as dry as the desert down there just half a mile from the coast. Remember, we got your clothes off and hung them on that cactus to dry? (*Myra is down to her panties. Girl appears in window. Watches intently.*)
IRENE:	I didn't feel all that great about being naked out there. I just didn't feel safe in that kind of place. (*Pause.*) Remember how crazy we used to be? Just head for the desert, slosh down some Quaaludes with some luke-warm Cold Duck and ball your brains out under the Arizona moon, the New Mexico moon. But being naked down there scared me. I felt like there was someone watching us all the time . . . (*Girl disappears.*)
BILL:	But your bra looked pretty cute hanging from that prickly pear . . .
MYRA:	(*Laughing. Half-dressed.*) That wasn't a prickly pear, Bill, that was a barrel cactus. You couldn't hang much of anything on a prickly pear . . . have you been drinking, Bill?
BILL:	Oh, I suppose I've wet my whistle once or twice this afternoon. Is that against the law, officer?
MYRA:	(*Putting on hat and glasses. Making a gun of her hand.*) Well why hasn't anyone offered me a drink, if the drinking has already started?
BILL:	(*Light hissing sound, becoming louder.*) I guess I hadn't thought of it as serious drinking.

IRENE: Why don't you offer Myra a drink, for God's sake!

BILL: What the hell is that hissing sound? There's not another leak in here is there?

IRENE: I don't hear any hissing sound. Do you, Myra? (*Hissing sound gets louder.*)

MYRA: Hissing sound? What kind of hissing sound?

BILL: The kind a hot water pipe makes just before it's about to burst! I ought to know what hissing hot water sounds like! (*Sound stops.*) Now I don't hear it. I hope it's not going to be one of those hissing sounds that comes and goes . . .

IRENE: BILL, WILL YOU PLEASE ASK MYRA IF SHE'D LIKE A DRINK!! (*Pause.*) ARE YOU RECEIVING OUTSIDE SIGNALS, BILL?

BILL: Myra, can I get you something to drink?

MYRA: I'd like a very, very dry martini, up, with a twist.

BILL: (*Putting on thick cowboy twang.*) Honey, this martini's gonna be so dry it'll turn your mouth into a closed laundry bag! (*Myra laughs.*)

IRENE: Don't start with the cowboy routines, Bill.

MYRA: Go on, Bill, I'm ready for a few laughs.

IRENE: Don't encourage him, Myra! He'll drawl all night.

BILL: (*Pointing to Irene.*) Myra, this little girl over here makes mah tongue hard! Ain't she purty! (*Myra chuckles.*)

IRENE: Stop it, Bill. Fixated or kaploosie, he's got two speeds . . .

BILL: Myra! This girl's got me beatin' my dick in the *dust*! (*Myra crackles and repeats Bill's line.*)

IRENE: (*Bill gives her a bear hug.*) Stop it, Bill.

BILL: (*Irene laughs despite herself.*) I'd kinda like to wet my whistle right now . . .

IRENE:	Bill, stop. If you don't stop, I won't make the chili.
BILL:	One very, very dry martini, up with a twist, coming up.
IRENE:	Make one for me too, Bill. No wait, a margarita . . .
MYRA:	I'll have a margarita too!
BILL:	Salt?
IRENE:	Salt! (*Bill exits through passageway next to shower.*)
MYRA:	I wish I could get that girl's face out of my mind.
IRENE:	Where'd you pick her up?
MYRA:	Arroyo Beach . . . right where you and I used to swim . . .
IRENE:	She was at the beach?
MYRA:	She was swimming when we got there, way out behind the kelp.
IRENE:	She was swimming? She just bumped her old man off and went for a swim?
MYRA:	Listen, that's not the strangest story of the week. You heard about the five-year-old kid in Firebaugh who shot his father?
IRENE:	I read about it . . .
MYRA:	Well that was the third murder by someone under ten in the state this month! Only this time it wasn't with daddy's gun. This five-year-old bought a gun!
IRENE:	He bought it? Where'd he get the money?
MYRA:	Out of his father's wallet. He bought it from his brother. His nine-year-old brother!
IRENE:	Stop. Stop.
MYRA:	These killings come in waves. First a seven-year-old'll just pull daddy's gun out of the dresser and shoot his older brother. But then you've got this five-year-old who sees *that* on TV, and he thinks, shit, if a seven-year-old can bump someone off, why not me? All I

	need to do is pull the trigger, and I can go to the roller rink whenever I want! (*Pause.*) Why should kids be any different than anyone else?
IRENE:	Well did you have to go swimming to arrest this girl?
MYRA:	Now that would have been a new one! We just waited up on the cliff 'til she came in . . . It took quite a while . . . She was way out beyond the kelp . . .
IRENE:	Oh, the kelp! Remember?
MYRA:	Of course I remember. (*Irene and Myra are on opposite ends of the table. Irene puts on Myra's hat and glasses. Girl comes up in window and swims as Irene makes swimming movements.*)
IRENE:	(*Swimming motion.*) I'd call you on the phone after school and I'd say, Myra, let's go lay in Mama's lap . . . and we'd swim out there and float in the kelp . . . that kelp was so thick we barely had to move to stay afloat . . . the ocean was our bed, and we'd lay there holding hands and trading secrets, bobbing on our backs like two sea otters . . . (*Irene and Myra slowly move together through the following sequences.*)
MYRA:	You know the funny thing was . . . while I was watching that girl swim way out beyond the kelp, I forgot who she was . . . and I started to think that girl was you. She was a real strong simmer, she kinda swam the way you did. Well, I haven't seen you swim for years, but you don't forget how someone moves through the water anymore than you forget how they move on the ground . . . (*Girl goes down in window.*) Well, finally she came out . . . she was tall . . . Don said five-foot-eleven off the report . . . more and more of her kept comin' out of the water like some kind of goddess . . .

IRENE: Surfer girl . . .

MYRA: I guess so . . . but I couldn't arrest her. Usually, if it's another woman, I'll make the collar, and Don backs me up. But I couldn't do it. It would have been like I was arresting you . . . (*Irene and Myra are side-by-side.*)

IRENE: I know what you mean: Bill keeps getting these letters from this girl who says she's his daughter . . .

MYRA: Oh, you told me about that!

IRENE: Well, I think she is his daughter! He denies it, but every time he does, I feel like he's denying me . . . and I feel like I've written the letters! He doesn't read them, but I read them, and I can hear my voice in hers . . . (*Bill enters. Stands watching in passageway.*)

MYRA: Well, it's hard not to sympathize with someone whose voice sounds like your own . . .

IRENE: And once you start sympathizing, you sort of forget who you are . . . (*They put their arms on each other's shoulders.*)

MYRA: I kinda like forgetting who I am . . .

BILL: I hope I'm not interrupting anything.

IRENE: Bring those drinks over here, Bill. You're not interrupting anything at all . . .

BILL: Are you sure? That sounded pretty serious to me. Like it might be some kind of private women's matter.

MYRA: I'm dying of thirst, Bill, and you got the liquids right there in your hands. (*He hands Myra a drink.*)

BILL: You know me, Irene, there's not a jealous goddamn bone in this dried-out old body of mine . . .

IRENE: Bring me the drink, Bill! (*He hands Irene her drink.*)

BILL: Hey, you two are suckin' down those drinks like the desert sucks down chubascos!

MYRA: Chubascos? What are chubascos?

IRENE: Oh-oh. Now we're in for it . . . (*During the following speech, Irene dances to Bill's words and lures Myra into it.*)

BILL: Chubascos are those August thunderstorms out in the Mojave when the rain comes down like swimming pools dropping out of the sky. That rain comes down so hard and so fast that for fifteen minutes or more there'll be these deep pools all around you, deep standing water where there's hardly a drop of rain from one end of the year to the next. And if you can get your clothes off fast enough, you can actually take a quick swim in one of those pools. You can dive deep down to the floor of the desert, what was just a desert hollow not moments before. But you've got to be fast, cause it's so dry out there, that before you've had a chance to get used to that watery depth, that water will be sinking faster than you can imagine into the dryness of the desert. Hell, I've taken a dive and swum around in one of those desert pools and come up and touched bottom, and I could already feel that water draining down over my neck and my chest. That desert just drinks whole swimming pools down, and while you're drying off and putting your clothes on, the pool disappears completely. Turn around once and there's nothing but mud. Stay a few minutes longer, and there's not any trace of the pool at all. Just sand. Every grain as dry as the next from Barstow to Kingman.

IRENE: How about getting us a couple more, Bill?

MYRA: Get one for yourself too, Bill.

BILL: I wouldn't mind wetting my whistle again at all. My mouth feels kind of dry. My lips are dry. My whole head feels kind of dry. (*He touches himself, and they do as they move.*) And that's strange, because there's plenty of moisture in the air. My eyes feel kind of dry, and when I slide my hand along my face, my skin feels dry, and my neck feels even drier. My shoulders are rutted with sharp little cracks, my chest is just a saline crust, and below that it's just sand . . .

IRENE: Your system's not getting enough lubrication, Bill!

BILL: That's right, my system's not getting enough lubrication. I need to lubricate from the inside out. I'll get us some more drinks. (*Exits out passageway.*)

MYRA: (*Quickly, while Bill is gone.*) Well, how long has this girl been writing to Bill?

IRENE: These letters have been coming for months. I've got stacks of them. (*Gets stack of letters.*) Bill won't even look at them. And she writes so beautifully. Sometimes she'll even put a poem inside. Here, read this one.

MYRA: (*Reading while Irene dances. Girl comes up in window and doubles Myra's voice. Irene joins them for last few lines. Music.*)

"Ash white as bird lime behind the house that you
     burned down,
Where the sheets flap as aggravation but not
     mournfully,
And the ranks of cabbage children bud and swell and
     pop
Big as melons, and we don't recognize a single face,
     but they
Are all taken and trimmed, whether in need or in
     anger.

And your little girl is just a curl of wildcarrot now,

Pushing up under the empty mugs, cooling her fever
with moss,

But not avoiding frank shadows. And the relatives
set up shop

For me. There's just one of them, a hag with sacks of
morels,

Which we dry on the bedspread abandoned by July.
The noon

Nudges in and pins us in to doll's dilemmas, the ones
you used

When younger to make the killers drop their tools.
But only

One of us remembers you. Only one of us awaits
you. (*Bill enters.*)

Only one of us knows who you are, where you are
and what

You mean and what you mean to be, but we don't
tell. Love says,

Stay still 'til he's ready. And that's enough. For today.

For today and every Tuesday of this month, as long
as I can

Still water the garden, stiff with pride, hoping you'll
call me."

BILL:	What's that you're reading there, Myra?
IRENE:	It's a letter from your daughter, Bill.
BILL:	I don't have any daughter.
IRENE:	That's not what your ex-wife says.
BILL:	You don't know my ex-wife.
IRENE:	But I know you and it seems believable.
BILL:	Well she should sue me and try to prove it in court.
	That woman was pregnant every day of her life. She

didn't feel right if she wasn't pregnant. If she couldn't get it from one man, she'd get it from another.

IRENE: She says you've got a teenage daughter.

BILL: Would you believe her before you believe me?

IRENE: But look at this stack of letters, Bill. The least you could do is answer the girl.

BILL: I can't control the lives of people who've been lied to. I can't control that. I know where I've been. I'm not some king in a fairy tale who kills his daughter without knowing who she is. I don't have any children. I've never had any children. And I never will. There are too many damn children in the world already, wandering around half-starved with no one to feed them. My mother made me, and it was a big mistake. She already had Phil. She didn't need no Bill. Well, I'm not adding to that pile, you understand? You got women out there get pregnant just to pass the time, that's not my fault. And they give birth to girls who get pregnant just to pass the time and that's not my fault either. No one can blame me personally for any of the tragedies of this world. As long as there's no tragedy here in the orange grove, that's the best I can do. This little domain is all I can control.

IRENE: Control! Control! We don't even know whether we're going to be here tomorrow or not. Avakian wants us to leave. I know he does. People used to own the roofs over their heads. My mother and father did. They had a roof and it was their own. We're renters, Bill. You're forty years old, and we're still renters! They can throw us out whenever they want!

BILL: That girl is not my daughter! Just because you live with a woman doesn't mean you're responsible for everything that slides out from between her legs. I'd like to be Phil: kiss 'em once, hug 'em twice, and send 'em on their way. No one blames you for anything. A lot of people would like to be Phil. He comes and goes like a summer squall, so everyone's real glad to have him around. You were even wishing that Myra was Phil. WELL MYRA WAS NOT PHIL!! (*The three rush to opposite places, drain their drinks. Pause.*)

MYRA: Well, of course I wasn't Phil. Would that I were.
Would that I were instead of who I am.
Or is it who I be? Would that I were
instead of who I be? Does that sound right?

BILL: I know Phil will be able to bring that bridge back.
I'd rather have amnesia than what I've got.
With amnesia the whole plot disappears.
A kind of Novocain covers your reruns.
If you don't remember anything, you don't know
who you are at all. You're someone
who feels cold. Someone who feels hungry.
When you want a bowl of soup you come out
of the fog on the most bone-chilling day
in early December into the warmest café in town,
and you say, I'll have the pea soup and the corn
    bread,
and they bring it right away. They don't care
if you're Bill or Phil as long as you can pay.

IRENE: And that pea soup will be good.
Those people can cook. I learned my cooking
from people like that.

MYRA: I learned to dance from people like that.
I learned to raise my arm and turn. (*She does so.
    Irene joins her.*)

IRENE: And then you taught me, Myra. Remember that?

MYRA: Of course I remember. How could I forget?

BILL: I haven't yet learned to raise my arm and turn.

MYRA and IRENE: O come on, Bill! Take a chance! You can do it! You're a natural!! (*Myra tries to show Bill how to dance. He moves clumsily. Irene establishes a steady movement in the opposite corner. Music.*)

IRENE: (*While moving.*) You hear water in the desert a long way off.

The rustling of the ocotillo won't cover it.

The stirring of the yucca won't muffle that sound.

Dogs will howl, and that will bring coyotes

to their calling too, but there will always be spaces,

pauses between thoughts, and that will be the water,

a long way off. A long way off.

MYRA: (*Coming to stir the chili, leaving Bill in clumsy dance.*)

And inside those pauses, there'll be pauses too,

when one kind of wind will rattle a dead saguaro.

They look so timeless and indestructible,

standing in the desert with their arms held high,

a cactus so cruel and patient, you'd think

they could do without water at all. And then

you find one dried up and humbled. And you see

what it was: a skin for holding water. A body

for holding water. But the water is gone.

And soon the shell of that saguaro will be gone as well.

All trace of it. All trace of it.

IRENE: (*Irene and Myra lead Bill to the chili.*) Come and stir the chili, Bill.

MYRA: Stir this chili, Bill. Put your heart in it.

We'll keep an eye out for your brother.

(They exit out screen door, but do not pass window.)

BILL: *(Silence. Stirs chili.)*
When I saw my
father dying I
closed the door be-
hind me and held on
to an iron rail
so I
wouldn't go down. *(Pause. Stirs.)*
I looked into the
mirror over the
sink, waiting
for the tears
to drown out my face,
but there were no tears.
(Pause, stirs chili. Tastes it.)
And when I came back
to where my father
was dying, my mother
was trying to feed him
some soup, but his mouth
couldn't hold it, it spilled
out of his face, down over
his sallow neck, and I
knew that it was ending. And
he looked in my
eyes and said, Bill,
why don't we get the hell
out of this motel, and I said,
why don't we, Dad? It's
time we were gone. *(Pause.)*

And then he took
my hand and pressed it
with the little strength
he had left and said, you're
not Bill, you're Phil. You think
you're Bill, but you're
really Phil. And then
he died. He was smiling.

IRENE: (*Entering with Myra, Mrs. Avakian just behind.*)
How's the chili, Bill?

MYRA: Do you want relief?

MRS. AVAKIAN: (*Putting head in window, then entering.*)
Sorry to barge in on you folks again,
but Bill, I ran into your brother Phil down the road,
hip-deep in mud where his pickup run in the ditch.

BILL: Oh no.

MRS. AVAKIAN: Now you know that place where the creek
run over the road this past spring?

BILL: I sure do.

MRS. AVAKIAN: Well Phil's hip-deep in mud down there
and he asked me if I wouldn't drive up here
and say he'll just be a little late.
He had some people down there helpin' him,
and he said he was almost out,
but that truck of his was just up to the hubcaps
on one end and spun across the road on the other.
I've said to Ernie every spring for thirty years
we need to put a little bridge in there.
Hell, some years there wouldn't be any road in there
at all.
You'd come over that little rise and there'd just be

a little river down there in the hollow.
Well, that's the thing about this place,
ten months a year just as dry as a lizard's nose
and then those rains come in . . .
Hell one time when I was a kid
one of those storms come down all of a sudden
from off the San Marcos ridge way up in the bosky
    there.
I was sittin' with my sister Eileen
on that embankment over by Johnny Weester's,
well what used to be Weester's that Sunkist got now,
and one of Weester's kids was down wading in the
    wash,
and she had a little nip-eared terrier we called
    Chicken Breath
cause that dog had gotten into our chickens a
    number of times,
and every time it came around my dad said he could
    smell chicken
on that dog's breath, so we just called it Chicken
    Breath.
Course Weester's little girl Doreen didn't like that too
    much:
she was the sister of the guy that's got the liquor
    store
over there in Lancaster where the new interstate is
    goin' through,
I forget what the hell his name is, Bobby Weester or
    Dwayne Weester . . .
BILL, IRENE, MYRA: Dickie Weester? Was it Steve Weester? Mike
    Weester? Dave Weester?

MRS. AVAKIAN: No, it was Dean Weester! Dean Weester, that's
right, you know the guy I'm talking about, he used to
have a liquor store over here too . . .

BILL: Oh I know Dean Weester all right!

MRS. AVAKIAN: So there! I thought you knew Dean Weester!
(*Girl is in window. Goes slowly down.*)
Well this was Dean Weester's little sister Doreen,
and she and this dog Chicken Breath were splashin'
and rompin'
down there in the wash and havin' themselves a
helluva time
and that water was about hip-deep and runnin'
pretty strong
and me and Eileen we could see it was stormin' up
there in the bosky
cause it got as black as an oil stain up along that
ridge
like someone just drained the crankcase right outta
the sky.
And we told this Weester girl she better get up on the
embankment
and sure enough that water rose a foot or two in no
more than 10 minutes
and this Doreen Weester got scared as hell and
managed to pull herself out
and got up on the embankment with us but that little
nip-eared dog
had already drifted quite a ways down the wash
and we run along the embankment all three of us
yelling to that dog
but it was just a little bitty thing and it couldn't fight
the current

and this Doreen Weester she just lost her senses and
   jumped back
into the wash just before it runs into the river to save
   that damn dog
and before you could say I told you so they were
   both struggling
just to keep their heads above water and there wasn't
   a damn thing we could do
well once we tried to reach out to them with a
   branch (*Lights go down.*)
but that Doreen Weester was struggling so hard
she didn't even see the branch
we had the branch out there but she never saw it
   (*Blackout.*)
and then they just went under
first the dog (*Pause.*)
and then the girl
and we kept running along the bank
'til we couldn't run anymore
and we didn't want to tell anyone
cause we were sure they'd blame it all on us
but we run to the Weester's howling all the way
and when we finally got to the Weester's there was
   no one there
the place was deserted
we just sat there knowing there was one dead dog
   and one drowned girl
in that river and we were the only ones that knew.
Well, you know what they say,
can't have oranges without water.

(Phil enters in the dark. Mrs. Avakian is gone. Phil is completely covered in mud. Lights come up very fast.)

BILL: It's the mud man my brother!

PHIL: Hey, if there wasn't no mud, we wouldn't be able to crawl in it!

IRENE: Phil, you look like one of those big earthworms that gets flooded out when it rains . . . and then it lays there wiggling on the ground trying to find its hole!

PHIL: Trying to find my hole! That's good!

MYRA: Would you like to take a shower, Phil? Then we could see what you really look like!

BILL: *(Phil has been wiping off and taking hits off a bottle.)* I've got a change of clothes you could wear right here.

PHIL: Oh come on! Your clothes would never fit me, Bill!

BILL: Of course my clothes would fit you, Phil! We're nearly the same size! We could be twins! Hell, we always wore one another's clothes! Don't you remember what a hard time dad had telling us apart we'd be switchin' shirts and shoes so often? We were practically interchangeable. Don't you remember that?

PHIL: *(Pause. Looks at Bill.)* No. I don't remember that at all. I don't even recall wearing anyone's clothes but my own.

BILL: I'm offering you a change of clothes, Phil . . . I'm offering you something comfortable to step into out of the goodness of my heart . . .

PHIL: *(Threatening to smear mud on Bill.)* You are? That's really brotherly of you, Bill! But I want to get a look at that heart of yours first . . .

BILL: Don't you rub that mud on me, Phil!

PHIL: Whatsamatter, Billy, don't be afraid of a little mud. It's just old Mama Earth, you know . . .

BILL: Phil, if you get mud on me I'll . . .

PHIL: This is your mud, Bill!

BILL: Get away from me, Phil!

IRENE: Rub it on him, Phil! Bill can afford to be a little muddy!

PHIL: I'm just returning this mud to its rightful owner! I didn't have this mud on me 'til I sunk down in it right there on your road! You own this mud!

BILL: We don't own that mud, Phil, we rent it . . .

PHIL: Holy motherfucking Christ on a crutch! You mean to say I'm covered in rented mud! I'll have to scrape it all off and put it back where it came from, every last gob! Now who's got the mudsucker? Is it you, Irene?

IRENE: Get those muddy paws away from me Phil!

PHIL: Do you hear that? Muddy paws! Gimme that mud-sucker, Irene, before I wrap my muddy tail around you!

IRENE: Get away from me, Phil! Bill get this muddy dog of a brother of yours away from me!

BILL: Hey, I got no more control over this bloody dog than any coyote's brother has over him!

PHIL: Muddy dog want mudsucker to get bloody mud off my muddy ass!

IRENE: Try Myra, Phil . . . The Highway Patrol always got their mudsuckers handy. In case of a muddy emergency.

PHIL: That's right! Why didn't I think of that!

BILL: Because you're a bloody muddy dog, Phil! You lack the power of reason! (*Mona passes window, slowly enough so very pregnant belly is visible. She looks in, then enters, holding door open.)*

PHIL: Myra! Gimme mudsucker! (*Pause. Stop. They look at each other. Mona watches.*)

MYRA: (*Getting up on table.*) Well, come and get it you big dog! I got it right here underneath my dress. (*Phil gets down on the floor and crawls toward Myra, making dog sounds.*) Now take it easy. I don't want any of that mud on me. Just reach up real gentle and don't touch my legs and don't touch my dress, and I'll drop that mudsucker right in your hand. (*Phil grunts assent.*) Now don't touch my leg and don't touch my dress, or the little mudsucker won't fall out!

PHIL: I no touch. Dog no touch lady. Dog want to be good . . .

MYRA: That's it. Nice and slow. Now don't touch my legs now!

PHIL: Dog no touch lady leg! (*Phil has hand up under Myra's skirt. Mona slams door.*)

MONA: Now I've seen all of it!

PHIL: Mona!

MONA: Lookin' for somethin', Phil? Lose your toothbrush?

PHIL: Mona! I'm sorry! I forgot!

MONA: Oh I don't mind laying out in the heat!

PHIL: I just forgot for a second, Mona! We were just fuckin' around!

MONA: Oh I can see how you were fuckin' around!

PHIL: Mona . . .

MONA: A hundred and three in the shade, flies and mosquitoes fryin' on the windshield, and this little girl about to bubble up out of me, and where does he go? "I'll just be a minute," he says, "to make sure there's room for one more." (*Touching her belly.*) Room for one more.

IRENE: Of course there's room for one more . . .

BILL: Any friend of Phil is a friend of Bill.

MYRA: Come on in and take a load off . . . chili's almost ready . . .

MONA: Well there better be enough for two more, cause I'm eating and drinking for two these days, me and my little daughter here . . .

IRENE: How do you know it's a girl?

MONA: Oh I knew right away.

PHIL: We had a sonogram done!

MONA: Sonogram! I knew it was a girl as soon as I was pregnant. This is to replace the one you lost on me, Phil. I told you that. I told you that a thousand times!

PHIL: Mona, I'm sorry. I was just on my way out . . .

MONA: (*Nudging Myra.*) You were just on your way in, Phil. I got eyes! Not that I lay any claim on you. I don't lay any claim on nothin' in this world. There's a top and a bottom to this here planet. Me, I occupy the bottom. But that's OK. That's where most of the people are. (*Baby jumps. She clutches her belly.*) Calm down little dewdrop!! You ain't ready for reality just yet.

MYRA: Why don't you introduce us to your . . . friend, Phil?

MONA: Don't you go callin' me a friend of anyone! You know what the last person I called a friend did? He cut my only daughter's head off!

PHIL: Mona, control yourself! You promised you wouldn't do it here!

MYRA: Did this get reported to the police?

MONA: The police! That's a joke.

BILL: Is this the truth, Phil?

PHIL: She's just a little disturbed . . . because of the baby . . .

MONA: (*To Irene.*) Is that the kind of world we live in? One day he's just the kid next door, then the next day he says I'm hidin' Mexicans in my house! Says I got wetbacks hidden behind my sofa, and he goes runnin' through the house with one of those big old machetes they use down there in Mexico for splittin' coconuts . . .

IRENE: That's unbelievable! When did this happen?

BILL: What the hell is she talkin' about . . .

PHIL: Don't listen to her . . . She'll come out of it . . .

MONA: Only this wasn't no goddamn Mexican this was Dickie Wells, and I'd known him since he was a boy and Eileen seen him comin' with that big ol' machete, and she dives behind the sofa . . .

IRENE: Oh, my God!

MONA: And Dickie Wells yells, "There's a fuckin' wetback now!" And he cuts the head right of my little Eileen! (*Pause.*)

PHIL: Mona . . .

IRENE: This can't be true. This just can't be.

MONA: You think this is just news stories. You think this kind of thing doesn't really happen to real live people. Well let me tell you something. Afghanistan is only a dream. That's what they feed you to take your eye off the eight ball. The real war's right here in El Centro, California. You tell me this story ain't true, Phil.

PHIL: It isn't true!

IRENE: I hope to God it isn't true!

MYRA: If this happened in El Centro, I'm sure I would have heard about it.

MONA: North America, South America, it's all the same, Russia, Japan, Band-la-desh, I-ran, I-raq, Uzbekistan, Amarillo . . .

PHIL: You promised, Mona . . .

MONA: . . . Albuquerque, Gallup, Yuma, Firebaugh, there ain't no difference. Not for me there ain't. Wherever I was on the face of this earth, my life would be the same. (*Pause. Tenderly, confused.*) Did I ever have a daughter, Phil?

PHIL: You had a daughter, Mona, no one disputes that . . .

MONA: Well, do I have a daughter now??? Can you see a girl of nineteen standing here beside me?

PHIL: She's away on vacation, Mona. She's fine.

MONA: Are you saying all this is just a lie? Are you telling these people this is all a lie!?

PHIL: Well it's not exactly a lie, but it's not exactly the truth, either.

MONA: You tell them you didn't see your daughter Eileen's head rolled under a chair while her body just lay there under the couch!

PHIL: I never had a daughter with you, Mona.

MONA: That girl was the spittin' image of you, Bill, and you know it!

PHIL: My name's not Bill, it's Phil . . . This is Bill, Mona, my brother Bill. Try to get small things straight first, then move on to more complex issues.

MONA: He looks just like you, Phil. The same red hair. The same blue eyes.
He coulda been Eileen's father as well as you.
(*Pause.*)
Do you think I could have a glass of water?

BILL: Of course you could have a glass of water.

IRENE: Ice cold water comin' right up . . . (*Pours water slowly in large glass. Hands it to Mona. Mona drinks it thirstily, spilling some of it over her. Pause.*)

MONA: Do any of you folks have any children?

IRENE: Well, Bill has a daughter by a previous marriage . . .

BILL: Irene, you're not gonna start on that shit again!

PHIL: None of us has any children!

MONA: You're damn right we don't have any children, 'cause when they cut the head off your neck, the blood don't circulate properly . . .

BILL: (*Leading Phil toward shower.*) Let's get you out of those clothes and wash some of that mud off . . .

MONA: (*Laughing.*) It just kinda drains right out right there on the floor . . .

PHIL: There never was any blood, Mona!

IRENE: Wouldn't you like to sit down, honey?

MYRA: Take a load off your feet?

BILL: I'll get this shower cranked up . . .

MONA: It just drains out right there on the linoleum and then you have to mop it up! (*She goes into a heavy labor spasm as Phil undresses. Irene and Myra hold onto her.*)

MYRA: I think we should get you to a hospital!

MONA: Oh no! No hospital! I'm days away. And I don't have no ID . . . They wouldn't take me with no ID!

BILL: (*To Phil.*) Is she all right? She looks really close . . .

PHIL: She's weeks away . . . She always pulls this act when she wants you to listen to her stories . . .

IRENE: Maybe a cold towel . . . Myra?

MYRA: I'll get it . . .

BILL: Is the kid yours, Phil? Who's the father?

PHIL: I don't know, Bill. We were livin' together down in El Centro. And then I got this well drillin' job with Bobby Walls out in Burn . . .

BILL: Out in the desert over by Yuma?

PHIL: Right.

MYRA: (*Drenching Myra's brow with cold water.*) Here you go, honey . . . (*Mona moans.*)

PHIL: Bobby promised me we'd hit water in less than three weeks. Three weeks! You know what happens. You're drillin' and you can almost smell the water! And then you hit some rock, and the bit breaks off and I'm holding Bobby Walls by the ankles while he hangs down head first in the hole and gets that sucker welded. By the time I pulled him out he looked like he'd been shit out of the earth! (*Mona groans loudly.*)

MYRA: Are you sure this baby hasn't dropped yet. This really feels like labor to me . . .

MONA: I'm just a day over eight months . . . if I been countin' right . . .

IRENE: You feel like you're about to pop . . .

MONA: I know I been countin' right . . .

MYRA: (*Wiping her brow.*) That feel a little better?

MONA: (*Shallow labor still.*) MMMnnnnnn.

PHIL: You know how it goes. A few more days and we'll hit water. And then it's four weeks, no water, five weeks no water. And you know the drillin' business, no water, no pay.

MYRA: I think you're about to have this kid . . .

MONA: The last one was early, so I know this one's gonna be late. I know I counted right . . .

PHIL: It was nine fuckin' weeks before we hit water, ten hours a day drillin' that sucker. And by the time I got back Mona's in the sack with a guy named Earl, so-navabitch I used to do business with! So you tell me whose kid it is, Bill, I don't know! (*Getting in shower.*) Woooo! This sucker is hot! (*Bill returns to maps. Myra regains composure and looks out window.*)

BILL: You know, Phil, I've been wanting to ask you something about that trip we took . . .

PHIL: What you say, Bill?

BILL: I've been wanting to ask you something about that trip we took down south . . . When we saw that little girl on the bridge, remember?

MONA: What were you saying about that daughter of Bill's?

PHIL: I can't hear you, Bill!

IRENE: Well, this girl has been sending him stacks of letters . . .

BILL: What are you telling her now, Irene?

MONA: That daughter of Bill's is out there!

BILL: Oh for Christ's sake!

PHIL: I can't hear you, Bill!

MYRA: What are you talking about?

MONA: I know that girl is gonna come! That daughter of Bill's is out there sure as I got a girl in my belly!

BILL: I can't believe this! (*Returns to maps.*)

MYRA: I think I better stir this chili . . .

MONA: Can you feel that girl out there?

IRENE: Of course I can feel her! Any woman could!

MONA: How about you, honey?

MYRA: What girl are you talking about? (*Steam from shower starts to cover stage.*)

MONA: (*Whispering.*) Bill's daughter.

MYRA: You mean outside? What do you mean?

MONA: (*To Irene.*) Here, you sit down. And let me get behind you. And let me put my belly up against your head. Maybe my girl will help you see Bill's . . . (*Pause.*) Can you see her now? (*Girl lurks in doorway.*)

IRENE: I can feel her, but I still can't see her . . .

MONA: Just take it slow . . . Men hide these girls away, but we can find them if we take our time . . .

IRENE: There's just a lot of mist so far, but something's moving around in there . . .

MYRA: What do you mean something's moving around in there? Can you really see something?

IRENE: I can't tell if it's a tree or a person standing in the mist . . .

MONA: Take your time . . . don't scare her away . . . she'll come when she's ready . . .

MYRA: Are you really seeing something, Irene? (*Girl is gone.*)

MONA: Why don't you come over here and sit by me too?

MYRA: Oh, all right. Just let me turn this chili down . . . (*Myra comes and sits down. Mona puts belly against her head.*)

IRENE: I can't tell if they're big saguaro cactuses or people with their arms held over their heads . . . there's still too much fog . . . like ground fog in the desert . . .

MONA: How about you, honey?

MYRA: It looks like the fog that rolls in off the ocean, just at dawn, when you can hardly see the waves . . . I think I can hear someone swimming out there though! Is that Bill's daughter? (*Girl watches through steam.*)

IRENE: But I see big tall saguaro cactuses, Myra, like down in the desert! She can't be in both places!

BILL: Phil! I've been wanting to ask you about that trip we took!

MONA: These are places she's moving through . . . ocean and desert both . . .

PHIL: What you say, Bill?

MONA: Places on the way . . . you're seeing her at different times . . .

BILL: When we saw that little girl on the bridge, remember!?

MYRA: It looks like Arroyo Burro Beach to me . . .

IRENE: There's a fast little creek running through the sand! It looks like the place where I nearly drowned . . . scraggly creosote hanging over the edge . . . is there someone down there? Is that Bill's daughter?

MONA: Take your time . . . she's still got a lot of growing to do . . .

PHIL: (*Poking his head out of shower.*) You know every time I get in a steamy shower like this, it reminds me of gettin' sent down to the jungle . . . protectin' those bananas for Uncle Sam, remember?

BILL: What? I was asking you about that bridge, Phil, on the trip!

MYRA: It is Arroyo Burro Beach, Irene! Where we used to swim! I can see the dark form of the kelp way off the shore.

IRENE: It's little Cuchara Creek, Myra, where Phil had to pull me out!

MONA: Wait for her shape to be clear . . . you've got to be patient!

BILL: The bridge where we met that little girl, Phil!

MONA: Don't try to see what's not ready to be seen.

PHIL: Everyone was joinin' the Guard to keep their ass from getting shipped down there, remember? (*Girl begins swinging in window.*)

BILL: Phil, I've heard every one of your goddamn war stories a thousand times! The war is over!

PHIL: And then the suckers mobilized the Guard! Sent my ass down there to haul jet fuel through the jungle! Pacify the snakes! (*Head pops up. Pointing fingers at Bill.*) You remember that don't you, Bill?

BILL: I'm tired of war stories, Phil. Everyone is tired of them!

PHIL: See, this mist would come in down in the jungle, hot as steam comin' out of the ground . . .

BILL: There isn't anything you can tell me about that war I don't already know, Phil . . .

PHIL: We'd have to truck that jet fuel right through the soup! That's right on the equator see, middle of Mama Earth . . .

BILL: Phil, I wanted you to help me remember this bridge . . .

PHIL: I remember one Sunday my driver José, he asks me if I wanna go to Mass before we roll . . .

BILL: I don't want to hear about the war, Phil. I'm sick of the war.

PHIL: Mass! Can you dig it? That sucker José never prayed for anything before unless it was for some fresh snake pussy! But he's scared because of that mist, see?

BILL: (*Coming to shower. Face to face with Phil.*) I know José was scared, Phil! We were all scared! Anyone who tells you he wasn't scared down there is a fuckin' liar . . .

MONA: (*To Irene.*) You should be able to see her now . . . there's the desert . . .

IRENE: Oh I can see her! She's walking along the edge of that creek. She's got such long, thick, red hair, she looks just like Bill! She's so pretty!

PHIL: Ridin' shotgun through the jungle on a truckload of jet fuel, 10,000 gallons of jet fuel behind your head, if you get hit you don't lose an eye or a leg . . .

BILL: You get erased! You vaporize!

PHIL: And it wasn't the snake regulars you was worried about.

BILL: It was the fuckin' snake people, man, the whole fuckin' country!

PHIL: Any young snake chick could roll a Molotov cocktail under your ass and blow you off the planet! (*Comes out of shower. Dresses in same clothes as Bill. They circle as he dresses.*)

IRENE: She's so pretty! She's pickin' flowers and ferns and twining them in her hair just like we did when we were kids . . . (*Girl is gone.*)

MONA: There's the ocean . . . I can see her swimming . . . You should be able to make her out . . .

MYRA: Oh, she looks just like you, Irene. The same steady stroke. If I didn't know it was Bill's daughter I'd be sure that it was you . . . and she's swimming right where we used to swim . . . way out beyond the kelp . . .

IRENE: But the girl I see's about to cross that creek! She's too young to swim!

MONA: Take it easy: one girl's getting older, one girl's getting younger. Let her find the shape she wants to be . . .

BILL: So this Sunday there's ten times as many people as we usually see, jammin' the roads in both directions,

	only you can hardly see them because of that mist. I'm ridin' shotgun. Got to check out every one of these sucker snake people. And all of a sudden this woman steps right out of the jungle!
MYRA:	Now she's wading in, Irene! She's a big, strong girl!
BILL:	She wasn't on the road, man! She just slithered off those tall jungle weeds like she was waiting for us!
MYRA:	More and more of her keeps comin' out of the water!
BILL:	She couldna been more than sixteen or so . . .
PHIL:	Those were the ones that really scared you, man, the young snake chicks!
IRENE:	Oh I knew this was gonna happen! She's gonna try to cross that stream on the log! She has no idea how deep it is!
BILL:	Any other day I'd have known there was a baby in there!
PHIL:	Coulda been a baby, coulda been a grenade!
BILL:	(*Phil is now completely dressed in the same clothes as Bill.*) I couldn't see in that fuckin' mist! So when she reached down between her tits, I fired! The blast knocked her right off her feet into the air! And something flew out from under her dress, but I couldn't see what it was. I didn't want to see! And then Paco stopped the truck. And he backed it up. He's not supposed to do that, man.
PHIL:	You never back up. What's done is done!
BILL:	And there she was, dead on the ground, and the baby on the ground beside her . . .
PHIL:	How could you tell in a mist like that?
BILL:	I shot through the baby and got the mother too. Same bullets!

MYRA: Wait a minute! Are you sure that's Bill's daughter comin' out of the water? She looks just like the girl we arrested today!

BILL: I'm so ashamed I did that, man.

MONA: Arrested?

BILL: Dad didn't raise us to be killers.

MYRA: Girl we arrested for drowning her father . . .

PHIL: It coulda been me, man, it coulda been any of us . . .

MONA: You're a cop?

MYRA: Yup, Highway Patrol, does that bother you?

MONA: Why should it bother me? I ain't done nothing wrong.

PHIL: Don't cry, man. You'll get me cryin'.

MYRA: You just seem kinda bothered that's all . . .

BILL: I got to cry, what else can I do?

MYRA: Did someone really cut your daughter's head off? (*Quickly, to Irene.*) Wake up honey, the real story's out here . . .

MONA: Well, Phil don't like me to tell it this way . . .

IRENE: What are you saying about Phil?

PHIL: (*Sitting down to maps.*) You got to help me with this bridge, brother. If we can remember the desert, maybe the jungle will fade away . . .

MONA: You see it happened in a motel . . .

BILL: Here, close your eyes, 'cause it was almost dark when we got to that bridge . . . (*Bill stands behind Phil. Puts his hands over his eyes.*)

MONA: Phil don't like me to talk about it . . .

BILL: I'll keep the light out . . . and we'll see if we can't get that bridge to come back . . .

MYRA: Phil's not gonna hear it . . .

IRENE: Phil's busy with Bill . . .

MONA: See, Phil and Eileen and me were staying in this mo-
         tel . . . the El Camino Motel . . . it's on the frontage
         road right there in Burn . . . you know where Burn
         is?

MYRA: By Yuma, out in the desert.

MONA: We went out there to meet this guy named Earl . . . he
         had some stuff he wanted Phil to sell for him . . .

MYRA: What kind of stuff?

BILL: Can you see the path now?

PHIL: I can see the path, Brother.

MONA: There was only one room left in that motel, see . . .
         and there was only one bed in it, and so we all had to
         sleep together in that one bed . . .

IRENE: Not Earl too!

MONA: Oh no! Are you crazy? No way! Forget it! That Earl
         would never sleep with Phil! Mona and Phil and Eileen
         weren't hardly people as far as Earl was concerned.
         He just wanted us to do his dirty work.

MYRA: What kinda dirty work?

PHIL: I can feel the coolness of that water now!

BILL: It's me and you man, headed straight for that bridge!

MONA: And our Eileen, I mean my Eileen, she'd been havin' a
         real hard time keepin' her water in at night. I think it
         had to do with Phil . . .

IRENE: But Phil's always been so nice with kids . . .

MONA: Well somethin' happened to him down in the jun-
         gle . . . he couldn't stand the smell of piss . . .

IRENE: But that wasn't Phil down in the jungle, that was
         Bill . . .

MONA: Well I get the two of them mixed up sometimes . . .

BILL: Can you see the bridge yet?

PHIL: I can hear the water, but I can't see the bridge . . .

BILL: Stay with it . . . I'm with you . . .

MONA: Anyways we woke up one morning all together in that motel room, and Eileen had peed up that bed like you wouldn't believe . . . I guess she'd been drinkin' more Dr. Peppers than we knew . . . and that bed was soaked, I mean saturated . . .

PHIL: I can feel the water, but I can't see the bridge . . .

MONA: And Bill woke up just drippin' in Eileen's pee!

IRENE: You don't mean Bill, you mean Phil!

MONA: Well maybe I'm just a little confused. Anyway, Phil woke up just drippin' in Eileen's pee. And he just hit the roof. And that's when he started makin' her march around the bed . . .

IRENE: March around the bed?

MYRA: I heard about this . . . this was reported last week!

MONA: Oh this wasn't last week! This wasn't reported. He'd march her around the bed, and he'd pull out that belt, and she'd be yellin', "don't hit me, Phil, don't hit me!"

BILL: Can you see the bridge yet?

PHIL: I can see the girl, but I can't see the bridge . . .

BILL: Well, if she's not on the bridge, where the hell is she?

PHIL: She's in a motel room . . .

BILL: Motel? What motel?

MONA: She'd yell, don't do it, Bill, and then he'd let her have it!

IRENE: Phil! Phil!

BILL: We stayed in the pickup! Don't you remember that?

PHIL: It's the El Camino Motel I see . . .

MONA: One time she wouldn't get up, and I tried to stop him!

BILL: El Camino Motel? You mean in Burn?

MONA: I said that girl's not breathing, Bill, don't hit her again!

BILL: I never did a thing to that girl, and you know it, Mona!

MONA: I saw what you did with my very own eyes!

PHIL: Myra, come here and take a look at this map. There's something here that doesn't make sense.

IRENE: (*Stirring chili.*) Yeah, go over there and help him out, Myra. He's trying to find his way into the present.

BILL: I never hurt that girl, Mona! You're always trying to make connections between one thing and another, so everything looks like some kind of plot. But there isn't any plot!

MONA: It's in your interest to say there isn't any plot, then no one can follow your story!

PHIL: Look, here's where we parked the pickup at the edge of the barrio . . .

BILL: Why would it be in my interest to say there isn't any plot? Plot or no plot, my life would be the same!

MYRA: Right . . . there's the lake, Lago Viejo . . . and there's the curve where that big house was with the big dogs . . .

IRENE: Avakian wants us out of here, I know he does . . .

MONA: You tell me you didn't march my daughter around that bed!

BILL: Now Mona, this has gone just a little too far!

PHIL: Avakian's nearly dead, Irene! He's not gonna kick us out with his very last words!

MONA: El Camino Motel ring any bells!?

BILL: I've had enough out of you, Mona!

IRENE: We're nothing but renters. You're forty years old and we're still renters!

MONA:	Did I ever have a daughter?
IRENE:	They can kick us out any time they want!
MONA:	Are you saying I never had a daughter at all!?
PHIL:	That girl is not my daughter!
BILL:	You had a daughter, Mona. No one disputes that!
PHIL:	Just because you live with a woman doesn't mean you're responsible for everything that slides out from between her legs!
MONA:	They took Eileen away from me because of what you did in that motel. Put her in a home. Said I wasn't fit to raise her myself.
BILL:	Mona, it isn't true!
MONA:	You think I couldn't see the handwriting on the wall!? They were selling those girls to A-rab businessmen! Eileen's shacked up right now with some A-rab sheik in I-raq!
BILL:	SHE'S NOT SHACKED UP IN IRAQ AT ALL, MONA!!! (*Pause.*) I just got a letter from her the other day.
MONA:	Where is she? Where's my little baby?
BILL:	She's fishing with her boyfriend up in Idaho, Mona! I told you that!
MONA:	You didn't tell me! You never told me! Give me that letter!
BILL:	(*They slowly pass the letter, hand to hand to Mona.*) Mona, that girl has been sending you stacks of letters. You never look at any of them!
MONA:	(*Stares at letter.*) You know I don't know how to read.
MYRA:	Here, let me read it for you, honey . . . we'll get to the bottom of this story once and for all . . .

MONA: (*Handing Myra the letter.*) You'll read me every word of it. Exactly like she wrote it?

MYRA: I promise. (*Girl up in window. Others gather around Myra. Movement.*)

MYRA and GIRL: There's no outlet to this lake where I lie
in my little aluminum boat and let the light
wind of evening rock me from side to side.
I'm no longer a baby, and I'm hardly a bride,
but the mist that plays over my body and holds me
grows whiter and whiter as the moon rises
above the trees. Something so innocent
throbs underneath me, like water breathing
in cisterns or wine sleeping in heavy barrels
or the slow roll of the tide that swells the lake
against the shore. And I am in something, and on
something, and of something, and outside
of something all at once, complete
but unfinished, distinct but unnoticed,
when another mother I don't know at all
is born in the milk of the night and makes my dream.

And then out of this whiteness a kind of nameless
calling, a kind of songless singing, a slow
and gentle rubbing of hands, thickens the air
where I float, and there are no more shapes
to locate my turning, not even a star to anchor
my gaze. And I am not one person, but many,
neither dead nor yet alive. I am nothing
but your daughter, and I keep on being born.

MONA: It's gonna come now! It's my girl coming back! She's ready now!

IRENE: Oh my God help me clear the table!

MYRA:	Water! Heat water!
PHIL:	I'll take care of the water!
BILL:	What the hell did I do with those paper towels?
MYRA:	Irene, get my emergency kit out of the back of the cruiser!
IRENE:	Is it open?
MYRA:	It's open! Right by my rifle! I'll get these sheets over and under her. (*Mona groans.*) How close are you honey?
MONA:	Oh, I'm a lot closer than I thought! She's in my water now! I can feel her pushing down! (*Sounds of water heating, steam rising. To Bill.*) Is this kid yours? Are you the father?
BILL:	Mona, I really don't think this is the time to worry about whose kid this is!
MONA:	Well, I wanna get the matter settled before she gets here . . . and there isn't much time!
BILL:	Don't you think you should just concentrate on having this baby right now, Mona?
MONA:	But are you gonna accept this girl as your own is what I wanna know!
BILL:	Of course I'm gonna accept the girl as my own! I told you that! I told you that a thousand times!
MONA:	Well, what if she ends up lookin' like Earl!? You're not gonna turn your back on her?
BILL:	I accepted your last kid as my own, didn't I, Mona!? And I wasn't even around when she was born! (*Irene comes in with emergency equipment. Girl comes up in window.*)
MONA:	Well where were you?
BILL:	I didn't even know you when that kid was born! It was years ago!

PHIL: Listen, Mona, if my brother here doesn't want to be the father of your kid, I'd like to volunteer . . .

BILL: Who do you think you are!? You can't be the father of this kid! You've never seen Mona before today!

PHIL: It's just a feeling I have! I feel like a father!

IRENE: Well can you believe that!? I've wanted to have a kid with you for years. And you won't recognize your real kid as your own! But someone else's kid comes along and you can't wait to be a father!

PHIL: Well I feel different, now! Maybe I'm not the father of this kid, but I feel like the father of some kid. I feel like there's a kid of mine around here somewhere . . .

IRENE: (*To Phil.*) You know, I don't even know who you are anymore!

MYRA: (*Mona groans.*) Never say never be ready! (*Looking out over audience.*) And there's big nimbus clouds heaped up on the horizon. Just right for a birth!

IRENE: I'm feeling a little sick to my stomach . . .

PHIL: You've been sick to your stomach for the last week or so!

MONA: She's in my water now! She's in my water now!

MYRA: Water flows in double spirals down the center of a stream . . . Just stay loose and that kid will swim on out! I was trained in this!

IRENE: Did anyone hear a bucket falling in a well?

MYRA: That's your stomach, Irene! How long ago did you have your last period?

IRENE: Well, actually I'm about ten days late . . . How did you know!?

MYRA: And you're as regular as the moon, Irene!

IRENE: Oh my God, you don't think I'm pregnant, do you?

MYRA: (*Mona moans.*) Have we got that water boiling yet?

PHIL: Little bubbles rising to the surface, reaching the top of the roll!

MYRA: Has anyone ever been born before? Well, this is what it looked like!

IRENE: (*To Phil.*) Baby, I think I'm pregnant. I'm over ten days late!

PHIL: No wonder I feel like a father, Irene!

IRENE: I knew that diaphragm wasn't in right. Remember I told you!? Remember I was worried?

PHIL: Of course I remember, how could I forget that?

IRENE: We were right over here on the edge of the table!

BILL: Instruments boiling, Myra! Ready any time!

MYRA: Just take all the air in as far as the breakers. Exhale, then play the fool at the foam's edge to keep it close . . .

MONA: I'm with you, honey . . .

IRENE: That had to be the night you wanted to make love standing up, right in the middle of the month!

PHIL: You wanted to make love standing up, not me, Irene . . .

IRENE: You know, I recall we both wanted to make love standing up . . .

PHIL: Doesn't make much difference now . . .

MONA: (*To Bill.*) You know I never would have slept with Earl at all if you hadn't stayed down in Burn for so damned long! I thought you'd forgotten me!

BILL: I told you we hit rock and the bit broke off, Mona! I had Bobby Walls hung upside down by the ankles in that well 'til he got the sucker welded!

MONA: Well you coulda called me! I got lonely!

BILL: By the time I pulled him out of that hole, he looked like he'd been shit out of the earth! (*Mona moans.*)

IRENE: (*To Phil.*) Remember I had you up against the wall, and we were both laughing?

PHIL: I saw you put that diaphragm in, Irene!

IRENE: I know I put it in, babe! But sometimes when you make love standing up the diaphragm wiggles loose and the cum goes squirting in over the top . . . I'm sure that's what happened!

MYRA: (*Mona moans. Girl up in window.*) There's a green, green island, just across a milky sea. Can you make it out?

MONA: Oh sure, no problem.

MYRA: Whole flocks of cormorants rushing along the shore, now push!

IRENE: Well I'm glad we got something growing now, honey.

PHIL: If we had to make a kid this was the way to do it! (*Everyone groans with joy. Baby is born.*)

MYRA: But look at this pretty little swimmer! No trouble at all. A strong little girl. Just ready to be born. (*They pass the baby slowly, hand to hand to Phil at end of table. The three women sit in chairs holding babies.*)

(*Mrs. Avakian enters. Looks for a moment at babies.*)

MRS. AVAKIAN: Well, Ernie's gone and it's a blessing!
            He closed his eyes and said, I'm leaving now, Eileen.
            I've got the tree I hollowed out, the one I was born in.
            It was right where I left it on the San Marcos Creek the day my mother let me wash up here,
            and I'm gonna squeeze my dry old seed inside it now and float on over. It's good to be inside this wood again,

to feel this world getting smaller and smaller.
I'm moving off for now, Eileen, he said.
I'm floating through the orange grove,
and I can smell the trees on either side
and I can feel the dark lake coming closer and closer,
and I'm happy, Eileen,
cause I got so dried out back there on Earth!
And then he yelled, Eileen! And I said, what is it,
     Ernie?
And he said, don't raise the rent on Phil,
I want him to stay. And I said, you don't mean Phil,
     Ernie,
you mean Bill. And he said, Phil, Bill, what difference
does it make? And then he died. He was smiling.

(*Women move gently from side to side. Mrs. Avaki-*
an remains still and observes. Bill and girl slowly pass
back and forth in window looking at each other. Mu-
sic. A sense of time passing through the following
speech.)

PHIL: I have looked away from you for so very long,
         I cannot believe you are truly my daughter.

         Is there a moment left to receive
         your breathing body into my hands,
         and hear your dear sighing curl in my ear?

         I have kept the sight of you from my eyes for so long,
         I have crossed my arms against my chest for so long,
         keeping your shadow from leaning on my heart,
         I do not know if I can unbend them now,
         and start to take in who you really are.

I am so used to your almost being, nearly being,
not quite being form, I feel my feelings
will slide from me now, like the half-dead scales
of an outmoded animal, and leave me nothing
but a dried-out sack of skin.

I have run from you so long in my dreams, kept you
    out
of my fantasies for so very long, felt your ghostly
fingers touch my neck as I fled from nightmare to
    nightmare,
I must become a father to know you now,

Cross over this bridge where you are waiting to
    shape me
and follow the curve of your own shining water,
where you flow lightly and brightly over the path
of my error, the traces of my fear,
and the map of my regret.

MRS. AVAKIAN: (*Brief silence. Movement stops. Bill and Girl face each other.*) Well, that's all very well, Phil, but I think it's time we got down to this chili!

IRENE: Oh, my God, the chili, Bill! I thought you were watching it!

BILL: Oh, it's all right. I just gave it a stir. (*To Girl.*) Wouldn't you like to come in and have some chili with us? (*She nods.*)

MRS. AVAKIAN: (*Girl enters, embraces Bill. Brief tableau.*) Well, these chili dinners are getting to be a real tradition around here. (*She embraces Girl. Others move toward table, serve chili.*) Hello sweetie. (*Pause.*) It sure is nice of you folks to have me over as often as you do. (*Girl sits at table and watches Irene nurse. Mrs. Avakian sits at table.*)

PHIL: Hey, you're family, Mrs. Avakian!

MRS. AVAKIAN: Well, thank you, Phil.

MONA: All these kids are gonna be callin' you Gramma, Eileen.

IRENE: (*To Girl.*) You like to watch her feeding, don't you honey? Hold her for a second, will you. Got to get this girl a fresh tit . . .

MRS. AVAKIAN: You know you've got a babysitter anytime you need one, Irene . . .

IRENE: Oh, don't you worry. As soon as this girl's ready to go on the bottle, it's back to the dog track for me!

MYRA: (*To Mrs. Avakian. They are eating the chili.*) You've done so much babysitting already, Eileen, I don't see how you could do any more!

MRS. AVAKIAN: Listen, if these children hadn't come along when they did, I don't know what I would have done with myself!

BILL: Oh come on, Mrs. Avakian!

PHIL: You work a sixty-hour week running this orange grove!

BILL: You work longer hours than we do!

MRS. AVAKIAN: Oh stop, stop. If you two hadn't known how to tap into that aquifer, we'd have lost this place to the bank! A lot of small growers went down this summer. Besides, you can't work twenty-four hours a day . . . you got to come home sometime. And there's nothin' I hate more than an empty house!

MONA: Bill, this chili is unbearable! Is there anything to drink?

BILL: Glass of O.J. comin' right up!

MYRA: Wooo, this is hot. You better watch out there, Irene. Hot chili gets in your milk, you know!

MONA: That'll wean the little suckers fast!

MYRA: I found out the hard way!

IRENE: Don't you worry about this little girl. I've been getting her used to my spicy milk!

MRS. AVAKIAN: Wooo-wooo-wooof! My god in Heaven, this chili *is* hot!

BILL: Drives out the parasites!

MRS. AVAKIAN: Well, pass me some of that orange juice, will you, Bill?

PHIL: I can feel my parasites leaving me now! OOOOOeeeee! This is gutburner chili!

BILL: (*Passing drinks.*) I told you you overdid it this time, Irene!

IRENE: Bill, you were the one that kept roastin' those jalapeños and choppin' 'em up and throwin' 'em in!

BILL: Are you sure you're not thinking about my brother Phil, Irene? People get us confused sometimes.

IRENE: I don't have any problems telling the two of you apart, Bill! The only person who can't remember who he is is you!

MONA: Emergency! Emergency! O.J.! O.J.! O.J.!

MYRA: My God, this is hot!

IRENE: It goes right up into your ears!

PHIL: Look at the sweat runnin' off my face, man!

BILL: It doesn't taste that hot to me. I don't know what you're talking about. (*They look at him incredulously. Pause. He suddenly reaches for his drink and gulps it down.*) Jesus H. Keeriiist! (*They all drink moaning 'til the heat subsides.*)

IRENE: You know this kinda reminds me of the time we were out by the beach walking past the Mexican restaurants after we'd all had dinner, and there was that light summer fog that comes in sometimes, and we stopped and sat down and listened to the waves comin' in, and your Ernie said, well, you never know how many more moments you're gonna have like this, so you better look around and see who your family is . . .

MRS. AVAKIAN: That's right. I remember that . . . (*They all look around at each other.*)

MONA: I think we better look around and see who our friends are, too, while we're still feeling good, and the taste of the chili is still in our mouths, and there's a steady silence in the orange grove, just the creek running slowly against the low muddy banks . . . (*They all look around at each other.*)

BILL: Well, I think we ought to have a toast to Ernie Avakian! Without him, we wouldn't be here.

PHIL: That's right! Without him I'd still be drillin' for water down in Burn!

IRENE: Bill would still be bent over those goddamn maps!

MONA: I'm ready! A toast to Ernie! You do it, Eileen!

MRS. AVAKIAN: Oh, I couldn't do it! I'm no good at speeches! (*General laughter.*)

MYRA: No good at speeches! Do you hear that?

MRS. AVAKIAN: You know how tongue-tied I get when I have to talk in public! (*Laughter again. Pause.*)

BILL: We owe this meal to Ernie, Mrs. A.

IRENE: Tell us something about him, Eileen. You know we never got to know him real well.

MRS. AVAKIAN: Oh Ernie was just Ernie!

PHIL: Come on, Mrs. Avakian. Tell us something to remember this occasion by.

MYRA: I bet you've got one special memory. (*Pause.*)

MRS. AVAKIAN: Well, there was this one time . . .

MYRA: Oh, I knew it! She was just being dramatic!

IRENE: Now don't make fun, Myra! (*Pause.*)

MRS. AVAKIAN: Well, it was in this house. This is where Ernie and me lived when we first got married. And I just found out that I was pregnant. This room was the whole house back then. We slept over there by the window. And one night, we're lyin' in bed, and Ernie says to me, you know, Elieen, if my mother hadn't been so ugly, why I'd be dead. And I said, Ernie, what the hell are you talkin' about! And he said, well, if she'da been good lookin', they'd have raped her 'til she was dead, and I'd have died without her milk. And I said, what the hell are you talkin' about, Ernie! And he said, we're from Armenia, you see. 1917, they killed my father, my brothers, but my mother, she run away with me. I was four years old, and she run from one end of Turkey to the other holding me. And every Armenian girl they raped and killed, all except the ugly ones. The ugly ones got to Syria, the ones so old no one wanted to rape them, just those women they left alive, them old and ugly women and me, Baby Ernie. (*Brief pause. Lights begin to go down, very slowly.*) When she got to Aleppo, she had no clothes on. The only thing she had on was me. (*Pause.*) And then he didn't say nothin' for a long, long time. I thought he was asleep. And then it started to rain, and he said, you know, we had an orange grove over there. And I said, where's that,

Ernie? And he said, over there, in Armenia, we had an orange grove. (*Pause.*) Well, here's to Ernie.

ALL: (*Toasting.*) Here's to Ernie! To Ernie Avakian!

BILL: He gave the world a lot of juice.

IRENE: He was good to us for no reason at all. (*Dim light for a moment as they drink. Fade to black, soft sound of water for a moment in the dark.*)

Hot Lunch Apostles

Sheila Dabney, Raymond Barry, Tina Shepard, Jack Wetherall, and Bimbo Rivas in a scene from *Hot Lunch Apostles*.

This play was first presented by The Talking Band and La Mama ETC, Ellen Stewart, Artistic Director, New York, April 1983.

The cast:

BARNEY:	Raymond Barry
ROD:	Jack Weatherall
PHOEBE:	Tina Shepard
EDGE:	Bimbo Rivas
LOOP:	Ellen Maddow
SLIDE:	Sheila Dabney
CYCLONE:	Harry Mann

Set by Marjorie Bradley Kellog.
Music by Harry Mann, Ellen Maddow, and Sybille Hayn.
Directed by Paul Zimet.

Characters

BARNEY, white, ex-marine, early fifties, barker and manager
EDGE, Barney's Latino right-hand man, forties and grizzled
ROD, a white male stripper, 30s, formerly in regional
    Shakespeare
LOOP, white female, 30s, utterly orderly when not hysterical
PHOEBE, geek and stripper, 30s, formerly "in film"
SLIDE, homeless black woman, happy to find work as stripper,
    20s
CYCLONE, a saxophone player

(*A traveling carny show, sometime in the future, but not the distant future. A remote rural route, vaguely Western U.S., but with place names intended to sound like anywhere. The front of the stage should indicate the flimsy trappings of fly-by-night carny. The stage itself should be deep enough so that three distinct playing areas can be employed simultaneously, divided only, when necessary, by transparent bead or other curtains. This way, midstage is visible and can be employed as playing space when action is occurring frontstage or way at the back. Likewise, the back part of the stage can be used to perform acts away from the audience, as if the audience were backstage. This allows the maximum possibility of "framing" scene by scene, particularly important when "sacred" acts are juxtaposed against "profane," or when "repulsive" acts are performed against backstage dialogue that turns the audience's interest back upon itself. Thus, as much as possible, no act is merely "performed," but enclosed, qualified or counterpointed by action or image on another part of the stage.*)

Nativity Scene

(*Wise Men—Barney and Cyclone—begin singing offstage. Lights come up on Joseph and Mary—Edge and Loop. Angel—Rod—is above on ladder. Phoebe is on hands and knees as sheep. All sing, but Phoebe, who makes sheep sounds during singing. Wise men enter bearing gifts: a horn, a small chair, a loaf of bread. Phoebe begins laughing, Loop hits her to quiet her down, but her laughter becomes uncontrollable as Barney pulls a baby bottle from his pocket.*)

BARNEY: All right, hold up! Listen, you guys better start gettin' serious about these Jesus scenes! It's not the fuckin' food stamp Nineties anymore. It's the fuckin' flat rot 21st century. We can't make it on pussy, sickos and yuk-yuks anymore. We gotta diversify. There's fifty million jobless people out there, beggin' for a shot at burlesque and squat. The competition's gotten vicious. You got legitimate actors doing this work. Lookit Rod here. (*Rod sings phrase of holy song.*) Lookit Phoebe. You got pregnant housewives in Kansas City fuckin' donkies just to feed the kids. I'm telling you, this gospel shit is our only shot. So the next time you get the giggles while we're doin' the holy pitchers, I want you to clear your screen a little and flash a gash close-up on what your life's gonna be like if our Jesus show

	don't make it. I want you to picture yourself with a big steamin' bowl of rock soup in your hands. And that means you, Phoebe.
EDGE:	Barney's right. We were barely makin' it at the gate.
BARNEY:	That's right, Edge. But with Rod as Christ, we'll kill 'em.
ROD:	What?
BARNEY:	I said with you as Christ, we'll knock 'em dead.
ROD:	I'm not playing Christ.
BARNEY:	You'll play Christ and like it.
ROD:	I'm not playing Christ. I've been humiliated too many times to take on that kind of role again. (*Pointing at doll below.*)
BARNEY:	I'm the director here! I do all the casting! Let's do it one more time. We got five weeks to Liplock.

(*They sing again. Light fades to blackout. Front curtain closes. Music. Phoebe comes through curtain and does her strip on the apron. She appears as quickly as possible after end of Nativity scene. Blackout after her strip. Curtain opens on Rod's female-to-male strip. Both strips should be raunchy to the verge of the ridiculous. Curtain closes on Rod. Loop and Barney on apron. Rod and Phoebe visible and audible behind curtain. They get into their Fungushead costumes during pitch. Rod as Rev. Vernal Mirrors, Phoebe as Fungushead with a rope around her neck. During pitch, Phoebe makes intermittent vomiting sounds.*)

BARNEY:	You've heard about her, you've read about her, and now you're gonna get a chance to actually see Phoebe B. Peabody herself, no holds barred.

LOOP: Two dollars is our special depression price. It's sad, it's really sad. Two dollars.

ROD: If I were tickled by the rub of love,
A rooking girl who stole me from her side . . .

PHOEBE: Roll it down, lover boy. No ticky, no pussy.

BARNEY: For only two dollars—just one quarter the price of the soupiest movie in town—you can look all day at this tortured woman, incurably addicted to the most horrifying drug ever known, the dreaded mucaloid.

ROD: Shall it be male or female say the fingers
That chalk the wall with green girls and their men.
How'd I look?

PHOEBE: Great. Everybody got a little something.

ROD: You work on the confusion. I'll get it cookin' as much as I can, and then I make it funny. If they don't laugh, you're in trouble. I'm glad your act is next. I always feel safe in these sacred costumes. Remember that cowboy that came screaming through here last year? "Where's that fuckin' faggot? I'm gonna chop up his dick and feed it to mah wife."
Because I do not hope to turn
Because I do not hope to turn again
Because I do not hope.

PHOEBE: Kill a faggot. Shorest way to heaven.

ROD: Listen, it's better than L.A. At least out here you can see the killers coming. L.A: Stick a tongue in your mouth and a knife in your neck.

LOOP: See what the dreaded mucaloid did to Phoebe. It's really sad, come back as many times as you want.

BARNEY: And you'll want to come back, 'cause what happened to Phoebe could happen to Daddy's little girl. You all know what crack can do to the human mind; you've

	all had nightmares of finding young Bobby with a big, fat, needle of heroin dangling out of his arm, but these drugs are like lollipops compared to mucaloid.

LOOP: Hear Phoebe talk. Watch Phoebe vomit. It's really sad. Two dollars.

PHOEBE: I'm glad you're back. I'd be throwing up for real if I had to do this every night without you.

ROD: I had to come back. The only jobs left were snap 'n swallow. There. There. The very, very Reverend Vernal Mirrors. Ready to console.

PHOEBE: You better not get too convincing. Barney's still hot to nail you to the cross.

ROD: Listen: I'll play Minnie Mouse. Sausage and Cream if things get tight, but no Last Supper. That's a serious part. I'd have to think about it. I'd have to think of all the times I've had the shit beat out of me.

PHOEBE: Barney gets an idea in his head, it's like Hiroshima in slow motion.

ROD: You said burlesque. I said fine. Geek is fine.

PHOEBE: I didn't mean to get you into this.

ROD: "Oh, Egypt, thou knowst too well
My heart was to thy rudder tied by the strings,
And thou shouldst tow me after."

PHOEBE: Tell me about it.

BARNEY: Mucaloid addicts call themselves fungusheads because of the puffy, fungus-like growth around the jaws. Their hair falls out in scraggly patches. Their skin turns blotchy yellow and the body is covered with little bulbous sacs that constantly break, ooze and slowly reform. Fungusheads call 'em love knobs.

LOOP: See Phoebe the Fungushead. She's sad and special. Only two dollars.

BARNEY: And now, here's Phoebe. And with her, Dr. Vernal Mirrors of the Eternal Conception Church of Hollywood, California!

ROD: Within moments of anal infusion, the mucaloid user experiences spasms of intense nausea for forty-eight hours. This is accompanied by a violent burning sensation in the mucous membranes, while razor-edged black disks whiz across the line of sight in constantly shifting patterns. Fungusheads call this "getting high."

PHOEBE: Skirt she made me was disease
Scorpions in the panties
They never come out
Bras to keep you quiet
Rags to plug you up
Kill a baby boy the first born
And feed the corn his blood

ROD: For many of us at God's Blood Mucaloid De-tox Center, Phoebe has been a real inspiration. She has reminded us that the way to God is not a primrose path of lollipops and box lunches, but a violent wrenching of the guts, so that we must tear our bodies to shreds and spit out our souls before we can join the Holy Spirit in permanent joy, in permanent bliss.

PHOEBE: There was an angel on an airplane:
It was Air Force One.
He had the killer baby then
And the bottom split open
And the big atomic baby got dropped
And every one of those men burned.
And every one of those women
Who were pregnant burned too.

Only the virgins were saved.
They were vomiting and their vomit
Saved them. That Bomb could not
Get them. They were afraid enough.
They were afraid enough.
They were afraid enough.

(*Curtain closes on end of speech. Lights down. Phoebe and Rod exit. Lights up for next scene.*)

The Arrival of Slide

(Slide tries to dig some non-existent crumbs out of a paper bag, stealthily crosses in front of the audience, floor level, is almost up the stairs when she surprises Loop at the edge of the apron. Loop is scared and goes at once into two voices, one harsh, hysterical, the other snide, coquettish. When she completes the "loop," she speaks in her natural voice.)

SLIDE: Can you run a mouth gash on me? It's the bottom of the ninth.

LOOP: What?

SLIDE: Biscuits, crackers, old bread. I'm dust to dust, snag it?

LOOP: I didn't take the eggs, honest! They were gone when I got back.

SLIDE: I didn't say anything about eggs. Dog food's the same as hash. Don't stick me. I'm close. I mean it. Give me some food.

LOOP: I'm not your waitress, but I'm your half-sister and that's the same. Even if there's no father when the baby is born, they still call the lady a mother. As long as she swells up real big before it slips out, she qualifies and no one can take her coupons away and no child can send his mother away ever.

SLIDE: (*Sitting on steps.*) Come to suckle at the funny farm . . .

LOOP: Please don't fall! Please don't move too fast. If the words don't catch up with the pictures, I'll go black. If you fall, you'll be down there below me and you won't be able to hear me and there won't be any audience and if there aren't any witnesses . . .

SLIDE: Just a piece of bread . . .

LOOP: Anyone could do anything to you! If a mother is alone with a baby and she wants to hurt that baby, she can. The baby can't protect itself. First, the mother tries to feed the baby, but the baby won't stop crying, so then . . .

SLIDE: I'm hungry, please . . .

LOOP: Please don't fall! If you fall, I'll fall with you. Don't move too fast in any direction. If one person is more alive than another, then the one who's under sinks and the one who's above has to look away and then she's a liar and her lie makes her hungry and she wants to eat.

SLIDE: Do you have any food?

LOOP: Of course I've got food.

SLIDE: Give me some. I'm starving.

LOOP: (*In her natural voice.*) Well, I don't have any real personal food of my own, but Barney bakes this bread and he's Al's brother and they're both really good guys. Al's not here right now; he's up in the mountains selling dope, but he helps us out if things get rough, and Barney always keeps enough bread for whoever's hungry. It's over there by the Jesus props. Eat some. Eat as much as you like. But not too much! 'Cause there might be an emergency, but eat enough, 'cause that's what Barney says bread is for—to keep you from dying.

(*Barney and Phoebe enter. Barney is reading from the Bible.*)

BARNEY: "Then turning to the woman he said to Simon: 'Did you see this woman? I came into your house. You did not give me water for my feet. But she washed my feet with her tears and dried them with her hair . . . '"

LOOP: Psst. Barney . . .

BARNEY: Who's this, Loop? Your long-lost sister?

LOOP: She's not my sister, Barney. She's just another hungry person. She's real good lookin', Barney.

PHOEBE: Bread make you feel better? How long since the gash?

SLIDE: Where'd you pocket that leg?

PHOEBE: This is carny, honey. All kinds'a customers. We pocket all the legs. How long?

SLIDE: Four big round ones. I've been goin' from door to door. Rich houses, plenty of food inside. Those rich motherfuckers bark you bad. Work a suburban street, they call one another before you get there. Two cars in the driveway. You stand on the porch and ring the bell; they don't even answer. Cocksuckers don't have the blood to say no.

BARNEY: You wanna work?

SLIDE: Hey man, there ain't a vulture in this country who don't wanna work.

BARNEY: Well, we got a job for you if you're not too shy.

SLIDE: Shy? Hey man, I was on my way to bein' a singer be-
            fore the rot got flat. I like gettin' up in front of people
            and doin' my stuff.

BARNEY: Well, we got a job for a stripper. Let's have a look at
            you. Take your clothes off.

SLIDE: I'm a really gash dancer. Really gash.

PHOEBE: Come on, Barney. She's wasted. Don't make her do it
            now.

BARNEY: There's no room for virgins on this particular bus. I
            ain't got time for guessing games. This ain't the senior
            prom. Now strip or burn.

SLIDE: Oh roll it down, top man. Shit. I been beggin' for six
            months; you can look at my tits with a microscope.

BARNEY: Take the bra off.

PHOEBE: Leave her alone, Barney. You're not blind. She'll do.

SLIDE: Hey, no need to get Christian. I seen top man before. I
            seen top man soon as Mama stopped cryin' right there
            on day number one.

BARNEY: Well.

PHOEBE: You'd make a good cop, Barney. You're in the wrong
            business.

BARNEY: You shut the fuck up, Miss College Degree.

PHOEBE: Don't mind Barney, he used to train gorillas. You're
            an ape, Barney. You got a dick for a brain.

BARNEY: You don't like it, go back to making snuff movies. I'm
            running this show. I make the rules here. This ain't a
            fuckin' orphanage. It's a pussy show. Why is no one
            able to understand this simple fact but me?

(*Barney exits.*)

PHOEBE: You have any bags?

SLIDE: No. Nothing. Not a thing.

PHOEBE: Come on.

(They exit. Curtain closes for Scoobie-Doo. Barney and Edge at opposite sides of the apron. Loop and Cyclone come through curtain and play saxophone, clarinet Scoobie-Doo theme. Then Rod, Phoebe, and Slide break through curtains in strip costumes. Edge crosses in front of all during his pitch, alternating his lines with strippers' singing and movement.)

EDGE: Now we're gonna put it together for you baby.
Everything you're hot to see I don't mean maybe.
Everything you're hot to touch, hot to taste, check it out.
No one leaves hungry, no one's left in doubt.
Can a virgin mamma fool the doctor? Is the nurse a little queer?
Step into the tent. Satisfaction guaranteed!

Was pussy a problem for J. C. himself? He's in the audience tonight.
We got routines for every taste and need. Check it out.
No one leaves hungry. No one's left in doubt.

No money for the movies? TV repossessed? This is the cheapest show since those Jewish comedians had a hit with the Messiah.
If a virgin has a baby boy, could the boy become a girl?

Or less? Or more?
No education needed, no college degree.
We take it down to basics, satisfaction guaranteed!

(*Last chorus of Scoobie-Doo theme. Singers, Cyclone exit. Barney and Loop remain for Scheduling I. "Getting Closer" music.*)

BARNEY: You got the list, Loop?

LOOP: I got the ones I remembered, Barney. Not the ones I forgot, but the remembered ones.

BARNEY: Let's see: Medicine Bow on the 10th. Geeks, tits, burlesque. Okay. Backstage after 10. No gospel, no hot lunch. Good, that's simple. That was a good show last year.

LOOP: That's always a good show, Barney.

BARNEY: Bad Bluff on the 12th. Same show. Cut 'n Shoot on the 14th. What's Cut 'n Shoot?

LOOP: Cut 'n Shoot's the place with the alfalfa dehydratin' plant just north of Kolmar. There was a strike last year, so we didn't go. Too many cops.

BARNEY: Right. Cut 'n Shoot on the 14th. Big on geeks, tits up, fags up, backstage anytime. A good straight show. Henrietta on the 18th. I hate that fuckin' place. One smell of pussy can get you crucified in Henrietta. Preachers got dogs out there sniffin' for pussy. Won't we have that gospel shit ready by then?

LOOP: It won't be ready 'til Liplock, Barney. Jesus is still just a little baby.

BARNEY: Well, can't we just skip Henrietta and come back with a gash crucifixion next month?

LOOP: Burn's an extra 70 miles by way of Aftosa, and you
          know what that's like.

BARNEY: Okay. Henrietta on the 18th. Morality geek, family
          burlesque, holy songs. Terrific.

LOOP: The girls like it, Barney. Puttin' it on instead of takin'
          it off.

BARNEY: Okay. Burn on the 21st. Full geek, sex end, fags up,
          tits up, no gospel, no hot lunch. Hey, wait a minute.
          Why no hot lunch in Burn? That's railroad, ain't it?

LOOP: Duck Lake's only 12 miles. You got oil, you got gobble
          girls. It's not worth the hassle.

BARNEY: Liplock on the 25th. Our gospel debut!

(They exit. Music ends.)

Crossifix

(Phoebe is trying to stow the cross under the stage. Loop joins her from backstage.)

PHOEBE: This is the stupidest idea I ever heard of!

LOOP: Barney's never failed us yet.

PHOEBE: He's failed me plenty of times.

LOOP: Well, he keeps our show together. Every idea he's had has worked so far.

PHOEBE: Holy rollers tryin' to bust us for years.

Jesus freaks used to be a joke.

Now they run the country.

And we're going to join the crusade?

Plus we got Rod in a rage at having to play Christ.

LOOP: Well, Barney says a good performer can perform anything.

PHOEBE: Barney says, Jesus says, Moses says.

LOOP: Well, Barney says if you can serve hot lunch, or give gash for a ticket, you can be crucified. One act's the same as the next.

PHOEBE: Listen, Loop. Don't tell me what Barney says. I don't want to hear what Barney says. He's been reading that damn Bible day and night for weeks.

LOOP: It's not such a bad story. 'Member when they put what-sis-name in the little basket? The little baby to float away? 'Member that one?

PHOEBE: Moses.

LOOP: Right, Moses. And then in that Jesus deal Barney was reading where that gobble girl comes in and washes Jesus' hair with her feet?

PHOEBE: Loop. She washes his feet with her hair.

LOOP: She does? Well that's too bad. I had it all pictured the other way around. Like Jesus was lying on the floor, snag?

PHOEBE: Snag, snag.

LOOP: Right. So Jesus is limp stretch on the floor, and this really gash gobble girl has this big bucket of hot water . . .

PHOEBE: I told you this was stupid! He said he measured it!

LOOP: Well, let's try it this way.

PHOEBE: I tried it this way.

LOOP: He said he measured it. Didn't you say he said he measured it? And if he measured it, it would fit, if he said it . . .

PHOEBE: Don't tell me what he said, Loop!

| LOOP: | I didn't take them, You took them. I saw you take them. Those were my underwear. They're not even your size. You'd need a crowbar to get into my panties. | PHOEBE: | Loop. Don't start that, Loop. Help me . . . Loop, the sockets . . . Plug in the sockets . . . Barney! Barney! |

(Barney enters.)

You took them.
I know you took
them. I saw you
looking at them
when I brought
them home.
You're crazy.
You're sick. I'm
leaving.
I saw you watching
me. You think
everything I buy is
yours. I work and
you lap it up.
What would I
want with your
underwear?
You took my
girdle. You can't
deny that. You
took my eggs. You
can't deny that.
You took my sixty-
watt bulb.
You're lying.
Deny. Deny. Deny.
Your mother was
a liar and she
raised me. And her
mother was a liar
and you're a liar
too! It runs in the

BARNEY: Come help me with
Loop. She slipped
and I can't get her
out.

Well, get Rod. He
knows the routine.
I gotta get this
Messiah stuff ready
for Liplock.

PHOEBE: Rod's got a
customer!

BARNEY: What happened?

PHOEBE: The cross doesn't
fit. I got mad.

family. I'm not a liar. You're a liar. The judge will be here soon. He gets off at five. He'll see right through you. He'll find my bulb. Oh Jesus! Jesus motherfucking Christ on a crutch! You've got eggs on your breath. Steal 'em, crack 'em, fry 'em. Slop 'em down. Work like a dog and look what happens. Oh god, you're gonna make me crazy. You didn't have enough eggs of your own. You broke your own eggs. Holy Mary Mother of God!	BARNEY: You can't get mad at her. You'll scare her. She'll freak out. Can't you use a little self- control? PHOEBE: The cross is too wide. BARNEY: It's not too wide! It is not too wide. That cross is not too wide. I mea- sured that cross myself. That's a custom-made cross. Plug in the sockets, Loop.

LOOP: Yes, Barney. We seem to be having a little trouble with this cross, Barney.

BARNEY: (*During this speech, the others drift on stage.*) Now. If you'd just slid it in like I told you. Get in there, you son of a bitch. Spread those goddamn fuckin' legs. Gimme a break. I know I measured this thing right. If they hadn't crucified the wise-assed son of a bitch in the first place, but no! He couldn't cool out for a while. He had to stick his face in it. Open up, you hypocritical gobble girl, or I'll break you open with my . . . (*He breaks the cross.*) Is there a place in the Bible we can use a broken cross? Maybe the cross breaks with Christ on it and the Romans decide enough is enough . . .

PHOEBE: Shut up, Barney. You're going to land us all in jail. You can't fuck around with the Bible out here.

BARNEY: Or maybe we could have something about this carpenter see, who makes defective crosses. And he's torn. He's torn. Hey Edge! Edge. Come over here. We gotta rehearse the Pilate-Caiaphas scene. You direct it just like I told you, okay? This is your chance, Edge. To be a director.

EDGE: All right! Okay, everybody, listen up. Barney's going to play Christ, and I'm going to play Barney. We're going to do the Pilate-Caiaphas scene. This is where Pilate washes his hands of the entire Jesus affair. (*To Rod.*) Caiaphas. (*To Loop and Phoebe.*) You two are gonna be the high priests. Angry. Grumbling. Okay. (*To Cyclone.*) You. You're gonna be a witness. You bring Jesus in and say "This man claims to be the Son of God!" Right. Got it? Okay. (*To Slide.*) Sweetheart, come over here. Your line: "This man says he can tear down the temple and rebuild it in three days." All right. Barney! What are your lines?

BARNEY: And from now on, I will be the right hand of power, coming . . .

EDGE: Right. I want you all to practice over here. (*To Rod.*) You're the high priest.

ROD: Can I use these lines in the Bible?

EDGE: Good. Use those lines. Then when you're done being Caiaphas, you're gonna whirl around over here and become Pilate. Very Roman. There's gonna be some water and I'm gonna play the messenger. Okay, everybody. Let's go!

PHOEBE: Wait a minute! Why are we grumbling?

EDGE: It's a question of power. Power. If you accept this man to be the Son of God, what do you lose? Your jobs at the temple. All right! Bring him in.

ROD: Where is this man who calls himself the Son of God?

(*Cyclone and Slide throw Barney down.*)

LOOP: Don't cross yourself, Rod. You're supposed to be Jewish.

BARNEY: Forgive them, Father, they know not what . . .

EDGE: No, Barney! Not yet.

ROD: What say the witnesses?

CYCLONE: This brother claims to be the Son of God!

PHOEBE and LOOP: Aaah!

SLIDE: This man says he can tear down the temple and rebuild it in three days.

PHOEBE and LOOP: Aaah!

ROD: How answer ye these accusations?

BARNEY: Forgive them Father, they know not . . .

EDGE: Not yet, Barney!

ROD: Answerst thou nothing? What is it which these witness against thee?

BARNEY: Forgive . . .

EDGE: Come on, man. Stay down!

ROD: I abjure thee by the living that you tell us whether you be the Christ, the Son of God!

EDGE: Now, Barney, now. Up, up.

BARNEY: And from now on you will see me sitting on the right hand of power, coming into the clouds of heaven.

PHOEBE: He said that?

ROD: (*Checks his Bible.*) Blasphemy! Blasphemy! Take him to Pilate!

> (*He whirls around to his Pilate position. The priests and witnesses spit on Christ.*)

EDGE: That's it. Spit on him! Really spit! Excellent! Now to Pilate.

PHOEBE and LOOP: Arrr, narr. Get over there, etc.

ROD: Art thou the King of the Jews?

BARNEY: Ehhh. Unng.

EDGE: I'm the messenger. Don't trial this man, he's a holy man. Your wife had a dream. Wash your hands of it.

ROD: Whom will ye that I release unto you? Barabas or Jesus who is called Christ?

CYCLONE and SLIDE: Barabas! Barabas!

ROD: What shall I do then with Jesus?

PHOEBE: (*To crowd.*) Crucify him.

CYCLONE and SLIDE: Crucify him! Crucify him!

ROD: Water! Bring me water!

LOOP: Rod, here!

ROD: Oh.

BARNEY: Forgive them, Father. They know not what they do.

ROD: I am innocent of the blood of this just person. Take him away.

CROWD: Get out of here. Throw him in the shithole, etc.

BARNEY: You motherfuckers! You'll pay for this! I'll get you for this!

EDGE: Barney! You can't play Christ.

BARNEY: What d'ya mean I can't play Christ?

EDGE: You're too big for the part, Barney.

BARNEY: What d'ya mean I'm too big!

EDGE: It's your hair, then, Barney. Something's wrong!

BARNEY: My hair? What are you crazy? I'll wear a wig! I'm a great Christ! All right, I'll tell you what: we'll have an audition. See if one of you guys can do a better Christ than me. You first, Edge.

EDGE: Nothing personal, Barney. (*Strikes Christ pose.*)

BARNEY: Next!

(*Loop does her Jesus.*)

BARNEY: Oh, Jesus. Next.

PHOEBE: That was nice, Loop.

(*Rod does his kinky Jesus.*)

BARNEY: Ooh. Very good. Write that one down for Liplock, Edge. Next.

(*Cyclone does his Jesus.*)

BARNEY: Next!

(*Slide does her Jesus.*)

BARNEY: Could you put a little more energy into it?

(*She raises her hands slightly higher. Phoebe does her Jesus.*)

BARNEY: Oh, that's good. You see that? That is facial expression. Very good, Phoebe, but you're all still missing something. He wouldn't just hang there. He'd get up on that cross and resist. You fuckin' Jews! You goddamn Jews! I'll make you all burn in hell! I'll make you all feel guilty. You Jews! You cocksucking Jews! See? He wasn't a pantywaist. He was a Man! All right. Now I want you all to work on your holy scenes. Get all the moves down, all the words. Over and over and over until you get it right. Edge and I gotta do a pitch. Come on Edge, we got an audience waitin'.

Garbage Eater

(*Barney does pitch behind back curtain facing away from audience, as Edge gets ready to "eat garbage" and others form an angel under a white cloth with Rod's face showing. They sing a Bach chorale, midstage, facing audience. The angel breaks down when Loop "loops" (Loop 2.) just as Edge goes on. After Barney tells them to take a break, Phoebe sings and does vaudeville dance, and Rod sits on a box as Jesus while Slide washes his feet with her hair. Loop sits on Barney's lap and then imitates Phoebe's song and dance.*)

BARNEY: Ladies and gentlemen, these are hard times. A lot of us have had to do things we never thought we had to do just to stay alive, and things are gonna get worse. And just to make the future a little less frightening, you're going to get a chance to see what very few people have ever seen: a professional garbage eater. Ambrosio Esperanza. He's just inside the tent. Two dollars. See how to survive when your food stamps run out. Prepare for the future. Two dollars.

I know all of you are familiar with those aged, ragged, crippled, skinny, filthy people you see every day around the dumpsters and garbage cans and wondered if you could ever be reduced to such a humiliating state. Who knows what the future holds for any of us? Better be

	safe than sorry. If we have to eat garbage, let's be good at it. What Ambrosio has to tell you may someday save your life. Get Ambrosio's favorite recipes. Two dollars. And now, here he is. Ambrosio Esperanza, our professional garbage eater!
EDGE:	Thank you, Barney. Thank you.
LOOP:	Get your hands off me, you bitch!
	You don't want me in your dresser, do you?
	You don't want anything sliding open!
	Get your hands out of my drawer!
	You don't want the judge to see the evidence, do you?
	I'll break your greasy hands off I swear!
ROD:	Loop! Plug in the sockets! Plug in your sockets! Barney!
BARNEY:	Plug in the sockets, Loop.
LOOP:	Yes, Barney.
ROD:	I said that. Didn't I say that?
LOOP:	If I remember my part and it's
	dark it's okay, and if there's light
	and I forget my part, it's okay,
	but if it's dark and I forget my part . . .
BARNEY:	Don't get into it. Take a break, everybody.
LOOP:	Sharing, Barney. Sharing.
BARNEY:	Sharing. Right. You got it, Loop.
EDGE:	The first thing you got to do to be a professional garbage eater is get over the idea that anything is rotten. (*Music begins.*) Take this chicken for instance. Stinking, moldy, full of maggots. But to the professional garbage eater, this is dinner. Mmm. Delicious. Use your imagination! Take this cardboard, for instance. Sprinkled with a little battery acid. Goes down smooth as oysters. I call it my cardboard taco.

ROD:	I knew there was a reason I wanted to play Christ. Don't worry about those hypocrites, my dear. Your sins are forgiven.
EDGE:	Old napkins!
ROD:	So are mine.
EDGE:	Just keep chewing.
PHOEBE:	(*Singing.*) I used to dance 'til I was dead on my feet in the good old, bad old days.
EDGE:	Dioxin artichokes. We got fields of them. Eat all you want.
PHOEBE:	(*Singing.*) Kept my head in a drunken, pleasant daze and played with the very best.
EDGE:	Learn to bark like a dog. Sometimes people will throw you scraps.
PHOEBE:	(*Singing.*) And the twenty-dollar bills were crispy you bet. And every man I knew was mad to drink where I was wet. Before the kingdom crumbled, and the rot got flat, it was bad, but it was good.
EDGE:	Watch old people in a cafeteria. Sometimes they die before they finish their soup. A meal is a meal, thank you, thank you.

Scheduling II

(Lights up on apron.)

BARNEY: Got the cow towns ready, Loop?

LOOP: We just stay on 85 'til we cross the river.

BARNEY: Oskaloosa, kinky Gospel, Monolith, Prairie View, Bocachita. What kinky gospel we doin' now, Loop?

LOOP: St. Theresa strip.

BARNEY: I don't want no St. Theresa in Bocachita.

LOOP: Wasn't no trouble last year.

BARNEY: I don't wanna push my luck with those fetus freaks.

LOOP: Sharing, Barney. Sharing.

BARNEY: Don't get into it, Loop.

LOOP: I didn't take the eggs, I swear!

BARNEY: Plug in the sockets, Loop!

LOOP: Yes, Barney. You're a comfort to me, Barney. If you're ever interested in a woman, just let me know.

BARNEY: I appreciate it, Loop.

LOOP: For you, I could remember it, Barney. First you take off all your clothes. Then you lie on your back. Am I right so far?

BARNEY: You got it, Loop.

LOOP: Then you spread your legs wide and make your mouth into a little pouty hole. Right? Am I right so far?

BARNEY: So far, so good, Loop.

LOOP: Then I say, "Oh Jesus God, I want you to fuck me. Oh Holy God, I want you to fuck me so bad." Ain't it like that?

BARNEY: It means a lot to me, Loop. As soon as I get done with this gospel stuff, I might be tempted.

St. Theresa Pitch

(*Barney and Cyclone stand S.L. in front of the curtain. Rod and Edge are in the background.*)

BARNEY: Can the suffering of a Saint touch something deep inside us?

Will the ecstasy of St. Theresa turn you on?

She's got more holes than you've ever dreamed of.

St. Theresa here's gonna show you how a young girl comes

when she's wounded by God himself.

St. Theresa Strip

(*Slide appears on the apron in a white robe, Loop and Phoebe with her singing religious music. The initial impression is of beauty and sacredness. Rod and Edge are midstage behind the singers. During the Rod and Edge dialogue to follow, Slide thrusts at herself with the arrow as they continue singing, and uses the arrow to take her clothes off. At the end of her strip, she exposes her breasts with the arrow and licks the shaft of the arrow as the scene ends. Strip and singing should be timed to cover exactly the conversation between Rod and Edge.*)

ROD: How can you be such a Jesus Freak and blaspheme like you do? You're worse than Phoebe. Aren't you afraid God's going to send you straight to hell?

EDGE: Listen man, on the judgment day, God's gonna send me straight to heaven on a non-stop. All the saints and priests and nuns and preachers, they gonna be waitin' for the local, and I'm gonna be all alone on the express. Well, it ain't gonna be crowded. And when I get there, Jesus is gonna call on me, by name, and he's gonna say, "Hey Edge! Come over here and run some of that funny shit on me, man." 'Cause that's gonna be a heavy day: the whole Earth's gonna be groanin' in pain. And all the bark motherfuckers that never gave a shit about anyone else are gonna be twisted up and bleedin', and Jesus is gonna need some gash jive to keep from freakin' out, and I'm gonna run it on him! 'Cause Jesus don't get to laugh 'til the Judgment Day. All the rest of the time while we're laughing to keep our heads straight, he's got to watch all the suffering, all the torture, he's what checks out all the bullshit, snag? He keeps the record, and the record is sad, snag, like this music. This music is sad. We're still hunting one another down. Lookit that arrow. Pussy for sale! But that's the truth. That's where the saints are really at. So far this is it.

ROD: But listen, if you believe in sin, I can't think of anything worse than making fun of the Bible.

EDGE: Listen, anytime you tell the story of Jesus, any way you tell it, you're telling the same story. The sicker you make the story, the more the light of the story shines through.

ROD: Try telling that to those preachers out there.

EDGE: That's the false prophets! If Christ came back right now, do you know who he'd hang out with?

ROD: Who?

EDGE: He'd hang out with us! No one else would notice him. But we'd see him. We'd see him 'cause we know how fucked up things really are.

(*He exits. Rod sits for a minute. Then he also exits.*)

Teachings

(Cyclone and Loop play saxophones from opposite ladders. Barney puts a cloth on Edge, and they become his disciples: during Teaching 1, walking behind him, during Teaching 2, seated in a group as Edge turns his back to the audience. In Teaching 3, Edge is on a box and the disciples are in front of him at midstage, as he speaks over them to the audience.)

Teaching 1

ROD: Don't think I've come to bring peace to the earth.
That's not what I'm here for.
I've come to bring war.

I've come to set son against father, daughter against mother, bride against mother-in-law.

Whoever loves his father or mother more than me, is not good enough for me. Whoever loves her son or daughter more than me does not deserve me. Whosoever is not with me is against me.

Teaching 2

If your leg makes you hesitate, cut it off and throw it

away. For it is better to stumble through life on one leg than to walk with both legs into everlasting fire.

And if your eye leads you astray, pluck it out, and throw it on the ground. For it is better to go through life with one eye than to be thrown with both eyes into the mouth of hell.

Teaching 3

On the judgment day, I will say to those on my left, fall sinners! Into the endless fire that the devil has waiting for you. For I was hungry and you did not feed me. I was thirsty and you offered me nothing to drink. I was a down-and-out stranger, and you gave me no shelter. I was naked and you gave me no clothing. I was sick and you did not visit me. I was a prisoner and you scorned me.

And those sinners will beg for mercy saying, "Lord, when did we ever see you hungry, or thirsty, or a stranger in rags, or sick, or in prison, and not take care of you?"

And I will answer them saying, "Anytime you fail to do these things for even the lowest beings on earth, you failed to do these things for me!"

(*All exit. Lights up on Barney and Loop. They stand on the apron at opposite ends.*)

Schedule III

BARNEY: Where we serving lunch, Loop?

LOOP: Every town in the cum zone, Barney.

BARNEY: Radium on the 27th, hot lunch all the way, Sausage 'n Cream, backstage full time. A good straight show. Sealy on the 30th.

LOOP: That's where we pick up the wheat harvest. Combine crews. 110 degrees in the cum zone by then, Barney. Three weeks, four stops, dependin' on the weather.

BARNEY: Right. Aftosa, Burn, Wagon Tire, Brush and Millers Incline. Gobble girls'll be ready for the gospel by then.

Sausage and Cream

(*From apron, Barney moves directly behind rear curtain, facing away from audience for pitch. As he does his pitch, Rod is seen just on the other side of the back curtain, praying. When Rod goes on (also behind back curtain, facing away from audience.) Loop mimes his dance and sex gestures on the other side of the curtain, back to audience. As Rod dances, Slide sings as she massages Phoebe. They are midstage, facing audience. The front curtain is open. As soon as Rod's strip is ended and Slide's song is over, Rod comes backstage and joins Phoebe, and Slide goes on to do hot lunch. Loop sits on rung of a ladder, puts on halo from Doctor's Office and holds baby doll on her knee in Madonna pose.*)

Sausage and Cream Pitch

BARNEY: Now it's time for all you ladies who wanna taste o'
cock to put your money down.

Direct from Las Vegas, the Fabulous Rod Rim
If God had a dick, he'd look like Rod
Five bucks to suck, twenty-five to swallow
Don't be shy, grandma
Rod's the dick of your dreams
You'll feel like you're suckin' on a baby's fist
I'm not talkin' about pie in the sky
This pecker is for real
Rod's the God of sausage and cream
Quick while hubby's pickin' his nose
Wrap your mouth around Rod
And suck your way to paradise

Slide's Song

Like a wind from the coast
crashing down among the oak trees,
love shattered my mind,
Sweet sister, that day.
I was stone sober
hard as hard men
had taught me to be.
I was stone sober
'Til your love made me drunk
and soft enough to be free.

(*Rod finishes strip. Slide exits, begins stripping behind back curtain.*)

ROD: Come! Let's have one other gaudy night.
Call to me all my sad captains,
Let's fill our bowls once more.

PHOEBE: Why Jesus, you're in Roman drag again!

ROD: The expense of spirit in a waste of shame is lust in action.

PHOEBE: Couldn't you save a little for me, my lord?

ROD: I must retire from thrashing awhile.

PHOEBE: Someone got a mouthful, you're as limp as . . .

ROD: Limp! What mean ye? Let us inquire

	more carefully and find by what harsh measure. But sire! Thou art dickless entirely!
PHOEBE:	What dick I need I have. A sudden thirst!
ROD:	Strumpet! Drain me not of my vocation!
PHOEBE:	But when will you rise again, noble Rod?
ROD:	When you and Slide are finished with the boys.

(*They kiss.*)

ROD:	I forgot it was Slide's hot lunch debut.
PHOEBE:	You're not going to get that Jesus look.
ROD:	It's not a Jesus look.
PHOEBE:	We all go through it. And we all get over it.
ROD:	Yeah, I know. That's what bothers me.
PHOEBE:	Rod, if you turn religious, I'll go crazy. I can't stand that look.
ROD:	What look are you talking about?
PHOEBE:	I saw you praying before you went on.
ROD:	I wasn't praying. I was rehearsing. Look, as long as I've got to play Jesus, I want it to be good. I'm not going out there and make a fool of myself. I've got a right to pray if I want to.
PHOEBE:	You were praying.
SLIDE:	(*Entering scene through back curtain.*) Oh God, my cunt feels like a toilet. I feel like a restroom in a fucking truckstop. I'm gonna split. This is sick. And now I'm sick.
PHOEBE:	Take it easy, Slide. If you leave, it only gets worse. Remember how you got here.

(*Barney enters.*)

BARNEY: Good work, Slide! Sticky shoes out there lined up already. (*Slide is crying.*) What'sa matter?

PHOEBE: What do you think is the matter, Barney? Did you ever see anyone serve lunch for the first time without breaking up?

BARNEY: Yeah. What was the name of that colt butch we debuted in Hoboken? Irene? Darleen? No diapers on that pussy.

PHOEBE: Doreen.

BARNEY: Doreen, right. Bark Doreen. Bark butch, but she could pin a faggot.

PHOEBE: Doreen's dead.

SLIDE: I wish I was dead. I wish I was a muthafuckin' piece of dead meat, 'cause that's what I feel like, a piece of dead meat with a brain. Shit! I might as well go out and fuck dogs now. Fifty ball-headed motherfuckin' ghosts throwin' up in my hole.

BARNEY: Take it easy, Slide.

SLIDE: Don't touch me. And don't look at me.

BARNEY: Pretty baby, roll it down.

SLIDE: Pat the dog. You think I'm a dog? You're disgusting!

(*She slaps him. He grabs her.*)

BARNEY: You need to clear your screen, Slide. You need to roll it down. I am the man here, snag? I don't pull it out unless I have to, but if I have to . . .

SLIDE: Oh, gash cowboy's gonna cut his meat.

(*Slide steps on Barney's foot.*)

BARNEY: You wanna rub gash pussy? I'll show you some cock. You'll squat and spread. (*Barney hits Slide.*)

PHOEBE: Get out of here, Barney!

BARNEY: You want to leave, too? Go ahead. You'll go right to the top out there. Thirty million beggars, but with your talent, you'll go right to the top.

PHOEBE: Barney, if you don't shut up, I will leave and I'll take Slide with me. Without us, you'd be broke in a week.

BARNEY: All right. Roll it down. I didn't come here for blood soup. I brought you something to ease the pain. Diplomatic pouch. Non-stop mica sparkle. Open your nose a little. Get her out there. Calm her down. Virgins always draw a mess of babies. Let's get it while we can. Five minutes. Meet my pitch.

(*Barney exits behind back curtain for his pitch.*)

SLIDE: I'm gonna gas up, 'cause I will snuff a motherfucker before I do that again.

PHOEBE: Have a hit with me before you go. It'll be a while before you get any shit as good as this again. Barney's private stock.

BARNEY: Now it's time for all the fruit cakes and wilting flowers to head on home. The only people I'm talking to now are the men who can take the heat. 'Cause that's what you're going to get if you step inside this tent: 100 percent certified all-American pussy piping hot. Two bucks a plate just head for the gate. We're serving lunch right now and there's only one thing on the menu and we serve it up tenderized, spread, juicy fresh, and ready to be chewed.

SLIDE: (*Snorting up.*) Thanks. I sure can use this.

PHOEBE: I know I can use it. I'm gonna have to serve lunch by myself all night.

SLIDE: Mmm, that's a load. Charge on gash motherfucker. Make my tongue hard.

BARNEY: Our girls strip to please, not to tease.

SLIDE: Listen Phoebe, doesn't it fuck with your head doin' that? Mouth after sloppy mouth?

PHOEBE: Not anymore. It freaked me out at first, but I'd been hooking for a couple of months when Barney took me on.

SLIDE: You turned tricks? Come on.

PHOEBE: You remember '08?

SLIDE: Yeah, I remember.

PHOEBE: Hot lunch was easy comin' out of that. Besides, Barney and I were together back then.

SLIDE: What? Oh come on.

PHOEBE: We were tight for years. We still are.

SLIDE: You two?

PHOEBE: You probably think Barney is the same as what he does.

SLIDE: Isn't he?

PHOEBE: No, not at all. Have another hit.

BARNEY: I know all you guys been ripped off at the girlie shows
                before.
            Pay big bucks for sucks and find some flabby,
                maggoty old crack behind the curtain.
            But here we make no false promises.
            I'm not talking about the life to come,
            I'm not talking about some artsy-fartsy postcard
                madonnas,
            I'm talking about living flesh, hot pulsing pussy.

More gash grace and beauty than you've ever seen
  squatting right on your fucking face.
Don't hang back, don't hesitate.

SLIDE: I still don't believe it doesn't fuck with your head.

(*They snort up.*)

BARNEY: You're goin' to be ecstatic. One taste of snatch sends
you straight to heaven.

PHOEBE: Listen, Slide. What you gotta understand is when you
serve hot lunch, that's not you out there. That's your
job. That's what you do to eat. Some people sell their
brains for a paycheck, some people sell their backs.
It's not who they are. You sell your pussy. It freaks
you out because you think it's wrong. You think your
pussy is sacred.

SLIDE: Oh gimme a break. I'm not exactly the Virgin Mary,
you know. Whoo! This shit is like ice. I feel like there's
a wind blowin' through me. Like there's nothin' out
there and there's nothing in here but wind. Like a fast
black car on a straight, black road, only there's no car
and no road, just wind.

BARNEY: And now so you know that what you see is what you
get, I'm goin' to give you just a little preview. Come on
out here, Cream honey!

PHOEBE: Save me a line for break. Take the rest with you. I'm
gonna miss you, Slide.

SLIDE: Snag.

(*Phoebe exits through the back curtain.*)

BARNEY: This here is Cream! Total control.

Cool and slow on the outside,
inside is a raving beast, a cat in heat,
a boiling sex machine.
Take a look at those moves.
Starting to get a little hard down there?
How about giving these boys a look at your snatch,
    Cream honey?
Now! Is there any red-blooded American male here
    tonight who can truly say he doesn't want to pull
    Cream down on his face and get a good deep taste
    of pussy?
You'd like that, wouldn't you, Cream honey?

PHOEBE: Yes I would, Barney.

BARNEY: Did the last show really get your juices running, Cream
    honey?

PHOEBE: Yes it did, Barney.

BARNEY: Are you ready to serve these boys some lunch, Cream
    honey?

PHOEBE: That's what I'm here for, Barney.

BARNEY: That's what she was made for!
And now I want to show you a little girl
who's gonna blow you over!
I've watched a lotta girls dance in my day,
but this coffee-colored girl just turns me into a
    puddle a cum.
Come on out here, Slide honey!

(*Slide hesitates.*)

BARNEY: And here's Slide! If you like your lunch down on the
    ground with lots of steamin' hot sauce, you're gonna
    like Slide.

Show 'em where you do your cookin', honey.
Are you feelin' good and horny tonight?

SLIDE: Yes, Barney. Good and horny.

BARNEY: I'm tellin' you, you boys have never
seen a pussy like this before.
It's a pussy miracle.
A dripping pussy miracle.
Just a few places left inside.

Agony in the Garden

(*Rod crosses stage right when Slide goes out for Barney's hot lunch pitch. When pitch is over, he gets on top of box and prays, joined immediately by Loop, Phoebe, and Slide, who gather around him and sing as his apostles. Enter Edge, holding Bible.*)

EDGE: And he went out and proceeded according to his custom to the Mount of Olives. And when he had reached that place, he said to them: "Pray that you do not come to the time of trial." And went on his knees and prayed. And an angel, from the sky, was seen by him, giving him strength. And as he came into his agony, he prayed the more intensely, and his sweat became like drops of blood falling on the ground.

(*Edge retreats.*)

ROD: Father, if it is not possible
          while I live on this earth
          for this bitter cup of hatred
          to pass me by, but I must
          drink it, and let men treat me
          as they will, then I will drink it
          because it is your wish.

BARNEY: (*Offstage.*) The one I kiss will be

the one you want to kill.

ROD: Wake up my friends and pray.
My betrayer is near. When he gives me
his kiss, I must leave you.

(*Barney enters.*)

BARNEY: Master, I bring you my love.

(*Barney kisses Rod on the lips.*)

EDGE: (*Offstage.*) Seize him!
BARNEY: Rod, your Christ is getting really good.
ROD: Thanks, Barney.
BARNEY: It really tore me up. I used to be Catholic, you know.
All right! Ready for Liplock.

Last Supper

(*Actors move immediately to set up for Last Supper, putting on biblical costumes. Slide sings "Think, Sinner, Think" as the table and boxes are put into place. As actors are seated, they continue to talk to one another, focusing the image of rehearsal and performance. On cue, actors move into frieze of Last Supper.*)

ROD: (*As Christ.*) Verily I say unto you that one of you will betray me.

(*They shift twice again, turning to look at each other, and then holding for a moment.*)

ALL: Is it I, Lord? Lord, is it I?

EDGE: (*As Judas, rising toward him.*) Surely it is not I, Lord!

ROD: You have said.

(*Pause. The actors shift slightly. Slide begins singing, tentatively.*)

ROD: Two days from now, I will die.
Nothing you or I or any man can do
Can keep me from being crucified.
The priests and rulers of this land
Must kill me or lose their power.
But you, my dearest friends,

You do not need
to betray me. You Peter,
closest to me of all:
Three times you will deny me
before the cock crows.

SLIDE: (*As Peter.*) It is not so, master.
I would die before
denying you.

ROD: Even so. I wish to remain
with you as you are: Whenever
you eat this bread, it is my body
that lives in the grain and feeds you.
Whenever you drink this wine
and feel the flush of joy
that is yours for the drinking,
that is my blood you will drink,
shed so you will remember
how once a man lived as I did
and for living as I did
was killed.

(*He stands. Scene ends.*)

Peter Scene

(*Table and boxes are cleared immediately. Christ (Rod) is brought in by Barney and thrown to the floor. Peter (Slide.) is above on a ladder. The mockers circle Christ. Rough atonal saxophone solo under the voices. Girl (Loop.) climbs below Slide on ladder. Others continue to circle Rod.*)

LOOP: You were with Jesus, weren't you?
           The one who says he's the Son of God.
           I saw you praying with him in the garden.
SLIDE: I don't know who or what
           you're talking about. Go away.
LOOP: You're one of them.
           You're scared to go inside.
           That's why you're hiding.
           You're a follower of Jesus.
SLIDE: I'm not one of anything.
           I'm not hiding.
           I don't even know who this Jesus is.
LOOP: I can tell by your accent.
           I can tell by your smell.
           You talk like him.
           You all smell the same.
SLIDE: I don't know what the hell
           you're talking about.

I swear on the head of Moses
I never saw the man before.
Now, if you don't shut your mouth-

(*The cock crows.*)

I'm going to have to shut it for you.

The Mocking

(*Slide begins to cry, mouth wide open, almost no sound. Loop joins mockers. They strip Rod, put a red cloth on him, a crown of thorns. They circle him with low, threatening laughter, hit him, spit at him.*)

PHOEBE: I am the King of the Jews!

BARNEY: (*Thrusting his pelvis forward.*) I am the power and the glory!

LOOP: Oh Father, Father, come and save me Father!

(*Barney comes to Rod as if to comfort him, then thrusts him hard to the floor. Slide cries out on ladder, then holds her face in a silent cry.*)

ROD: Daughters of Jerusalem,
do not cry for me
but for yourselves and your children. Listen:
the day is going to come when people will say,
"Blessed are the aborted dead babies,
the wombs that are barren,
blessed are the breasts that give no milk."
If you think this day is terrible-
a day is going to come
when people will pray

to the oceans, Please drown us!"
and to the mountains, "Please, smother us!
Come down on us!
leave no trace!"

If they do these things to me
when the wood is still green
and people take joy in living,
think what will happen when the wood
is dry, and living itself becomes a burden.

Crucifixion

(*Actors form three painterly images of the crucifixion, the first
silent, the second, with Christ still on the cross. Phoebe moans
repeatedly and throws herself to the floor. The third image is
of Christ being taken from the cross. Slow flute and clarinet
music. Final image breaks and table and door are set up for
Doubting Thomas and final scene while Barney and Loop do
final scheduling.*)

Last Scheduling

BARNEY: We never could have done it without Rod. Those people thought he was the real Jesus. I was starting to feel a little creepy myself.

LOOP: Oooo, the bread and the blood and the wine and the body. I forgot who I was when he was sayin' that!

BARNEY: Listen, if we packed 'em in killin' Christ, think what a fuckin' smash we're gonna have when we get that resurrection in. Edge says it's kinda the hot lunch of the Bible. Do we have time before Aftosa?

LOOP: Well, we got a hot lunch turn, geeks up, in Firebaugh on the 12th. Same thing in Bastrop the next day. Girls'll be pretty tired.

BARNEY: Fuck those pussy pits. We made more doin' gospel last week in Liplock than hot lunch gets us in a month.

LOOP: I never knew there were so many nice, clean people. And they all said "thank you" too. I could hardly get all that money in the box and the dollar bills weren't all wet and sticky.

BARNEY: We can rest up a little, buy some clothes, get Thomas the Doubter down, get loaded, relax, then we'll really be ready for Aftosa.

Doubting Thomas

(Disciples become still for a moment as Rod climbs the ladder as Christ returning. All are present but Phoebe, who plays Thomas, and is offstage.)

ROD: Peace be with you my friends.
    I have returned from death
    to breathe my spirit into you.
    You are now my apostles:
    Whomever you forgive
    will be forgiven,
    whom you refuse to forgive
    will bear the stain of sin
    until final judgment.

    (He comes off ladder and they touch him. He runs out. They rejoice, "He came back! We're saved! He is the Son of God! There is a life to come!" During the upheaval, Thomas knocks on the door. They become quiet.)

EDGE: It's Thomas. He'll be so happy to hear.

    (He opens the door for Phoebe. She enters.)

PHOEBE: They're looking for us everywhere.

I crawled on my hands and knees.

EDGE: Thomas! Jesus was here!

PHOEBE: What?

EDGE: He breathed his spirit into us!

PHOEBE: But when?

SLIDE: He gave us eternal life!

EDGE: Just now when you went out.

PHOEBE: But that's impossible!

BARNEY: He showed us the wounds.

LOOP: He was here! He blessed us.

PHOEBE: You're making fun of me.
When I see myself the holes
from the nails in his hands and stick
my fingers into them and thrust
my hand into the gash in his side,
I'll believe you and not before.

ROD: (*Re-entering.*) Peace be with you, Doubting Thomas.
Stick your fingers here
into the holes in my hands
and thrust your hand here
into the gash in my side
and be not an unbeliever
but a believer whose glory
is one with my own.

PHOEBE: My Lord and God.
I can't do this. I won't do this. I can't stand it.

ROD: But what's wrong?

PHOEBE: Stop pretending to be Christ!
We've turned into a bunch of fucking liars.
This used to be an honest business.
We gave people what they paid for.
It was sick, but it was real.

	Now we got this soft-core wet dream.
	Jack off on Rod! He's the Son of God!
	Stick your fingers in his holes!
ROD:	Stop it, Phoebe.
PHOEBE:	People so starved for hope, they drool at the smell.
	And we serve it up!
	Do they make you squat on their faces for a piece of bread?
	Don't worry! After you're dead, you get another shot.
	Paradise! Just inside the tent. Two dollars.
	And you and I are the proof, Rod. See?
	I got my hand in your slit right up to the elbow.
	You've been born again!
	If you can do it, anyone can.
	Get your money before it's too late. Eternal bliss!
	Five bucks to suck, twenty-five to swallow.
ROD:	Stop it.
PHOEBE:	And that's not the worst of it, Rod.
	The worst of it is that you're getting off on it.
	Leave 'em crying in the aisles.
	A pimp for God!
ROD:	Stop it!
PHOEBE:	Shit. Maybe this is how it got started.
	Unemployed actor. Steady part. A routine to end all routines.

End of Thomas the Doubter

(*Rod exits. Actors mill around confusedly during the following speeches, except Loop, who crouches at once behind a box, and Phoebe, who stands by herself at the side. Eventually the others seat themselves at the table recalling, but not reproducing, The Last Supper. Loop remains hidden until her final speech.*)

SLIDE:	Bottom of the ninth.
	Suburbs bark you bad.
EDGE:	Look, Phoebe, I got no gospel,
	I got no job.
	We were barely makin' it.
BARNEY:	Why look a gift horse in the ass?
	We were out of intensive care.
SLIDE:	I'd rather flash than beg.
	I'd rather believe than squat,
	I'd rather pretend to believe
	than serve hot lunch any day.
	My bills are paid, snag?
	Paid in Full.
EDGE:	Check it out.
	This can't be the only world there is.
	If we don't have a dream, we're dead.
SLIDE:	Sam drone, uncle vultures on a rock soup gash from
	Coast to Coast.

You got your pain killers!

EDGE: I'll do it. You don't have to.

SLIDE: Stuck my fuckin' brother.

Pneumonia. No scrip. Tuberculosis.

Where's Jesus? Rod got a customer?

BARNEY: How the fuck do you know he didn't come back?

Were you there?

You think all there is

is what you can see?

(*Pause.*)

SLIDE: Where is he?

(*Pause.*)

BARNEY: Rod'll be back. We'll have a great fuckin' show.

I feel better around religion.

I don't know if I believe in it,

but it's better than what I had in my head before,

which was absolutely nothin', so what the fuck?

Real Acting

(Mid stage is half lit. Front and back curtains are closed. Rod is tied on crucifix. Barney and Edge have huge mallets and spikes. We can see them clearly, but focus is not sharp. Lights slowly come to full by end of scene.)

BARNEY: You really wanna do this, Rod?

ROD: I'm sure.

BARNEY: Are you ok with this, Edge?

EDGE: You really mean it, Rod? This ain't Hot Lunch.

ROD: I mean it. Yes. Do it.

EDGE: I'm in.

(They drive the spikes loudly into Rod's hands and feet. Rod moans but does not scream. They finish. Rod weeps. Edge exits with Barney, opening curtain.)

BARNEY: Phoebe! Phoebe!

(Phoebe rushes in, crossing paths with Barney.)

BARNEY: Still think you're God? Rod wants to talk to you.

(Phoebe strides toward Rod. At first she thinks he's refined his act.)

PHOEBE: Beautiful. Total geek. You're the best. I've always believed in you.

(*She suddenly realizes it's real. Stops short. She raises her arms. The image is one of horror, repulsion, and devotion.*)

PHOEBE: No. No. No, no, no, no, no, no, no!

(*She falls flat. Blackout. Barney closes the curtain.*)

Last Loop

(*Loop pops up behind center box and sits.*)

LOOP: (*Harsh voice.*) Every baby that comes into this world
is the same as every other baby.
Even if there's no father
and it's breathing, that baby
all by itself needs milk.
Even if there's no mother;
somewhere anything living
needs to be fed. Feeding
is what does it. Anywhere you see them,
big stacks of eggs cracked open with the
yolks running into the pan is what
I was once and am now because
of living, and will be too. Dead, I mean.
  (*Coquette voice.*) I saw you eating those eggs.
You weren't really knocked up.
You saw me do it and then you pretended.
I showed them the blood.
You can't shut the drawer forever.
  (*Harsh voice.*) I don't want anyone to say I'm
    stealing.
I don't want anyone to fall down too soon.
Even if that baby has no relatives at all

when they shut the bulb off, there's a little light.
So you can tell if that baby's still breathing.
Even if it's sleeping, that baby will be breathing.
At least I hope it will.
Anything could kill it! It has a hard time living!
There's too much blood! There's not enough milk!
The blanket slipped off! It was cold!
(*Normal voice.*) Well. That's all I have to say right
now. The real
Jesus couldn't be here tonight. That's Rod.
He's gone. But he might come back.
Oh God. Now I'm crying, and I don't know
why I'm crying, and I'm afraid
not of the end, but of the beginning,
when you have to start the story over
and you're crying because you don't
know what comes first. You're a person,
not a baby, but you're crying anyway,
and you don't know why.

(*Lights fade to black. Actors come through front bead-
ed curtain for curtain call as "Scoobie-Doo theme"
plays.*)

Pedro Páramo

Translated and adapted from the novel by Juan Rulfo.

Presented by The Talking Band and La Mama, ETC, Ellen Stewart, Artistic Director, New York, March, 1984.

The cast:

ABUNDIO, TILCUATE:	William Badgett
PEDRO PÁRAMO:	Raymond Barry
FATHER RENTERÍA:	Bimbo Rivas
EDUVIGES, DOROTEA:	Sheila Dabney
SISTER OF DONIS, MADRE VILLA:	Ellen Maddow
MUSICIAN:	Harry Mann
DOLORES PRECIADO:	Louise Smith
SUSANNA SAN JUAN, DAMIANA:	Tina Shephard
JUAN PRECIADO:	Jack Wetherall
DONIS, BARTOLOMÉ SAN JUAN:	Paul Zimet

Directed by Paul Zimet
Set Design by Jun Maeda
Music by Alice Eve Cohen, Sybille Hayn, Ellen Maddow, and
   Harry Mann.

Characters

PEDRO PÁRAMO, a wealthy landowner
JUAN PRECIADO, his abandoned son
DOLORES PRECIADO, his abandoned wife
SUSANNA SAN JUAN, his lifelong love
BARTOLOMÉ SAN JUAN, her father
ABUNDIO
DAMIANA
FULGOR
TILCUATE
FATHER RENTERÍA
EDIVIGES
DOROTEA
DONIS
SISTER OF DONIS
JUSTINA

Act I

Scene 1

(Juan and Dorotea lie embraced in a single grave in a raked, rough, wooden stage. Dorotea is very thin.)

JUAN: I came to Comala because they told me my father
was living there. Someone named Pedro Páramo.

(Lights go off on them. Lights up on the chorus of Indians who are squatting in clusters in different areas of the stage playing music. The overture ends after the Indians have moved to the two chorus areas on either side of the playing space. Dorotea slides under the stage. Trap closes. Light comes up on Juan, standing.)

JUAN: I promised to go and see him when she was dying:
she was about to die and I would have promised her
anything.

(Maria Preciado emerges from under the stage, accompanied by choral singing—her theme.)

MARIA: Don't forget to go and see him. His name
is Pedro. Pedro Páramo.
I know he'll be glad to meet you, my son.

JUAN: So there was nothing
          I could do but say that I would do it, and once I said
          I'd do it, I just kept on saying it
          even after it was hard to break free
          from her dying hands.

MARIA: Juan. Listen.
          Don't go begging him for anything. Just ask him
          for what belongs to us, what he was supposed
          to give us and never did. Make him pay
          for the way he forgot us, my son.

          (She recedes. Trap door closes over her.)

JUAN: I didn't think I'd keep my promise,
          but from that time on I began to feed myself
          on dreams and let delusions eat at me.
          I started to build my whole world on the hope
          that there was such a person as Pedro Páramo,
          the husband of my mother. Because of all this
          I came to Comala. *(Walking music begins. He
             walks.)*

CHORUS: It was in the dog days of summer
          when the hot August air is poisoned with the smell
          of rotting flowers. The road was going
          up and down and down and up.

JUAN: You know what they say,
          "It depends on whether you're going or coming:
          if you're going the road goes up and up, coming back
          it's all downhill."

          (Abundio enters. They walk together)

JUAN: What's the name of that village?

ABUNDIO: That's Comala, señor.

JUAN: Are you sure that's Comala?

ABUNDIO: I'm sure, señor.

JUAN: But why does it look so poor and sad?

ABUNDIO: Things have been rough in Comala, señor.

(Abundio walks off. Walking music stops.)

JUAN: I always imagined it would be like it was
             in my mother's memories. She was always
             sighing for her beloved Comala, praying
             she'd be able to come back, some day, but she died
             before her homecoming. Now I was returning
             instead of her, and I expected to see
             what she told me I would see.

(Maria emerges. Her theme.)

MARIA: When you come through the pass at Los Colimotes,
             there's a beautiful view of a green plain below
             with a touch of yellow from the full-grown corn.
             From there you can see Comala so white
             and shining it illuminates the earth in every
             direction.

*(She recedes. Abundio enters instantly. Walking music
begins. Juan and Abundio walk together.)*

ABUNDIO: And why have you come to Comala?
             Maybe I can help you in some way?

JUAN: I've come here
             to see my father. He lives here, they say.

ABUNDIO: There'll be a big fiesta
in your honor. It's been years since anyone came
        here.
They'll be happy to see someone again.

CHORUS: In the blurring reflection of the sun
the plain was like a transparent lake
steaming up into the sky, and through that steamy
haze you could see the grey horizon, and beyond,
a chain of mountains, and beyond that,
a distance beyond all distance.

ABUNDIO: And what does
this father of yours look like, if you don't mind
my asking?

JUAN: I don't know him. I've never seen him.
I only know they call him Pedro Páramo.

ABUNDIO: Ah, come on. Don't bullshit me!

JUAN: Well, that's what
they told me his name was, Pedro Páramo.

ABUNDIO: AHH!

(*The walking music stops at this exclamation, and
Abundio turns out of sight.*)

JUAN: I met him at Los Encuentros where the roads
going every which way come together. I sat there
a long time, not sure which way to go. (*Walking
        music. To Abundio.*)
Hey, where are you headed?

ABUNDIO: I'm going down, señor.

JUAN: Have you ever heard of a place called Comala?

ABUNDIO: That's exactly where I'm going.

(They walk for a few moments. Come to a dead stop. Their shoulders almost touch. Walking music stops as they do.)

ABUNDIO: Pedro Páramo is my father, too.

(The walking music resumes. They move.)

JUAN: We left behind the hot air above, and began to sink in
    a heat
    so pure there didn't seem to be any air at all.
    (To Abundio.) The air is on fire.

ABUNDIO: Yes, and this
    is nothing. Nothing at all. Relax.
    It's going to be even worse
    when we get to Comala. They built that village
    over the hot coals of the earth, right smack in the
    mouth
    of Hell. They say that when someone from Comala
    dies and goes to Hell, they come crawling back up
    here
    to get their blankets. Hell's too cold for them.

JUAN: Is Pedro Páramo really your father? Who is he,
    anyway?

ABUNDIO: Pedro Páramo is pure hatred. Hatred itself. He
    invented the word. They got it from him.

(Walking music stops and the Maria theme is sung.)

JUAN: I felt the wet photograph of my mother I kept
    in my pocket warming my heart as if she
    were sweating too. I found it

in the kitchen cabinet, in a stew pot full of herbs.
My mother hated to have her picture taken.
She said photographs were black magic.
And maybe it was true, because hers
was full of tiny needle holes, and near her heart
there was a hole so big you could stick your finger in.
I've got my finger in it now: I brought it with me
hoping it might help my father remember me . . .

(*The Maria theme stops. Sound of flapping paper and dry wind blowing.*)

ABUNDIO: Hold on. Take a good look. See that hill
over there that almost looks like a pig's bladder?
Now turn this way. See that ridge that looks
like a sharp, thin knife? Can you see it?
Now see that sierra that's almost too far away
for us to see? All of that is the Media Luna Ranch.
One end to the other. Like someone said,
all the land that the eye can chew and choke down.
And all that land is his. You and I are sons
of Pedro Páramo, all right, but the fact is,
our mothers gave birth to us stretched out on straw
    mats
on cold concrete floors. Then he'd take us all to town
in a cart to be baptized. Three or four of us at a time.
The same thing happened to you, right?

JUAN: I don't remember.

ABUNDIO: You lie like a whore.

JUAN: What did you say?

ABUNDIO: I said we're almost there, señor.

(They turn a corner and stop. Walking music stops.)

JUAN: But what's happened here? It looks so lonely,
            as if it had been abandoned.

ABUNDIO: Abandoned? It's been raped and left to die.

JUAN: And Pedro Páramo?

ABUNDIO: Pedro Páramo has been dead for years.
            I hope the maggots ate his eyes out,
            and then his lips, and then his face.

(Pause. He begins to go.)

            See where those hills come together? That's where
            my house is. If you want to stay there,
            you're more than welcome. But maybe you should
            stay, and have a look around. There might be
            someone still alive. Look for Dona Eduviges.
            You can tell her I sent you.

JUAN: But what's your name?

ABUNDIO: Abundio.

JUAN: Abundio what?

ABUNDIO: Abundio. *(Exits,)*

(Music.)

CHORUS: It was that hour when the children are playing
            in the dusty streets
            of every pueblo
            filling the afternoon with their calls,
            that time of day when even the black walls reflect the
                last
            yellow light of the sun and turn dark. That's what
                Juan

Preciado saw
in Sayula
yesterday afternoon at this
very moment. A flock of white birds cracked the still
    air
beating their wings, struggling to get free
in the light of the late afternoon.
Now he's here,
in this village
without sound. He hears his own footsteps fall
against round paving stones and echo behind him
as if he were following himself.
He sees empty houses,
doors faded and cracked, windows strangled with
    weeds,
weeds growing
through rooftops
in the last light of dusk.

(*A woman in a reboso passes. He sees her.*)

WOMAN: Buenas noches, señor.

JUAN: Wait! Can you tell me
where Doña Eduviges lives?

WOMAN: Right over there.
It's the house beside the bridge. (*Exits.*)

(*Juan turns, sees the house and then the door, is about
to knock when Eduviges appears in the doorway with
a lighted candle.*)

EDUVIGES: Please come in. I'm Eduviges Dyada. I've been waiting

for you. Your room is ready. Just come this way.

JUAN: (*Following her, stumbling with difficulty.*) What is all this stuff?

EDUVIGES: Junk. Odds and ends. People leaving town use my house

to dump the things they can't take with them.

No one ever comes back for it. The room I've got for you

is at the very end. I always keep it empty for you.

(*Turns to him with candle.*) So, you're Maria's son.

JUAN: Yes, but how did you know?

EDUVIGES: She told me you were coming. She said you'd be here today.

JUAN: Who said that? My mother?

EDUVIGES: Yes, your mother, Maria.

Well, here's your room.

JUAN: (*Looking around.*) But there aren't any windows.

There's no air. There's nothing to sleep on in here.

EDUVIGES: Oh, don't worry about that. Sleep's the best mattress

to have when you're tired. First thing in the morning

I'll fix a bed for you. It's not easy, you know, to get a room

ready on a moment's notice. You've got to know in advance.

And your mother didn't tell me 'til today.

JUAN: My mother? My mother is dead!

EDUVIGES: Ah, that's why her voice

seemed so weak, like it had to travel a long way to

get here. Now I understand. How long ago did she die?

JUAN: A week ago, today.

EDUVIGES: Oh, the poor thing, she must have felt
          abandoned. We promised one another we'd die
             together.
          We said we'd go together to keep our spirits up along
             the way.
          We were such good friends. Didn't she ever talk
             about me?

JUAN: No, never. Not to me anyway.

EDUVIGES: That's very strange. Of course, we were only young
          girls
          back then. But we were so close. So now she's gotten
          ahead of me. Well, I'll catch up. I'm the only one
          who knows how far away heaven really is; and I
             know all
          the shortcuts. *(Pause.)* Forgive me for talking to you
          like this. I do it because I think of you as my own
             son.
          Oh, many times I've said to myself, "Maria's son
          should have been mine." I'll tell you why later.

JUAN: Yes . . . I'm sure . . . I'm really very tired.

EDUVIGES: Come and have a little something to eat first.
          Just a tortilla . . . some beans.

JUAN: I'll come . . . I'll come later.

(Lights off them. She leaves. He sleeps.)

Scene 2

(Media Luna.)
(Storm music, then rain.)

CHORUS: Water slid from the rooftops, burrowing holes
in the sand
in the courtyard.
The storm was over.
From time to time
a breeze shook
the branches of the pomegranate trees
and glistening drops tapped the bare ground.
Then the chickens
strutted into the courtyard,
snapping up the wiggling earthworms
uncovered by the rain and swallowing them whole.

*(The light is on the young Pedro Páramo, sitting on
the toilet with his pants down.)*

PEDRO'S MOTHER: Pedro! Pedro Páramo! What are you
doing in the bathroom so long?
YOUNG PEDRO: Nothing, Mama.
PEDRO'S MOTHER: If you stay in there much longer, a snake's
going to come and bite you!
YOUNG PEDRO: Yes, Mama, coming. *(Pause.)*
I was sitting in there thinking about you,
Susanna. In the green hills, remember?
When we were flying kites that windy day?
We could hear the sound of the whole village
from up there on top of the hills, and the wind
was unwinding the string so fast I could

hardly keep up so I yelled, "Help me! Susanna,"
and then there were such smooth hands pressed
   against
my hands! "Let it out! Let it out!" I yelled,
and then we started laughing, and then we looked
into one another's eyes while the string
ran out between our fingers, and all at once
the string snapped with a little crack
as if a passing bird had cut it
with its wings, and then up there above
the paper bird tumbled in somersaults
'til it got lost in the green of the hills. Your lips
were all moist as if you'd been kissing the dew.

PEDRO'S MOTHER: Pedro! I thought I told you to come out of the
bathroom!

YOUNG PEDRO: Coming, Mama.

PEDRO'S MOTHER: Why are you taking so long? What were you
doing in there anyway?

YOUNG PEDRO: I was thinking.

PEDRO'S MOTHER: Well, can't you do your thinking somewhere
   else?
It's dangerous to spend so much time in the
   bathroom.
One of these days a rattlesnake's going to slide in and
   bite you.
Besides, I've got plenty of work for you to do inside.
(Exit)

YOUNG PEDRO: Miles from the earth, above all the clouds,
farther away than anything, that's where
you're hiding Susanna, you're up there
where I can't see you, where my words won't reach!

PEDRO'S MOTHER: Pedro Páramo! Get in here now!

Scene 3

(*Eduviges' house.*)

EDUVIGES: So, as I was saying, I almost was your mother.
She never told you this?

JUAN: No. I heard about you from the man
who brought me here, someone named Abundio.

EDUVIGES: Ah, good old Abundio. He was such a good
storyteller!
Everyone felt terrible when he went deaf. One of
those
rockets they use to scare watersnakes exploded right
next
to his head: BAM!! And from that time on he never
spoke again. He said there was no sense saying
things because
he couldn't hear a thing, so there was no pleasure in
talking
anymore. But that didn't keep him from still being a
good person.
He just didn't speak, that's all.

JUAN: But the man I met could
speak and hear perfectly well.

EDUVIGES: Then it couldn't have been him. And besides,
Abundio
is dead, I'm sure of it. So, you see, it couldn't have
been him.
Maybe it was another Abundio. The world is full of
Abundios.
Anyway, getting back to your mother:
there was this fellow

who used to work out at the Media Luna breaking
    horses. He
could stay in the saddle until the horse collapsed.
    And he wasn't just
good at breaking horses. He had another talent too:
he could stir your dreams. And your mother grabbed
    his bones
and wouldn't let go. And she wasn't the only one.
    One time I was
sick and he showed up and said, "I'm going to
    examine
you so you'll feel better." You can imagine what kind
of a doctor's examination that was: he'd loosen you
    up
and massage you all over: first your fingertips, and
then he'd start rubbing your hands, and then your
    arms,
and then he'd caress your legs. And while he was
    doing
this and that he'd be telling you your fortune and
falling into a trance, rolling his eyes and muttering
prayers and curses at the same time, and all the time
    he'd
be licking you like a gypsy and getting every inch of
you good and wet. Sometimes he'd end up
    completely
naked saying he was only getting undressed because
we wanted him to. And you know what? Sometimes
    he was right.
So the night of her wedding, this fellow comes to see
your mother, and he looks into her future, and he
    tells

her, "You better not go lovemaking with any man
    tonight
because the moon's in a really bad mood." So Maria
comes running in to me saying she can't do it.
It's her wedding night, right? And she's telling me
it's impossible to sleep with Pedro Páramo. And there
I am trying to convince her to forget what this crazy
    fool
said. "I can't do it," she says. "Please go in my place.
He won't notice." Now, I was a little younger than
    she
was, and a little shorter, but in the dark, we'd look
    about
the same. So I went. The darkness helped me, and
something else your mother didn't know. The fact
    was,
I liked Pedro Páramo, too. I went to bed with him
    full of
desire. I got right in bed and snuggled up to him,
but he'd been drinking all day. The only thing he did
    was
wrap his legs around me and snore. Before it got
    light I went
to see your mother. "Maria," I said. "You go in
    now."
"What did he do to you?" she said. "I wouldn't
    worry
about it," I said. I was disappointed. The next year
    you
were born. I wasn't your mother, but I didn't miss by
    much.
Maybe she was too embarrassed to tell you about it.

Well, the marriage didn't last. Before long her soft
eyes
grew hard as stone. Pedro Páramo got all her land
and drove
her away. *(Pause.)* When are you going to get some
rest?

*(Music of rain, the light leaves them, though they re-
main where they are.)*

Scene 4

(Media Luna.)

YOUNG PEDRO: The day you went away, Susanna, you went
darkened by the red of the afternoon sun,
like dried blood at dusk. You were smiling.
You said,
"I like it here because of you, Pedro,
but I despise it for everything else,
even being born here.
And now I'm going to leave it behind."
She won't come back. She'll never
come back. I'm never going to see her again.

Scene 5

*(Intermittent music of pounding hooves approaching and
departing.)*

JUAN: What is it, Doña Eduviges?

EDUVIGES: It's that damn horse of Miguel Páramo
                pounding up the road to the Media Luna.

JUAN: So someone still lives at the Media Luna, then?

EDUVIGES: No, nobody lives out there. It's just Miguel's horse
                going
                back and forth. You couldn't separate those two.

JUAN: Who's this Miguel?

EDUVIGES: Miguel Páramo,
                Pedro Páramo's son, Miguel. The only one he ever
                    raised.
                The horse goes running everywhere looking for him,
                    and it
                always comes home around this time of day.
                Maybe the poor thing's still too guilty to rest.

JUAN: What are you talking about? I don't hear any horse.

EDUVIGES: You don't?
                It must be my sixth sense then. *(Pause.)*
                Don't you hear it now? Of course you hear it!
                He's coming back . . .

JUAN: I don't hear anything.

EDUVIGES: Then it's just me again.
                Well, anyway, on this night I was already in bed
                    when
                I heard Miguel's horse, and then I heard Miguel
                    himself
                tapping on my window. It was no surprise
                to see him because there was a time
                he'd spend the night here sleeping with me
                'til he met that girl who sucked his brains out.
                "What happened?" I said to Miguel. "Did she
                throw you out?" "No, she still loves me," he said.

"I just got lost on the way to her village.
There was a lot of fog or smoke or
something. I went further and further,
but I didn't find anything. If I
told anyone else in Comala, they'd
just say I was crazy." "Crazy, no,"
I said. "You're not crazy Miguel, you're dead.
I told you that horse was going to kill you
one of these days." And he said, "All I did
was make my horse jump that stone wall so I
wouldn't have to go the long way round to get
to the road. I know I jumped it and just kept on
    going.
But there was nothing out there but a lot of smoke
    and fog."
"Your father's going to twist and turn tomorrow,"
I said. "Now go and rest in peace, Miguel.
And thank you for coming to say goodbye."
And I shut the window. *(Pause.)*
Have you ever heard the moan of someone dying?

JUAN: No, Doña Eduviges.

EDUVIGES: It's better that way.

(Pause. The candle goes out by itself. Blackout. Funereal music.)

Scene 6

(Music and funeral procession. The coffin of Miguel Páramo is borne and placed on the stage floor. The mourners retire, and with their exit, the music ends. Father Renteria kneels beside the coffin.)

FATHER RENTERÍA: There are air and sun and clouds in the sky,
and up there, above the blue heavens, are
hymns sung by sweet, angelic voices.
There is hope, in short, there is grace for us,
to balance out our grief. But not for you,
Miguel Páramo. You have died in sin;
you will never receive God's forgiveness.

(Pedro Páramo has entered unseen by Renteria and has overheard the above.)

PEDRO: Father, I want you to bless him. He was my son.
FATHER RENTERÍA: Your son was an evil man, Don Pedro. He cannot enter
the Kingdom of Heaven. God would despise
me if I interceded for the likes
of Miguel Páramo.
PEDRO: I know that you hated him, Father.
Maybe you were right. Your brother's murder. Some
people said it was Miguel. Then there's that business
about your niece, though that kind of thing's
very hard to prove.
I can't blame you for hating him.
Father, I'm asking you to forget those things.
Maybe God's already forgiven him:
why not be merciful and forgive him
yourself . . . and accept this gift for your church . . .

(Pedro drops a bag of heavy coins on the coffin. Pause. Renteria makes the sign of the cross over the dead body and mumbles a blessing. He picks up the money, and Pedro exits. Renteria goes to the altar.)

Pedro Páramo 247

FATHER RENTERÍA: It's all yours, Lord. He knows how to pay for
salvation. But only you know if this is the price of it.
As far as I'm concerned, dear God: please!
Send him to Hell and let him twist forever!

*(Music of bird whistles. Renteria's niece, Anna,
enters.)*

FATHER RENTERÍA: Anna, do you know who was buried today?
ANNA: No, Uncle.
FATHER RENTERÍA: Miguel Páramo. *(Pause.)*
You're certain that he was the one
who did it, aren't you?
ANNA: Yes, Uncle, I'm certain.
He grabbed me at night, in the dark.
FATHER RENTERÍA: But if it was dark, how do you know it was
Miguel Páramo?
ANNA: Because he said to me,
"I'm Miguel Páramo, Anna, don't be afraid."
FATHER RENTERÍA: But you knew he killed your father didn't
you?
What did you do to get away from him?
ANNA: I didn't do anything. He told me
he had come to ask for my forgiveness.
It was pitch dark, and I was so confused
because I wanted to hate him, but I kept
remembering what you told me about
being forgiving. So I smiled at him,
but later I thought he couldn't see my smile
because the night was so black I couldn't
see him. And then the next thing I knew,
he was on top of me and his hands were

all over me. "Make a sound and I'll kill you,"
he said, and he put his hands around my neck.
So I just stopped thinking.
Until I saw the morning light
through the open window, I felt like I was dead.

FATHER RENTERÍA: But you've got to be sure it was him!
Didn't you know his voice?

ANNA: I didn't know him at all. But I know
that right now he must be at the very
bottom of Hell: because that's what I prayed
with everything in my heart.

FATHER RENTERÍA: Just be thankful to God Our Father
for taking him off the earth where he did
so much evil. It doesn't matter now
if he's in Heaven or not. He's dead.

*(Anna exits. Bird whistles. Renteria names saints,
counting them like sheep. He falls asleep.)*

FATHER RENTERÍA: Santa Nunilona, virgin and martyr.
Santa Solome, widow.
Elodia and Nulina, virgins.
Cordula and Donato, orphans.
Santa Margarita, keeper of the faith . . .

(Enter Rosa Dyada.)

ROSA: Father, it's me, Rosa Dyada.
Father wake up, it's me, Rosa!
I've come to ask you again to save the soul
of my sister, Eduviges. We heard you
forgave Miguel, so we thought if you could

forgive him, maybe you'd reconsider
Eduviges.

FATHER RENTERÍA: No! Absolutely not!

ROSA: But Father, you know Eduviges
always served her fellow human beings,
she gave them everything she had,
she even gave them sons, every one of them.
She was such an affectionate person,
and they all just took advantage of her.

FATHER RENTERÍA: But she killed herself. That's against the will
of God.

ROSA: There was no way out. She had no choice.

FATHER RENTERÍA: How could she fail at the very last minute?!
She had so many deeds piled up for her
salvation! And she threw them all away!

ROSA: She didn't kill herself. It was grief that killed her.

FATHER RENTERÍA: Maybe with Gregorian Masses . . . but we'll
need help for those . . . we'll have to send for priests,
and that's going to cost money . . .

ROSA: Father,
I'm a poor woman, you know how poor I am . . .
there's no money . . .

FATHER RENTERÍA: Let's just leave things as they are then.
Let's put our trust in God.

ROSA: But Father,
you forgave Miguel Páramo!

FATHER RENTERÍA: NO!
You must leave now! I need to get my rest!

(*Rosa Dyada exits, and Dorotea enters, carrying a
block of wood. She is laughing.*)

FATHER RENTERÍA: What's this, Dorotea, drinking now, too?

DOROTEA: I was just at Miguel's wake, Father. Everyone just kept
passing me drink after drink; I made a fool of myself.

FATHER RENTERÍA: You've never been anything but a fool,
Dorotea.

DOROTEA: But listen, Father, I've really got something to confess
this time . . .

FATHER RENTERÍA: Dorotea, you couldn't commit a sin if you
wanted to.

DOROTEA: But Father, this time it's true . . .

FATHER RENTERÍA: All right, all right, let's hear it.

DOROTEA: I'm the one who used to get girls for Miguel Páramo,
Don Pedro's son.

FATHER RENTERÍA: But why? How could you do such a thing?

DOROTEA: I was hungry, Father, he promised to feed me . . . he
gave
me milk every morning . . . so I did what he told me
to do.

FATHER RENTERÍA: You brought girls to him!

DOROTEA: Sometimes, yes, other times I'd just talk to them.
Sometimes, I just showed him where they were,
you know, where they'd be alone . . .

FATHER RENTERÍA: There were a lot of them?

DOROTEA: There were so many I lost count. *(Pause.)* You could
forgive me,
Father. I know you could. I need to get to Heaven.
I need to see if my son is there . . .

FATHER RENTERÍA: My hands aren't clean enough to forgive you,
Dorotea. Heaven is closed to you now.

(Dorotea leaves.)

Scene 7

(Bird whistles and funeral music.)

EDUVIGES: Have you ever heard the moan of someone dying?
JUAN: No, Dona Eduviges.
EDUVIGES: Well, it's better that way.

> *(Pause. The candle goes out by itself. Eduviges leaves, Juan settles himself to sleep. Toribio is unseen.)*

TORIBIO ALDRETE: Go ahead! Kill me! Kill me if that's what
        you want! Life isn't worth shit anyway!

> *(Juan starts. He settles again. We see Toribio hanging.)*

TORIBIO ALDRETE: Just let me kick! You can hang me! You can
        kill me! But I've got a right to kick!

> *(Juan is fully awake. A woman carrying a candle appears.)*

JUAN: Is that you, Eduviges? What's going on?
DAMIANA: Please don't call me Eduviges. My name is
        Damiana. I heard that you had come.
JUAN: Damiana Cisneros? Aren't you the one
        who used to live on the Media Luna?
DAMIANA: I still live there. That's why it took me
        so long to get here. I want you to stay
        at my house. You'll be able to rest there.
JUAN: My mother told me about
        a Damiana who took care of me
        when I was born. Are you the . . .

DAMIANA: I'm the one.
         I've known you since you first opened your eyes.
JUAN: I'll go with you. Did you hear what was
         going on? It was as if they were killing someone.
DAMIANA: Maybe that was an echo that got locked up
         in here. It was in this room that they hung
         Toribio Aldrete. But that was a long time ago.
         I don't know how you got in here.
         There's not even a key to this room anymore.
JUAN: Doña Eduviges let me in.
DAMIANA: Eduviges Dyada?!
JUAN: Yes, her.
DAMIANA: Poor Eduviges. She must still be
         suffering then. You better come with me.
         Eduviges killed herself, you see . . .
         This was quite a few years ago, too.
         And Father Renteria refused
         to forgive her. We'd better get out of here.

         (*They exit.*)

Scene 8

(*Eduviges' bar. Eduviges plays the harmonium in the shadows. Toribio Aldrete and Fulgor sit at a table drinking. The music continues throughout the scene.*)

TORIBIO ALDRETE: Well, I'm really glad we can still talk man
                 to man, Fulgor. Because to tell you the truth,
                 I was getting a little worried about you since
                 you started working for Pedro Páramo.

FULGOR: Toribio, how long have we known each other? It was me who convinced Don Pedro to let you stay on the land.

TORIBIO ALDRETE: Well, I'm grateful to you.

FULGOR: Eduviges! Will you let me use your corner room tonight?

EDUVIGES: Of course you can, Don Fulgor.

TORIBIO ALDRETE: Nobody can say you're not a man, Fulgor.
(Laughing.)
You've really got balls. And I'm not just saying that because of the power you've got behind you.
I mean you've got your own balls. But that maggot you've got for a boss makes me want to puke.

FULGOR: I know exactly what you mean. (The harmonium music swells. Lights out.)

TORIBIO ALDRETE: Go ahead, kill me if that's what you want.
Life isn't worth shit anyway.
Just let me kick! You can hang me!
But I've got a right to kick!

(Light comes up suddenly on the image of Toribio hanging. Fulgor is gone, as is Eduviges. The harmonium continues. Toribio disappears like magic. Light comes up on Pedro.)

PEDRO: Susanna, I begged you to come back.
A full moon hung high in
the middle of the world. My
eyes were lost looking at you
scrubbed smooth by the moon.
Susanna, Susanna San Juan.

(Light off of Pedro; the harmonium stops. Light up for Damiana and Juan crossing the stage. Walking music.)

DAMIANA: Didn't your mother tell you about Pedro Páramo?
JUAN: No. She never mentioned him 'til she was dying.
DAMIANA: Isn't that strange. Well, I can tell you:
I used to take care of your father, too.
He left the Media Luna when he was very young.
He was a little monster. He stole. He wouldn't work.
Pedro couldn't stand taking orders from anyone and
he fought with his mother and father tooth and nail.
We thought they were going to kill one another.
And then one day he disappeared without
saying a word to anyone. He was gone for years
and we never heard a word from him. And
then his father died. We never thought we'd see
Pedro Páramo again, and all of a sudden he showed
   up
and started to run what was left of the Media Luna.

Scene 9

(Fulgor is knocking at the door. Pedro Páramo keeps Fulgor waiting, then lets him in.)

PEDRO: Come in, Fulgor. Sit down.
FULGOR: I'd rather stand up, Pedro.
PEDRO: Whatever you like. But don't forget it's *Don* Pedro
   now.
My father is dead, Fulgor. *(Pause.)* Well, let's hear it.

FULGOR: The story is bad. There's nothing left. *(Shuffling papers.)*
We just sold off the last cattle. We owe a ton of money.

PEDRO: Who do we owe it to?

FULGOR: Forty thousand pesos . . .

PEDRO: I didn't say how much, Fulgor, I said *who*. Try to listen a little more closely next time. Who then?

FULGOR: *(Reading.)* Let's see, there's the Preciados, the Fregosos,
the Guzmanes . . . there's no way we're going to pay them
all . . . now there are still some people around who
might be interested in buying the land. And they could
probably pay good money for it. And with that we could
pay off the debts.

PEDRO: One of those people interested in buying the land wouldn't
be you, would it Fulgor?

FULGOR: Me? How could it possibly be me? Pedro, where am I going
to get money . . .

PEDRO: *Don* Pedro.

FULGOR: Don Pedro.

PEDRO: All right, Fulgor. Who do we owe the most?

FULGOR: The Preciados. Your father always put them aside for
the last. He knew he could get away with it, seeing they had
no men left in the family. Now Maria Preciado runs

	everything there. She owns the Enmedio Ranch.
PEDRO:	Is she married?
FULGOR:	No.
PEDRO:	Today, you're going to propose to Maria Preciado.
FULGOR:	Oh come on! She won't marry me! I'm too old.
PEDRO:	You're going to propose for *me*, Fulgor. You're going to tell her that I'm in love with her, and on the way back tell Father Renteria to arrange the wedding.
FULGOR:	And what are we going to do about Toribio Aldrete? He claims part of the Media Luna is his.
PEDRO:	Does he trust you?
FULGOR:	Probably.
PEDRO:	Take him to town, get him good and drunk, and get rid of him.
FULGOR:	Don Pedro, I think I'm going to sit down.
PEDRO:	Listen, Fulgor, when you see her, tell Maria whatever you like, but make sure you tell her I love her. That's very important. Actually, I do love her, because of her eyes, you know what I mean?
FULGOR:	I know exactly what you mean. *(Pause.)* You know, I'm going to like working for you.

(Fulgor leaves Pedro and stops outside the door.)

| FULGOR: | How the Hell did that boy get so smart? |

(Lights change. The Maria theme is sung. Fulgor is seen standing behind Maria's chair, whispering in her ear.)

MARIA: Oh, now you're making me blush, Don Fulgor.
How could Don Pedro be interested in me?

FULGOR: Interested? He can't sleep thinking about you, Maria.

MARIA: Oh, you're giving me goosebumps,
Don Fulgor. I never would have imagined it!

FULGOR: He's been thinking about you from the moment he
came back. Now the time of mourning is
over, he wanted me to tell you right away.
Now, let's set the wedding date for the day
after tomorrow.

MARIA: Isn't that a little soon?
I don't have a thing ready. I have to order
a trousseau. And write my sister. No, it would
be better to send a messenger. But in any case,
I can't be ready before the eighth of April.
And today is the first. Yes, around . . .

FULGOR: Listen, Maria,
you don't understand. If it were up to Don Pedro, the
wedding would be *today*. We'll take care of
everything
for you, don't worry.

MARIA: But there are other things now,
Don Fulgor, women's things, you know. Oh, I'm so
embarrassed to tell you this. You're practically
making me faint. It's that time of the month.
I'm so ashamed.

FULGOR: Marriage has nothing to do with the time
of the month. This is a question of love, Maria.

MARIA: But you don't understand me, Don Fulgor.
FULGOR: I understand you completely. It's settled then;
             the wedding will be the day after tomorrow.
MARIA: Just give me a week, Don Fulgor, a week!
FULGOR: *(Leaving.)* Congratulations, Doña Maria!

             (He goes.)

MARIA: I've got to do something to make it go away
             sooner. Maybe if I heat up some water right now . . .
             But it's going to last three days. *(Pause.)*
             Oh, but I'm so happy! Thank you, God, for giving
             me Pedro Páramo, even if he gets tired of me later.

             (Fulgor is seen outside Maria's house.)

FULGOR: No one's going to believe what that boy pulled off.

             (Crossfade to next scene.)

Scene 10

(Comala—image sequence)
(Walking music.)

DAMIANA: This village is so full of voices! They
             get stuck in the cracks in the walls: when you
             walk, you hear other footsteps stepping
             in your own, and laughter so old
             it seems tired of laughing. Just now,
             on my way here, I met a procession, a wake.

A woman stepped away from the others and said,
"Damiana! Pray to God for me!" and she pulled
  back
the hood of her reboso, and I saw the face of my
  dead
sister, so I said, "Sixtina, what on earth are you
doing here?" But she ran back and disappeared
among the other women. So don't be shocked
if you hear a familiar voice now and then.

JUAN: So my mother told you I was coming, then.

DAMIANA: No, I haven't heard from your mother
for years. How is she?

JUAN: She's dead.

DAMIANA: Dead? Already? How did she die?

JUAN: I don't know. She just died.
Maybe she died from sadness. She used to sigh
all the time.

DAMIANA: Oh, that's very bad. Every time you sigh,
a little breath of life slips out of you. So she's
dead then?

JUAN: I thought you already knew.

DAMIANA: Me? Know? How could I know? I already
told you I haven't heard from her for years.

JUAN: Then how did you know I was here, then?

(*Walking music stops.*)

JUAN: Are you alive, Damiana? Tell me!
Are you really here?

(*She disappears.*)

JUAN: Damiana!
            Damiana Cisneros!
CHORUS: iana . . . iana . . . ana . . . na . . .
            sneros . . . sneros . . . neros . . . eros . . .

(*Silence. A man appears.*)

JUAN: What about you, are you? . . .
MAN: What about you, are you? . . .

(*A woman in a reboso passes rapidly, in the
shadows.*)

WOMAN: Buenas noches, señor, buenas noches.

(*Strange music and murmuring of the dead. People
pass, Juan watches.*)

FIRST GIRL: Look who's over there. Isn't he the one?
SECOND GIRL: It's him! Don't let him know you notice.
FIRST GIRL: Let's get out of here. If he follows behind, it's
            because he
            wants one of us. *(Pause.)* I wonder which one of us
            he wants.
SECOND GIRL: I'm sure it's you.
FIRST GIRL: That's funny, I thought it was you.
DOROTEA: *(To Juan.)* Give me some money. I need milk for my
            son.

(*She shows him her block of wood which she carries
as though it were a baby. An image of people crossing
a desert establishes itself as she speaks, and continues
past her exit to the beginning of the following speech.*

Macario is revealed by the passing of the desert peo-
ple. He sits on the ground, with a stick. Raucous clari-
net music, then a single crazily singing voice and the
beat of a drum. The singing stops, the drum continues
throughout the following. Macario speaks to Juan.)

MACARIO: I'm waiting for the frogs to come out of the sewer.
They were making so much noise last night that
Dorotea
couldn't sleep. So she told me to sit here with this
stick and kill every one I could. Frogs are green all
over. Toads are black. Eduviges says it's bad to
eat toads. But I eat toads and frogs and they taste
the same to me. I love Eduviges more than Dorotea.
Eduviges has got the little purse, but Dorotea's the
one
who feeds me. Eduviges eats first, and then she gives
us what's left. She makes two little mounds with
her hands, one for me and one for Dorotea, and
sometimes
Dorotea doesn't want to eat, and she gives one to
Damiana because
Pedro never feeds her unless he's drunk, and he
thinks she's Susanna.
I always try to steal from every woman, I don't care
who feeds me,
because I'm always hungry, and I never feel full,
and sometimes they let me drink from their tits,
and milk from a woman fills you up just like a frog.
Frogs and milk together would be like a meal real
people eat.
I don't feel like a dog when Damiana gives me her
food.

But Eduviges lets me drink her milk, and it's as sweet
   as
hibiscus flowers. She has little tits
full of milk right here where boys have ribs.
I've drunk goat's milk, and I've drunk milk from a
   sow
who just had baby pigs. But it wasn't as sweet
as the milk of Eduviges. She's good to me,
not like those people in the street who throw
rocks at me, and then my shirt has to be mended
and I have scabs, and Damiana has to tie
my hands together so I won't scratch the scabs.
Blood has a good flavor, too! What I'd really
like right now would be a nice warm squirt
of a woman's milk in my mouth, but when I'm not
eating what I really like is to bang my head.
My head is really hard! I like to start off
very slow like the drum I can hear out the window
in the church when the priest is yelling.

(*A faint roll on a gong, gradually increasing with the
drum, until both utterly drown out the rising level of
Macario's voice. He is throwing his head and torso
back and forth.*)

The road of good things is filled with light,
the road of bad things is dark, the road of good
   things
is filled with light, the road of bad things is dark,
the road of good things is filled with light,
the road of bad things is dark,
the road of good things is light,

the road of bad things is dark . . .

(*Juan is left pounding his head on the ground. Silence and darkening.*)

Scene 11

(*The house of Donis and his sister.*)
(*Juan is prostrate outside the house, Donis near him. The woman stands in the doorway.*)

DONIS: Who are you? What are you doing here?

JUAN: I came to look for my father. Please,
I want to go back where I came from.
Help me go back.

DONIS: Why don't you come inside
for a minute and rest?

JUAN: You're not dead, are you?

DONIS: He must be drunk.

WOMAN: He's just a little frightened.

(*Donis takes him inside as she talks.*)

WOMAN: We heard someone moaning and banging on our
doorstep,
and there you were. What happened to you?

JUAN: So many things have happened to me.
I'd rather just sleep right now, if you don't mind.

DONIS: Not at all. Lie down. Take it easy.
We were already asleep.

(She brings him a pillow and he lies down on the floor.)

WOMAN: Yes, please, sleep here,
You'll help us stay warm.

(Juan sleeps immediately, and the couple returns to bed.)

WOMAN: What kind of a man can he be?
DONIS: Who knows? Didn't he say something about
looking for his father?
WOMAN: That's what I thought he said.
Maybe he just got lost. Remember when those
men turned up here and said they were lost?
The ones who were looking for some place,
and you told them you didn't know where
it was? Some road? Some house? Some cows?
          Remember?
DONIS: I remember, I remember. Let's
go back to sleep.
WOMAN: It's almost light. You asked me to get you
up before dawn, so I'm doing it. Get up.
DONIS: What did I want to get up for?
WOMAN: I don't know
why. You told me last night to wake you up.
You didn't inform me why.
DONIS: In that case let
me sleep. You heard what he said. He's
exhausted. He wants to sleep.

(Pause.)

WOMAN: He just moved. If it happens again, he's going
to wake up. And if he wakes up, he'll see us here,
and if he sees us here, he'll ask questions.

DONIS: Questions?
What questions?

WOMAN: You know what questions.
And then he'll talk.

DONIS: Look, do me a favor:
forget about him, will you?! Anyone
can see he's too tired to move, nevermind talk.

(Pause.)

WOMAN: He's moving. Something's eating at him
from way down inside, and I know what it feels like
because the same thing happens to me. It eats at you,
and it eats at you, like you swallowed some acid.

DONIS: *WHAT* happens to you?

WOMAN: That.

DONIS: What the Hell are you talking about?!

WOMAN: It's just that seeing him . . . I mean when I see it,
I remember how I felt the first time you did it to me.
And how much it hurt. And how sorry I was that I
did it.

DONIS: What? What?

WOMAN: The way I felt as soon as you did it.

DONIS: Are you going to start that story *again*? We did what
we did.
Why don't you go to sleep and let me sleep, too?

(Pause.)

WOMAN:	It's light. I can see that man from here.
	And that means there's light, and that means the sun's
	going to be up any second now.
	And then he's going to see us here.
	Look at the way he keeps turning and turning.
	I'm sure he's committed some horrible crime.
	And we've given him shelter. And even though
	we only did it for one night, we did it;
	we let him hide out here, and sooner
	or later we're going to have to pay for it . . .
DONIS:	Come on! He's just a poor man like the rest of us.
	Look, if you don't want to sleep, why don't you
	get up and go somewhere?
WOMAN:	But where will I go?
	I know, I'll light the lamp, and then I'll go and
	ask him to come sleep in my place in bed with you.
	Would that make you feel better?
DONIS:	Okay, then. Ask him.
WOMAN:	I can't. He scares me.
DONIS:	Then go do your work and leave us in peace!
WOMAN:	I know. I'll light the lamp . . .

(*Light fades out. Music. Donis is gone, and Juan and the woman sit together on a bench. Midday light. Juan is nibbling some food.*)

WOMAN:	I'm sorry there's so little.
JUAN:	That's all right.
	I'll just eat a little something, and then I'll
	be on my way. How do I get out of here?

WOMAN: Which direction do you want to go?

JUAN: Any direction.

WOMAN: Well, there are a lot of roads. There's one that goes
to Contla. One goes straight over the mountains.
There's one to the Media Luna. And one more
crosses the whole valley. I wonder where that one
goes?

JUAN: It goes to Sayula.

WOMAN: Sayula! Think of it! I thought
Sayula was over here on this side. I've always
dreamed of making a little trip there. They
say there are a lot of people in Sayula.

JUAN: About the same as anywhere.

WOMAN: Really! Imagine that!
And here we are, so all alone, wanting
to know just a little more of the world.

JUAN: Where did your husband go?

WOMAN: He's not my husband.
He's my brother. But he doesn't want anyone to
know.
He went to look for a lost calf. At least that's
what he said.

JUAN: How long have you two lived here?

WOMAN: Forever. We were born here.

JUAN: You must have known my mother,
then, Maria Preciado.

WOMAN: Maybe *he* did. I don't know
anyone here anymore. I never go out. Ever since
he made me his woman, I've stayed locked up
inside. I'm so afraid they'll see me!
Wouldn't you be afraid of me? Tell the truth.
Look at my face. Isn't it frightening?

JUAN:	It seems like an ordinary face to me.
WOMAN:	Can't you see these purple stains like burn marks
	that cover me from head to foot? And that's
	only the outside. Inside of me
	there's a sea of mud.
JUAN:	But who's going to see
	you anyway if nobody lives here?
WOMAN:	That's what you think.
	They stay locked up in their houses,
	that's all. Oh, he's coming, did you hear?
	It's him.

(*Donis enters.*)

WOMAN:	What happened to the calf?
DONIS:	I still couldn't find it. But I picked up the trail.
	I'll get it tonight.
WOMAN:	You're not going to leave
	me alone tonight? I won't be able to stand it.
DONIS:	Tonight I'm going for the calf.

(*Pause.*)

JUAN:	I just found out you're brother and sister.
DONIS:	You just found out. Congratulations! I've known it
	for a long time.
WOMAN:	I told him so he'd understand about us, that's all.
DONIS:	So, what *do* you understand?
WOMAN:	Yes, what is it that you understand?
JUAN:	Nothing. I understand nothing.
	I understand less and less all the time.
	I want to go back where I came from.

I want to go now while there's still some light.

(*He leaves. Donis goes after and stops him.*)

DONIS: It's better if you wait.
           It's going to be dark soon and the roads
           are rough and tangled with brush.
           It's easy to fall or get lost out there.
           Tomorrow you'll be on your way.
JUAN: All right. I'll stay the night.

(*He turns to go back. Lights out then immediately up
again: dusk. Juan sleeps restlessly. Music.*)

CHORUS: Through the roof open to the sky he could see flocks
                   of thrushes
           passing overhead, and then a few clouds
                   crumbled by the wind.
                   And then the evening star.
                   And then the moon.
           And then he felt tired again with the heavy heat
               pressing down,
           dreaming the roads from Comala were covered
           with brush and sharp stones, and he stumbled
               against them,
           cutting his hands,
           and then he noticed that the opening
                   through the mountains before him
                   had closed up
                   like a wound.

(*A woman has entered the house and taken a sheet
from under the bed, then exited silently. Juan has seen*

her. Light changes, music stops. Donis and his sister come in from another room of the house. She carries a teacup. Juan is moaning, asleep.)

JUAN: . . . evening stars sleeping next to the moon . . .
roads are all closed up . . .

WOMAN: Here. Have some of this. It's orange blossom tea . . .
helps you calm down . . .

JUAN: There was just a woman in here. Did you see her?

DONIS: C'mere. Leave him alone. It's just another of those
damn religious people.

WOMAN: He's got a fever. We've got
to get him into bed.

(They get him up and put him on the bed.)

DONIS: Don't worry about him. These guys put themselves
in trances just to get attention. Look,
you can see he's stopped shaking now. That's
because he can hear what I'm saying.
I'm going for that calf, now.

(Donis exits. After hesitating in either direction, the woman gets in bed with Juan. Music.)

WOMAN: Can't you sleep?

JUAN: I'm not sleepy. Where's your brother?

WOMAN: He's out roaming around. You heard before where he
had to go: the calf. He won't come back.
He's been trying to leave forever.
He saw his chance, and he took it.

(Pause.)

Pedro Páramo 271

WOMAN: I left you a little something in the kitchen,
some tortillas and dried beef. There's not
much, but it should be enough to take the edge
off your hunger.

(*Juan goes to the kitchen.*)

WOMAN: That's all I could get for you. I got
it from my sister, traded her for two clean sheets.
She was the woman you saw in here who frightened
you.
I didn't want to tell you with Donis here.
I've had those sheets since my mother's time.

(*Maria Preciado appears. Juan sees her.*)

JUAN: Mother! Can't you hear me?
MARIA: Where are you, my son?
JUAN: I'm here in your village, with your own
people. Can't you see me?
MARIA: No, son, I can't see you.

(*She disappears.*)

WOMAN: Why don't you come over here with me?
JUAN: I'm going to stay
over here, in my own corner. That bed is hard as
rocks.
WOMAN: Donis won't be back. I could see it in his eyes.
He was just waiting for someone to come so he could
go.
And now it's your turn to take care of me.
Come on. Come sleep here with me.

JUAN: I'm all right, right here.

WOMAN: The ticks'll make a meal of you over there.

(He moves toward her. Music. He finally reaches the bed, lies down, then sits up. The music continues and the woman lies sleeping.)

JUAN: The heat woke me up. The heat and the sweat.
           That woman's body was covered with the crusts
           of earth that were melting into a pool of mud.
           I felt like we were swimming in the sweat that
           dripped from her skin: there wasn't enough air
           for me to breathe. So I went outside to get some
           air, but the heat kept after me: there wasn't any
           air, no air at all. I had to gulp the same air
           that came out of my mouth, holding it back with
           my hands so it wouldn't get away. I could feel my
           breath coming and going, each time less and less,
           until my breath was so thin it slipped through
           my fingers forever. Then I couldn't breathe at all.

(The music intensifies. Murmurings of the dead. Momentary blackout, then Juan sits with Dorotea in their grave. Peaceful music.)

JUAN: I remember that I saw something like clouds
           of foam making a whirlwind overhead, and
           then the foam rinsed through me as if I were
           full of holes and lost in a darkening fog.

(Blackout. End Act I.)

Act II

Scene 12

DOROTEA: Now you really want me to believe
you died of suffocation, Juan Preciado?
If there really wasn't any air that night,
how could they have carried you, never mind
bury you? For as you can see, they buried you,
you're buried all right, there's no doubt about that.

JUAN: What you say makes sense, Doroteo. You did say
your name was Doroteo, didn't you?

DOROTEA: It might as well be. It's Dorotea actually.
But who cares? Dead man, dead woman, it's all the
same.
You'd have been better off if you never
left home. Why did you come here anyway?

JUAN: I came to Comala because they told me my father
was living there. Someone named Pedro Páramo.

DOROTEA: Your father was Pedro Páramo?

JUAN: That's what they told me.
Illusion brought me here.

DOROTEA: Ah, illusion.
You really pay for that one.
I never even had a roof over
my head, but illusion, there's always plenty

of extra illusion around. I spent
my whole life looking for a son
who never existed and all because
of a dream. I had two of them, actually:
a blessed dream and a rotten dream.
I dreamed I had a son, a little boy
with tiny hands and feet and the sweetest
little mouth, and when I woke up
I really believed the dream was true. So I took
a piece of wood and folded it in my
reboso as if it really was a baby.
I took that piece of wood with me wherever
I went. I'd stop by the side of the road
where I was begging and pretend to feed him.
And then I lost him. I lost my son.
I kept unfolding my reboso over and over,
but I couldn't find him anywhere.
And that's when I had my rotten dream.
It took a rotten dream to get rid
of the blessed one. I dreamed I went
to Heaven to look for my son. I was sure
he'd gotten mixed in with the angels.
But all of the angels' faces were the same,
blank faces, no expressions at all, as if
each face were pressed from the same blank mold.
And I kept begging them to tell me
where my son was, but they'd walk right past me
like I wasn't even there, and then all
of a sudden one of those angels
walked right up to me and without saying a word
sank his fist deep into my stomach
as if he were sticking it in a big mound of wax,

and he pulled something out of me that looked
like a walnut all blackened and cracked.
"What you see here is the proof," he said. I tried
to tell him it was just my stomach
shriveled up by hunger but he just shook his head.
"These things happen," he said. "We made a
    mistake:
we gave you a mother's heart, but the womb
of a barren woman." So that's how
I realized I never had a son.

JUAN: But how did you end up in here with me,
            Dorotea?

DOROTEA: No one left in Comala to beg from.
            So I just sat down and waited for death. No one's
            going to notice anyway, I thought. I'm the kind
            of person who never bothered anyone. I didn't even
            take any space from the earth itself.
            I was so thin by then, that they just buried me
            in the same grave as you, and I fit quite nicely in
            the hollow of your arms. Only it seems to me that
            I should be the one who's holding you.

(*They exchange positions. Music of raindrops.*)

JUAN: What do you know about Pedro Páramo?
DOROTEA: Do you hear, up there, outside, it's raining.
JUAN: I feel like someone's walking over us.
DOROTEA: Now, now, forget about your fear, my son.
            Think pleasant things. You might as well.
            We're going to be buried here
            for a long, long time.

(*Lights off of them. Storm music.*)

Scene 13

(Media Luna.)
(Storm, then steady, soft rain.)

FULGOR: If this keeps up, we'll have the best crop yet.
           It looks good, Don Pedro, there's more than enough
           to fill the silos to hold us 'til harvest, and with a rain
           like this, what a harvest it will be!
PEDRO: Good. Look at those fields. And all that land is mine.
FULGOR: There's just one problem, Patron.
PEDRO: What is it, Fulgor?
FULGOR: It's your son Miguel, Patron. There was a woman
                here yesterday
           who said that Miguel had killed her husband.
PEDRO: Look, whatever he does just tell them that I did it.
           Besides, Miguel's not strong enough to kill anyone
                yet.
           You need kidneys as big as melons to pull that off.
FULGOR: This woman wasn't crazy, Patron. I know how to
           measure grief, and this woman had it by the kilo.
           I couldn't buy her off. I offered her one hundred
           bushels of corn to forget the whole business.
PEDRO: Who was this woman?
FULGOR: I don't know, I never saw her before.
PEDRO: Then what are you worried about? People
           you don't know are people who don't exist.

Scene 14

(Juan and Dorotea lie in grave. Music of raindrops.)

JUAN: Up there, outside, the seasons must be changing.
My mother used to say that whenever
the rains come to Comala, the air would be full
of green reflections and the smell of green.
She'd tell me how the cloud tide would come
and spread out over the earth, and how the earth
would change color with each movement of the sky.
She always wanted to come back here to die.
Maybe that's why she sent me in her place.
Well, I never did get to see those clouds. I wonder
if they're the same as the ones she saw back then.

DOROTEA: I couldn't tell you,
Juan Preciado. It's been so many years
since the last time I looked up, I've forgotten
the sky. And if I had looked up, what good
would it have done me? Heaven is so high
and my eyes were so tired of gazing:
it was enough to know where the ground
was. Besides, I really lost interest in Heaven
when Father Renteria told me I'd never get
to Glory anyway. He never should have told me,
because from then on, my life was nothing
but misery. It's better not to be born.
I mean it. For me, Heaven is where I am
right now.

JUAN: But what about your soul?
Where did it go?

DOROTEA: She must be wandering around

the earth with the rest of them. I don't worry
about that anymore. When I finally sat down to die,
I was relieved: I couldn't wait to leave earth
behind. But my soul couldn't stand it, begged me
to get up and keep crawling ahead as if she believed
there was still some miracle that could wash me
clean of sin. I'd had enough. I couldn't budge.
"This is the end of the road," I told her. "You'll
have to take care of yourself from now on." And I
opened my mouth so she could leave.
And she left. And then I felt something
thin and wet fall into my hands.
It was the thread of blood that tied her to my heart.

(*Light comes up on Susanna lying in a nearby grave.*)

SUSANNA: I'm sleeping in the same bed my mother
died in so many years ago. I'd sleep right
next to her in a little place she hollowed
out for me under her arms. I can still
hear the rise and fall of her breathing,
the shivers and sighs that lulled me to sleep.
None of this is true. I'm really here
thinking of time gone by to forget the loneliness.
And this isn't my mother's bed: it's a black
box like all the dead get buried in.
I know where I am, and it makes me think
about that time of year when the lemons are
ripe and the February wind
breaks the fern stalks
when they've dried up from neglect.
That's when my mother died. A little

downy hair was just beginning to grow
on my legs. I was so sad to think that
my mother would never see ripe lemons again.
It hurt me her eyes were closed to the light.
But what good would have come if I had cried?

JUAN: I heard someone talking, a woman's voice.

DOROTEA: Oh, that's Susanna San Juan. She's buried in
the big sepulcher. She was married to
Pedro Páramo.

JUAN: Married to Pedro Páramo?

DOROTEA: She was his second wife. He fell in love
with her when he was a boy. And even though
she left Comala, he waited thirty years for her
to come back. Some people said she was crazy. What
was she saying?

JUAN: Something about her mother.
I couldn't make it out very clearly.

DOROTEA: Look, if she
starts talking again, let me know. I'd like to
hear what she has to say.

(*A murmuring of voices. Others in the grave are dimly seen.*)

JUAN: Listen! I think she's saying something.

DOROTEA: That's not her. You'll get used to it. Those are
voices from farther away.

(*The voices continue; after a bit, Susanna speaks again.*)

DOROTEA: Listen, I think it's

her. You've got those good young ears, so
pay attention.

JUAN: I don't understand what she's saying.

DOROTEA: Well, listen harder.

JUAN: . . . Moaning. Nothing more. Maybe
Pedro Páramo made her suffer, too.

DOROTEA: Don't you believe it. He loved her
so much. After she died he spent the
rest of his life sunk in an armchair
looking out the window into the road
where they took her to the cemetery.
So ask yourself now if he loved her or not.

(*Blackout. Music.*)

Scene 15

(*Pedro is sitting in an armchair, Fulgor standing.*)

FULGOR: Patron, have you heard who's back in these parts?

PEDRO: Who's that?

FULGOR: Bartolome San Juan.

PEDRO: And . . . ?

FULGOR: That's just what I was wondering about.
What are you going to do?

PEDRO: You haven't
spoken to him yet?

FULGOR: No, I wanted to talk
to you first. Because he didn't even look
for a place to rent. He just rode straight up
to your old house, got down, and unpacked his bags

	as if the place belonged to him.
PEDRO:	There were two of them, weren't there?
FULGOR:	Yes.

Him and his wife.

PEDRO: It couldn't have been his daughter, could it?

FULGOR: Well, she was young enough to be. But from the way he treated her, I'd say it was his wife. *(He laughs.)*

PEDRO: Go get some sleep, Fulgor.

FULGOR: All right, Patrón. *(He exits.)*

(The chorus plays music and sings. The light is focused on Pedro.)

CHORUS: I've waited thirty years, thirty years for you
           to come back here, Susanna.
  I had everything it was possible to have, everything
           but you, Susanna.
  Do you know how many times I begged your father
           to come back, how many messages?
  I wanted to cry, and I did cry, Susanna.
           I felt that Heaven had opened.
  I wanted to run to you, to hold you
           in my arms.
  I've waited thirty years, thirty years for you
           to come back here,
           Susanna.
           Susanna San Juan.

(The light cross-fades from Pedro to Susanna and Bartolome.)

BARTOLOMÉ: Susanna, there's a certain kind of village knows all about

misery. You can tell you're in one of them just by
sipping a little of their tired air, poor and thin
like everything old. And this is one of those villages.
Pedro Páramo asks us to come back here. He lends us

a house, gives us everything we need. But we don't have to be
grateful for it. Do you know what he wants? I didn't
think we'd get all this for nothing. I told him I'd pay
him by doing some work. I tried to get him to see the old
mine still had some possibilities. You know what his answer
was? "I'm not interested in your mine, Bartolome. The
only thing I want from you is your daughter. She's the best
work you've ever done." Pedro Páramo loves you, Susanna.
He says you played with him when you were little.
He says you went swimming in the river together. If I had
known, I would have torn you to shreds.

SUSANNA: I don't doubt it.

BARTOLOMÉ: What did you say to me? You don't doubt it?!

SUSANNA: That's what I said.

BARTOLOMÉ: So you want to sleep with him?

SUSANNA: Yes, I do.

BARTOLOMÉ: Don't you know he's married? Don't you know he's had hundreds of women?

SUSANNA: Yes, I do, Bartolome.

BARTOLOMÉ: Don't call me Bartolome! I'm your father! *(Pause.)*
I tried to talk him out of it. I told him that
even though you were a widow, you acted like
your husband were alive. But whenever your
name came up, he closed his eyes as if the light were
too bright to bear. *(Pause.)* I can see it all coming.
Bartolome San Juan, a dead miner, and Susanna
San Juan, daughter of a miner found dead in
a shaft of the Andromeda. He's sending me out there
to die. There's nothing but evil ahead.
I see that now. That's Pedro Páramo for you.

SUSANNA: And who am I?

BARTOLOMÉ: You're my daughter. *Mine.* The daughter
of Bartolome San Juan.

SUSANNA: I'm not so sure about that, Bartolome.

BARTOLOMÉ: You're not so sure? The whole world is pressing
in on me. There are revolutionaries on every
road, trying to kill everyone in sight, so I
come here just to keep you safe and put
myself in the hands of a murderer for your sake,
and you say I'm not your father? Are you insane?

SUSANNA: Didn't you know?

BARTOLOMÉ: You're insane.

SUSANNA: Of course I'm insane,
Bartolome, didn't you know?

*(Blackout. Susanna lies in her grave. Pedro is dimly
seen, seated in his chair behind her, as the lights come
up.)*

SUSANNA: I loved to bathe naked in the sea with you,

Florencio. The water licked my ankles
and withdrew, circled my waist
with its smooth arm, and I let myself
sink into it, all of me.
I think you were a little jealous of the sea.
You'd say, I like you better at night
when we're in the same bed, under
the same sheets, just the two of us
in the dark. You were so silly, Florencio.
I loved the sea because of you.

(*Lights off on her, up on Pedro. Song.*)

PEDRO: Now I have you Susanna, you'll never leave again,
           you'll never leave. You have nowhere to go.
           Now everything I've wanted is mine, everything
           I want is mine. Nothing I've done was a crime. I did
               it for you.

(*Pedro speaks this with the singing. Fulgor enters.*)

           Fulgor, there's never been any other woman on
           earth like this. And I thought I'd lost her.
           I'm not going to lose her again. You tell her father
           to keep working those mines. It'll be easy
           for the old bastard to disappear out there . . .
FULGOR: It could be . . .
PEDRO: It has to be!!! She's not getting away this time.
           We have to take care of the unfortunate,
           the orphaned daughters of our dead employees,
           am I right, Fulgor?
FULGOR: We have to take care of our own,

Patrón. *(Pause.)* This is good. This woman's
brought the young stud back in you again.

(Blackout.)

Scene 16

(Comala market / Susana's bedroom, Media Luna.)
(The chorus sits as Indians on different parts of the stage, as at the
opening of the play. One member of the chorus sits in the regular
chorus location, and speaks. The others make music.)

CHORUS: Over the fields of the valley of Comala
         a light rain was falling.
         It is Sunday, and the Indians have come down from
             Apango,
         with their rosemary, chamomile, bunches of thyme.

         In the fields where the corn is just sprouting up
         men move over the drowned land,
         firming up the tiny shoots with their bare hands,
         trying to keep them from washing away.

         The Indians sit and shiver,
         not so much from the cold and dampness
         as from fear of hunger to come.
         Along the road from the Media Luna
         comes Justina Diaz.
JUSTINA: Maybe if I hang some rosemary in her room, it will
             help
         poor Susanna sleep. Everything's so expensive these

days. This puny twist for ten centavos, and not a bit
of odor in it.

CHORUS: When it starts to get dark,
the Indians get up slowly from their places,
walk out into the rain with heavy bundles,
and head back home.

*(The chorus returns to the two chorus locations. Light
onto Susanna's bedroom. Pedro is with the sleeping
Susanna. Justina enters.)*

PEDRO: Justina! Pack your things and get out of here.
We don't need you anymore.
JUSTINA: You may not need me,
but she needs me. She's sick, Don Pedro.
PEDRO: I'm going to take care of her myself from now on.
SUSANNA: *(Screaming.)* Bartolome?! Is that you? *(Pause.)*
What's the matter with you, Justina?
Why are you screaming?
JUSTINA: I didn't scream, Susanna,
you must have been dreaming.

(Pedro exits.)

SUSANNA: Justina, you know very well
I never dream. You have no consideration
for me. I couldn't sleep all night. You forget to put
the cat out and it keeps me awake all night.
JUSTINA: The cat slept with me. Right between my legs.
It was soaking wet, and I felt sorry for it, so I let it
sleep with me. It never made a sound.
SUSANNA: Well, not a sound exactly, it just made

a playground out of my bed, jumping
from my feet to my head, and meowing
softly as if it were hungry, so hungry!

JUSTINA: You're dreaming up lies, Susanna.
When Don Pedro comes back
I'm going to tell him I can't stand it anymore.
There are plenty of decent people around here
who'll give me work. And they're not maniacs like
  you,
and they don't annoy people like you do:
tomorrow I'm leaving and I'm taking
my cat with me so you'll be left in peace.

SUSANNA: You're wicked and you're damned, Justina,
but you're not going anywhere. You're not
going anywhere because you'll never find
anyone who loves you like I do.

JUSTINA: No, no, don't worry, Susanna. I won't go.
I won't leave you. Even if you make me scream
and curse, it doesn't matter. I'll always be here.

(*Susanna falls asleep and Justina leaves. Dream music.
Light comes up on Bartolome holding a lantern.*)

BARTOLOMÉ: Susanna! Susanna! Come here! I need you!

(*Susanna rises from her bed and goes to him above.*)

SUSANNA: All right, Papa, I'm coming.

(*Bartolome speaks as he puts a harness on her and
lowers her.*)

BARTOLOMÉ: I want you
    to help me find something at the bottom
    of this shaft . . . lower, Susanna, lower.
    Don't worry, I've got a good hold on you.
    Just a little lower, Susanna,
    and tell me when you see something.

    (Susanna screams.)

BARTOLOMÉ: Bring me what's there, Susanna!
SUSANNA: It's a skull, Papa!
    A dead person's skull!
BARTOLOMÉ: There should be
    something else near it. Bring me what you find.
    There's money down there. Round wheels of gold.
    Look for them, Susanna!
SUSANNA: But I can't find
    anything else, Papa!

    (He hauls her up, takes off the harness.)

SUSANNA: Papa, that skull in . . .
BARTOLOMÉ: Don't ask questions.
SUSANNA: . . . but Papa . . .
BARTOLOMÉ: Just forget what you saw, or I'll make you forget.

    *(Lights off on him. Susanna returns to bed. Music. She
    gets up. During the chorus, she stands.)*

CHORUS: The rain has stopped,
    but the winds stayed on.
    Pavilions of clouds grazed over the earth.
    Susanna San Juan listened to the night.

Pedro Páramo   289

The wind dragged the stars
back and forth
across the sky.

(Justina enters.)

JUSTINA: Susanna, your father is dead. He died last night.
They found him in the shaft of the Andromeda.
You're all alone now.

SUSANNA: So it was him.
It *was* him; he came back to say goodbye to me.

*(Exit Justina. Susanna goes back to bed. Father
Rentereia enters with a candle.)*

SUSANNA: Is that you again, Papa?

FATHER RENTERÍA: I am your Father, my child.

SUSANNA: I know you're dying from that flame in your heart.
(Pause.)
I know you've come to tell me my father is dead,
but I already know that. Don't wear yourself out
for my sake. I've got my sorrow kept in a good,
safe place. And watch out that flame in your heart
doesn't go out.

*(She moves to kiss or caress the flame. He blows it
out.)*

FATHER RENTERÍA: I came to comfort *you*, my child.

SUSANNA: Then goodbye, Father. Please don't come back.
I don't need your comfort. Why do you
come to see me anyhow,

when I'm already dead?

(*Blackout.*)

Scene 17

(*The Media Luna. Pedro is seated in his armchair. During the blackout there has been loud, incessant knocking. The light comes up. La Tartamuda is standing before Pedro.*)

PEDRO: Who are you? What do you want?

TARTAMUDA: My nininame is
La Tartamuda. I need to talk to Dedon Pedro.

PEDRO: You're
looking at him. Make it fast.

TARTAMUDA: It's about Don Fulgor.
They kikikilled him. We were out by the diditches
when a gang of memen stepped in front of us.
There must have been fififty of them.
And one of them yelled, "I know who this one is,
he's the foreman at the
     MemmmmememmimmemmMedia Luna."
They paid no atattention to me. But they told Don
Fulgor to get down off his horse. They said they were
rerevolutionaries. They said
they were going to take over the Media Luna.
"Get moving! Run!" they yeyelled to Don Fulgor.
"Tell your boss we'll be coming to see him."
Don Fulgor jumped down suwuweating and took
off running, and that's when
they shshshshot him, in the back,
with one fofoot in the air, and the uuuother
on the grgrgrgro . . .

PEDRO: Are you just going to
stand there with your tongue hanging out?!
Go tell them I'm waiting right here
whenever they want me.

(*She turns and starts to go.*)

PEDRO: Wait! You know El Tilcuate?
Tell him I need to see him right away.

(*She starts to go again.*)

PEDRO: Just what kind of "Revolutionaries" were they,
            anyway?
TARTAMUDA: I don't know. They didn't sssay wuwuwhat kkk . . .
PEDRO: All right, all right. Just tell Ticuate to
            get up here as fast as he can.
TARTAMUDA: Riright aaway, Papatrón, riright away!

(*She exits. Pedro goes to Susanna's room. Song.*)

CHORUS: What world is this woman living in?
                Now that I have her, where is she?
            Now that I've found her, how can I possess her?
                Susanna, Susanna San Juan.

(*Pedro goes back downstairs to his armchair. The light
fades on him. The beat of a drum.*)

Scene 18

(The drum continues. Song.)

CHORUS: All across the darkness
            through each town and pueblo,
            men with guns and torches
            ready to burn and kill.

            For a moment
            the poor drank the whole horizon,
            with thirsty eyes they drank.
            The earth turned dark with blood.

            (Incessant knocking. The lights come up on Pedro and two revolutionaries standing before him.)

PERSEVERANCIO: Are you Pedro Páramo?

            (Pedro nods.)

PERSEVERANCIO: Good. You own all this, huh?

            (Pedro nods.)

PERSEVERANCIO: We hear you wanted to talk to us.
PEDRO: Yes. Won't you come in, gentlemen? Damiana.

            (Damiana enters with stools.)

PEDRO: Please, have a seat.

            (Felipe sits.)

PEDRO: Perhaps you'd like something to eat?

(Damiana brings in a tray of food. Later liquor. Felipe indulges.)

PEDRO: So, what can I do for you?

PERSEVERANCIO: You've got eyes: this is a Revolution.

PEDRO: And?

PERSEVERANCIO: A Revolution! Isn't that enough for you?

PEDRO: But what's this revolution about?

PERSEVERANCIO: I'll tell you what this
           Revolution's about. And I'll make it nice and clear.
           We're rebelling against people like you
           because we're sick of seeing our children starve
           while you sit here up to your ears in gold
           and grain. First the government. Then we
           get rid of the rest of the bloodsuckers.

PEDRO: How much do you
           need to make your revolution? Maybe I can help . . .

PERSEVERANCIO: Help from you? Look, Pedro, we've been
             around here
           for a while, so don't try to pull . . .

FELIPE: Hold on Perseverancio.
           Let's see what the man has to say . . .

PERSEVERANCIO: Bullshit. We
           should take everything he's got, right up to the
           corn he's got stuffed in his pig's gut.

FELIPE: Take it easy,
           Perseverancio. How much money do we need?

PERSEVERANCIO: Well, the
           way I figure it, 20,000 pesos wouldn't be bad
           for openers. Or maybe the señor thinks that's too
             little.

Let's say 50,000 pesos, then. Is it a deal?

PEDRO: Look, I'm
going to give you 100,000 pesos. How many men do
you have?

PERSEVERANCIO: We've got three hundred men.

PEDRO: I'm going to lend you another
three hundred. Both the men and the money will be
waiting
for you within a week. How does that sound to you?

(Felipe nods.)

PEDRO: So then, gentlemen, within a week.
It's been a pleasure meeting you both.

*(Pedro and Felipe shake hands, Perseverancio exits,
Felipe follows. Tilcuate enters from the shadows.)*

PEDRO: Which one do you think was boss, Tilcuate?

TILCUATE: I'd say it was the fat one who didn't say much.

PEDRO: You don't usually make mistakes about things like
this,
Tilcuate. You've seen these revolutions before.
Well, I'm putting you in charge of this one.
But maybe you're not ready for a fight right now?

TILCUATE: Are you kidding?
You know me, Patrón: you know I can't wait
for the killing to start.

PEDRO: Good. I want you to get
three hundred good men and sign them up with these
"Revolutionaries." You know how to take care
of the rest yourself. *(Pause.)* And, Tilcuate,

you know that little ranch they call the "Puerta
Piedra"?
Well, it's yours from now on.

TILCUATE: I'd do what I'm doing just for the fun of it,
ranch or no ranch. But I appreciate it all the same.
It'll give my old lady something to do while
I'm out there playing around.

PEDRO: Just make sure you don't get too far from my
territory.
That way if others show up, they'll see we've already
got troops in the field. And come see me as soon as
there's news.

TILCUATE: I'll see you soon, Commandante.

(Blackout. Lively flute music.)

Scene 19

(The graveyard.)
*(Juan and Susanna speak concurrently. Juan is translating her
mumblings to Dorotea.)*

DOROTEA: What's she saying, Juan Preciado?

JUAN: She says she used to hide her feet between
his legs. Her feet were frozen like cold stones,
and he'd warm them up in his crotch like bread
browning in the oven. Then he'd nibble
her feet telling her they were like fresh,
golden loaves. She'd sleep snuggled up,
squeezing herself inside him, deeper and deeper
until she'd cry out without knowing what

was happening to her.

SUSANNA: I loved to . . . you'd say, "Give me those fresh
golden loaves!" . . . I'd squeeze . . . I'd sink
deeper and deeper . . . nothing ever hurt me like your
death, Florencio.

DOROTEA: Who was she talking about?

JUAN: Someone named Florencio.

DOROTEA: Oh, that's who she was married to before
she came back to the Media Luna.

(Susanna starts speaking again.)

JUAN: She says he was late coming home that night.
It was almost dawn. But she hardly noticed
because her feet were warm as if someone had
        wrapped them
in mittens. And when she woke she found them
covered with a magazine. She was lying there
staring at her feet wrapped up in that
magazine when they came in to tell her he was
dead. He must have wrapped her feet up
just before he died.

SUSANNA: . . . late coming home . . . almost dawn . . .
freezing . . . feet . . . so snug . . .
wrapped up . . . couldn't stay awake . . .
magazine . . . told me you were dead . . .
they told me you were dead.

(Blackout. Music.)

Scene 20

(*Susanna's bedroom. Justina is sponging Susanna.*)

SUSANNA: Tell me, Justina,
how many birds have you killed in your life?
JUSTINA: A lot, Susanna.
SUSANNA: And didn't it make you sad?
JUSTINA: Yes, Susanna.

(*Pause.*)

SUSANNA: Do you believe in Hell, Justina?
JUSTINA: Yes, Susanna,
I do, and in Heaven, too.
SUSANNA: I only believe in Hell.

(*Susanna seems to doze. Justina exits rapidly.*)

SUSANNA: What did he say? My Florencio? Was he talking about
my Florencio? You son of a bitch, God! You lousy rotten
son of a bitch! I asked you to take care of him.
I prayed that you protect him. But all you
care about is *souls,* and what I wanted was his
body! HIS BODY! Can't you understand that?
What am I supposed to do now with these useless
breasts without his lips to nibble them?
Tell me! Tell me, you bastards, what do I
do now? . . . oh, oh, mmmmmmm . . . oh, that's better
Florencio . . . that's much better now

mmmmmmmm . . . mmmmmmmm . . .

(*In her thrashing she has become undressed. Pedro, Renteria and Justina enter. Susanna is moaning uncontrollably. Pedro crosses quickly to her and pulls the blanket over her.*)

PEDRO: Susanna! . . . Susanna!

FATHER RENTERÍA: My daughter, I've come to give you communion.

(*She passes her orgasm as Renteria mumbles a blessing and puts a communion wafer in her mouth. She chews luxuriantly.*)

SUSANNA: Mmmmmmmmmm. That was really good, Florencio.

FATHER RENTERÍA: Just repeat after me: "My mouth is full of dirt."

SUSANNA: *(Laughing.)* That's right, Father.

FATHER RENTERÍA: Don't say, "That's right, Father," just repeat what I tell you to.

SUSANNA: Do I have to confess again? Haven't I confessed enough?

FATHER RENTERÍA: This isn't confession, Susanna. I've only come to talk with you a little: to prepare you for death.

SUSANNA: Am I going to die?

FATHER RENTERÍA: Yes, daughter.

SUSANNA: Then why don't you leave me alone? I know you're here to keep my dreams from me. How will I ever find them again? Why don't you just go away, and leave me in place?

FATHER RENTERÍA: I'll leave you in peace, Susanna,
        if you'll just repeat the words I say.
        Then you can go on sleeping. You'll feel as if
        you were singing yourself a lullaby.
        And once you fall asleep, no one's going
        to wake you up ever again, I promise.
SUANNA: All right, Father. If you let me sleep,
        I'll do whatever you want me to do.

(She sits up. The blanket falls off her naked body. She leans her back on Renteria's chest. He covers her with the blanket.)

FATHER RENTERÍA: My mouth is full of dirt.

(Susanna speaks simultaneously; different words, different worlds.)

FATHER RENTERÍA: My mouth is full of dirt. I drink cups
        of warm and foamy saliva. I eat clods
        of worm-infested earth. They choke my throat
        and scrape the roof of my mouth. My mouth caves in
        squirming in pain, bitten and pierced by my own
          teeth.
        My cheeks dissolve. The gelatin in my eyes
        turns liquid and runs down over my face.
SUSANNA: My mouth is full of you, my mouth is full of
        your mouth . . . your lips pressed against mine,
        hard . . . crushing me, biting me 'til I bleed . . .
        you lick my cheeks . . . my eyes . . . my face . . .
        Florencio! He held me in his arms and he loved me.
FATHER RENTERÍA: *(To Pedro.)* I don't know if she's repented or
        not.

And I don't know if there's anything to forgive her
for.
Susanna, you are going into God's presence.
For sinners his punishment is inhuman.

SUSANNA: Will you please
go away, Father. I feel very sleepy. Justina,
will you please do your crying somewhere else?

(*Music. Renteria and Justina leave. Pedro sits over Su-
sanna, who lies with closed eyes. Crossfade to the next
scene.*)

Scene 21

(*The graveyard—The Carnival Sequence—the grave again.*)
(*Dorotea talks to Juan.*)

DOROTEA: I was in Comala when Susanna died. Pedro Páramo
wanted
to give Susanna a funeral no one would ever forget.
Just at dawn the people of Comala awoke to the
ringing of bells: first the big bell in the cathedral
and then all the smaller bells, Sangre de Cristo,
Cruz Verde, and even the little sanctuary bell.
Noontime
came; the bells were still ringing. Midnight came;
the bells hadn't stopped. People had to yell to each
other just to be heard. After two days of ringing
everyone was nearly deaf. People thought there was a
fiesta going on and began wandering into the plaza.
They
were even drifting in from Contla and Sayula,
expecting

a big celebration.

(*Music of bells.*)

DOROTEA: And that's what they found. Even
when the bells stopped ringing the fiesta kept on.
There was no way to tell them Don Pedro was in
mourning. There was no way to make them go
    home.

(*Blackout. The bells ring very loudly. There is a grad-
ual increase in the number of instruments contributing
to a cacophony. The bells stop when the lights come
up suddenly and the instruments join in a unified, vi-
brant music. All the actors, including Juan and Doro-
tea, participate. Pedro is revealed, watching the pro-
ceedings from above . . . The Carnival ends with an
image of people crossing a desert, and Juan and Doro-
tea again in their grave. She speaks the following dur-
ing the strains of the last music and the passing of the
desert image.*)

DOROTEA: When they buried Susanna San Juan hardly anyone
    in Comala
knew that it had happened. They were all at the
    fiesta.
Pedro Páramo swore revenge on Comala forever. He
    kicked
us all off the land and burned up the equipment. And
that's when the weeds took over: weeds in the fields,
weeds in the barns, weeds choking the windows of
    empty
houses. You remember how deserted Comala looked
    when

you first came here? That's what happened.
Don Pedro said he was going to cross his arms
and let Comala starve. And he did.

(*Blackout.*)

Scene 22

(*Media Luna—Madre Villa's bar—Media Luna.*)
(*Pedro sits in his armchair, Susanna's blanket across his lap.*)

PEDRO: Old people never sleep. Hardly ever. Sometimes
           you seem to sleep a little bit, but you never
           stop thinking. That's all you can do is think. (*Pause.*)
           Well, it won't be long, now. It's been a long time
           since you left me, Susanna. The light was just like
           this light, not so red, maybe, but the same
           weak lightless light. I was sitting watching the
           dawn, and watching you go, right there, where the
               sky
           started to open to the light. I called out, "Susanna,
           come back! Susanna San Juan."

           (*The light leaves Pedro and comes up on the bar. Ma-
           dre Villa is sweeping and Gamaliel lies in a drunken
           heap, giggling. Abundio is trying to rouse him.*)

MADRE VILLA: Get up, you pig, you've got customers! Wake up!

           (*She prods him.*)

GAMALIEL: You bitch! I'd like to shit in the milk of your
mother. Fuck her! And fuck your father, too, the
sonovabitch.

And fuck you! And while you're at it, don't forget to
fuck me, too, because if there was ever shit to fuck,
that's it . . .

MADRE VILLA: *(Loudly.)* I'm sorry, Abundio, the poor thing was
up half the
night waiting on some drunks, and they kept pouring
drinks for him.

ABUNDIO: All that I want is a pint of alcohol.

MADRE VILLA: I hope that Refugia hasn't been having her faint-
ing spells again.

ABUNDIO: She's dead, Madre Villa. She died last night. And just
when I'd gone and sold my burros. I sold my burros
for
medicine, and then she died.

MADRE VILLA: I can't hear a word you're saying. *Did you say
something?*
What did you say?

ABUNDIO: I said Refugia is dead. She died last night.

MADRE VILLA: I *thought* I could smell death around her
somewhere.

Do you have people for the wake?

ABUNDIO: Not a one, Madre Villa. That's why I want
the alcohol,
so I can get rid of this pain.

MADRE VILLA: You want it straight?

ABUNDIO: Yes, Madre Villa. I want to get drunk fast.

MADRE VILLA: Abundio, because it's you,
I'm going to give it to you half-price.
I just want you to tell your dead wife,
the poor thing, how much I always appreciated her.

And I want you to tell her to always
remember me when she gets to Heaven.

ABUNDIO: Yes, Madre Villa.

MADRE VILLA: Make sure you tell her before she cools off, okay?

ABUNDIO: I'll tell her. I know she must be counting on
your prayers, too. She must have felt bad dying like
that with no one there to give her the last rights.

MADRE VILLA: Didn't you try to get Father Renteria to come?

ABUNDIO: I went looking for him. But they told me
he was off in the hills.

MADRE VILLA: Hills? What hills?

ABUNDIO: Off in the boondocks somewhere. You know he's
started a revolution of his own now.

MADRE VILLA: Not him, too!
May God protect us.

ABUNDIO: Revolution. No revolution.
What difference is it to us? Give me another one
for the road. The only thing I promise is that I'll
drink it with the dead one, my juicy little cuca.

MADRE VILLA: Get along then before you wake up my son,
and don't forget to give my message to your wife.

(Light fades on the bar as Abundio leaves it. He propels himself through a route that eventually takes him, with walking music, to the Media Luna. Light comes up on Pedro.)

PEDRO: Damiana! Go see who that is coming up the path.

ABUNDIO: Could you help me out with a little money to bury
my wife?
Give me some money so I can bury my wife. *(Pause.)*
All I want is a little money so I can bury my woman.

(Abundio stabs Pedro. As he withdraws the knife, Damiana sees what is happening. Her screaming and struggling with Abundio is mimed in slow motion. During the following speech, Abundio stabs Pedro many times, speaking softly.)

ABUNDIO: What the Hell is she screaming about?
She's making so much noise, I bet even my
dead woman can hear it. She's back there
on the bed, you know, I put her out on the patio
where it's cool so she won't rot too fast. Mi cuca,
last night we went to bed together and she was frisky
as a filly, biting me and scraping my nose
with her nose. You know who I mean, Refugia,
my wife, the one who had the little boy
who died just after he was born. I had to sell
both my donkeys just to get the doctor to
come. They cost so damn much, these doctors,
and then he told me the boy died 'cause she was
sick . . . mi cuca . . . she's out there now
keeping cool in the night breeze . . . she's
not rotting too fast, her eyes are closed,
she won't see the dawn, she won't see this dawn
or any other dawn. *(Pause. He shouts.)*
Give me a little something for Chrissake!

(He moves away, vomits.)

ABUNDIO: Pedro Páramo was my father, too. I'm drunk.

(Abundio exits. Music begins, gradually becoming very full.)

PEDRO: Susanna, I begged you to come back.

A full moon hung high in
the middle of the world. My
eyes were lost looking at you
scrubbed smooth by the moon.

(Pause while the music increases.)

PEDRO: I know that in just a few hours Abundio
will come back here with bloody hands,
begging for the help I refused to give
him. And I don't have the hands now to cover
my eyes. I'd have to see him. I'd have to
hear him 'til his voice faded out completely.

DAMIANA: It's me, Don Pedro. Do you want me to bring
you your breakfast?

PEDRO: No. I'll come get it myself. *(They enact the
following.)*

CHORUS: Then he leans on the arms of Damiana
Cisneros and falls pleading and pleading
from within but unable to shape a single word.
He beats the bare earth
with a single dry blow,
weak as a child, and then he crumbles to pieces
as if he were nothing but a pile of stones.

(Pause.)

CHORUS: The sun went turning over the things of the earth
and gave them back their forms,
the worn, tired earth, turned
and furrowed so many times,
warming a little in the early light.

(Blackout. Ends.)

About the Author

Playwright and poet Sidney Goldfarb is a Professor of English at the University of Colorado at Boulder, where he has taught creative writing since 1973. He is also the author of the following:

POETRY

Speech, for Instance
Messages
Curve in the Road

PLAYS

Tristan
Big Mouth
The Transposed Heads (drama, with Julie Taymor)
Huerfano
Music Rescue Service
Transposed Heads (musical, with Julie Taymor)
Bad Women (from an idea by Tina Shepard)

SCREENPLAYS

Juan Darien (with Julie Taymor)
The Tranposed Heads (with Julie Taymor)
The Flying Dutchman (with Julie Taymor)

Acknowledgments

Thanks to: Paul Zimet, Ellen Maddow, Roger Babb, Rocky Bornstein, Tina Shepard, William Badgett, Will Patton, Raymond Barry, Mary Shultz, Suzanne Baxstresser, Sheila Dabney, Harry Mann, Louise Smith, Jack Wetherall, Blue Gene Tyranny, David Greenspan, Julie Taymor, Eliot Goldenthal, Jenny Dorn, Barbara Dilley, Marcia Douglas, Vicki Cass, Stephen Dunham, Roger Echo-Hawk, Nana Gavidia, Michael New, Jim Kincaid, Enrique Hernandez D'Jesus, Jun Maeda, Salome Rodriguez, Peter Berge, Eva Heggestad, Jayne Anne Phillips, Tim Roberts, Julie Carr, George Quasha, Susan Quasha, Chuck Stein, Jenny Fox, Michael Flatt, Ellen Stewart, Ellie Covan, Matthew Maguire, Bruce Rayvid, Frederick Lahey, Elizabeth Lahey, Chris Affleck, Patty Collinge, John Lewis, Anne Hammel, Warren Motte, Kay Bloss, David Mauri, Richard Halpern, Joanne Kyger, Steve Katz, Peter Michelson, Marcia Lawther, Bob Hirschfeld, Suzanne Opton, Terry Rowden, Rhonda Garelick, David Simpson, Steve Gorn, Jeffrey Robinson, Elizabeth Robinson, David Henderson, Katherine Eggert, Reed Bye, Lannie Harrison, Bob Rubin, Joanne Kyger, Yvonne Puig, Robin Blaser, Clark Richert, Barbara Ittner, Elaine Baker, Chip Baker, Bob Hymer, Richard Gianone, Brenda Romero, Peter Warshall, Max Schott, Anselm Hollo, Jane Dalrymple-Hollo, Math Trafton, Rajika Puri, Yamil Borges, and, especially, Sara and Miranda Goldfarb.

Eternal Spirits: Linda Bohe, Bob Creeley, Ed Dorn, Rick

Fields, Armand Schwerner, Allen Ginsberg, Bill Alfred, Robert Lowell, Denise Levertov, Bimbo Rivas, Lucia Berlin, Phillip Whalen, Colin Walcott, Kobun Chino Roshi, Dante Bonacci, Lenny Rosenfield.

For Deeply Appreciated Support: The National Endowment for the Arts, The New York State Council on the Arts, The National Endowment for the Humanities, The Talking Band, Otrabanda Company, The University of Colorado at Boulder.

Breinigsville, PA USA
03 September 2009
223496BV00001B/1/P